WOMEN, CRIME, AND SOCIETY

WOMEN, CRIME, AND SOCIETY

A Critique of Theoretical Criminology

Eileen B. Leonard

Longman

New York & London

WOMEN, CRIME, AND SOCIETY

Longman Inc., 19 West 44th Street, New York, N.Y. 10036
Associated companies, branches, and representatives
throughout the world.

Developmental Editor: Nicole Benevento
Editorial and Design Supervisor: Judith Hirsch
Interior and Cover Design: Dan Serrano
Manufacturing and Production Supervisor: Robin B. Besofsky

Library of Congress Cataloging in Publication Data
Leonard, Eileen B., 1947–
Women, Crime, and Society.
  Bibliography: p.
  Includes index.
  1. Female offenders — United States. I. Title.
HV6046.L46   364.3'74   81–8148
ISBN 0–582–28288–8   AACR2
ISBN 0–582–28289–6 (pbk.)

Manufactured in the United States of America
9 8 7 6 5 4 3 2 1

This book is dedicated to my mother,
Marie C. Bresnahan
and my father,
Thomas C. Bresnahan

Contents

Tables and Figures

Preface

I

Theoretical criminology is incapable of adequately explaining female patterns of crime. Despite the public's obsession with crime, despite the morbid fear it arouses, despite the endless volumes written to account for it, sex, the most powerful variable regarding crime, has been virtually ignored. A curious oversight.

Women are typically noncriminal: they have lower rates of crime in *all nations, all communities* within nations, for *all age groups,* for *all periods of recorded history*, and for practically *all crimes.*[1] Still, this intriguing and significant information has been left unexamined. As Barbara Wootton (Adler and Simon, 1979: vi) notes:

> It is surely, to say the least, very odd that half the population should apparently be immune to the criminogenic factors which lead to the downfall of so significant a proportion of the other half. Equally odd it is, too, that although the criminological experience of different countries varies considerably, nevertheless the sex differentiation remains.

It is at least as peculiar that criminologists have consistently ignored this.

It is easy to beg the question by attributing this neglect to the low crime rate among women; but this very fact offers a dramatic opportunity to test our theoretical understanding of crime. A brief, if unsophisticated, example will illustrate this. Many people believe poverty causes crime. Yet, in any ghetto or poverty-stricken area, at least half the population is female,[2] and their crime rate is typically very low. Poverty alone does *not* cause crime, or this discrepancy would not exist. Criminology contains an articulate (and much more sophisticated) collection of sociological theories, each incisively explaining criminal behavior. Although the topic of women and crime needs an enormous amount of empirical and theoretical work,[3] I have attempted to examine various sociological theories and to assess their applicability or relevance to women.

Initially I thought it might be possible simply to add what had been overlooked, and to elaborate an analysis of women in terms of existing theory. I quickly discovered that this is impossible. Theoretical criminology was constructed by men, about men. It is simply not up to the analytical task of explaining female patterns of crime. Although some theories work better than others, they all illustrate what social scientists are slowly recognizing within criminology and outside the field: that our theories are not the general explanations of human behavior they claim to be, but rather particular understandings of male behavior. A single theoretical canopy has been assumed for men and women, although their social realities are extremely diverse. Thus, something quite different will be needed to explain women and crime, although any attempt to bring women within the pale of formal academic criminology must begin with a profound criticism of the theoretical state of the field itself.

II

This book begins by examining the existing literature on women and crime. Immediately, a disturbing, indeed sexist,[4] portrayal of females, both criminal and noncriminal, is strikingly evident. This image of women is discussed and criticized.

The second chapter analyzes the numerical involvement of women in crime, including arrest data from the F.B.I.'s *Uniform Crime Reports*, and court statistics. The types of crime women commit are examined, as well as how their crimes have changed over the past 25 years. Related statistics on the status of women (employment, income, and education) are discussed, in order to put women's criminality in perspective.

Any analysis of criminal statistics is extremely lax if it ignores the problems associated with these statistics. This is particularly true regarding the data on women, since charges of discrimination against women (which would increase their official crime rate) are countered by equally strident claims of chivalrous treatment (which would decrease their official crime rate). I will explore these issues and their relationship to the reliability of the statistics. This chapter also includes a discussion of women within the criminal justice system and criminal law, which further illuminates female patterns of crime.

The next five chapters analyze the major sociological theories of crime, and their application to women: Robert Merton's anomie theory, labeling, Edwin Sutherland's differential association, subcultural theory, and Marxist explanations of crime. Each theory is probed to see if it adequately explains the low crime rate among women and the increases presently occurring.[5] Every chapter begins with a straightforward examination of the basic assumptions and propositions of the theory under discussion. Although I believe it is impossible to remove all bias when discussing a theory, I have attempted to be as impartial as possible in my presentation, and have included numerous quotes to let the reader evaluate each theory and ponder its potential application to women. Thereafter, I discuss the major criticisms of each theory. Finally, the theory is applied to women.

III

This study should interest academic audiences, especially students of criminology, because it discusses and criticizes the major sociological theories in the field, illustrates their application, and focuses on the criminality of a previously neglected group. In addition, the book is extremely relevant for courses on feminism and women studies, since it concerns the role of women in modern society, their oppression, and the unexpected ways this relates to their involvement in crime.

But I anticipate a wider audience will be attracted to this work since it treats issues that deeply affect us, our daily actions, and our closest concerns. Few people have not at some point worried about crime, in personal terms — fearing for their own safety — and in larger measure as to what such apparent disorder portends for our society. Similarly, changing relationships between men and women have brought strain, confusion, and indecision about our behavior and what we expect of others. This study will not resolve these issues but will contribute to that tradition of social science that, at its best, helps us interpret profound social change (be it in crime or sex roles) and thereby offers a more fundamental understanding of our world and our place in it. Here alone lies the possibility of control over our lives — only by understanding the forces that shape us can we act on these forces and, sometimes, change them.[6]

Theoretical criminology, carefully studied, teaches us much about crime, why it occurs, and how it can be controlled. Theoretical criminology, carefully criticized, illustrates the blindness of social science regarding women, elucidates another example of sexism, and can make us more attuned to the position of women in a society that allows such oversights to exist and persist.

Finally, examining these theories enables us to reemphasize the importance of social structure, and the impact it exerts on human behavior. This sociological insight is absolutely essential to those seeking a more complete understanding of themselves and their social existence. Our pridefully individualistic society, however, stubbornly ignores the impact of social structure. Unfortunately, personal liberty is neither enhanced nor protected by shrugging off the effects of larger structures on individual behavior. (The slave is not released from bondage merely by believing he or she is free.) Indeed, an awareness of the power of social structure, and an analysis of the bonds that constrain as well as sustain us, is the first liberating step toward self-determination.

NOTES

[1]This paraphrases Sutherland and Cressy, 1960: 111.

[2]According to the Bureau of the Census, women and female children accounted for 58 percent of the 24.7 million persons below the poverty level in 1977. Women also maintained 49 percent of the families living below the poverty level that year. (*A Statistical Portrait of Women in the United States: 1978*, 1980: 2).

[3]In 1969 criminologist David Ward observed that our understanding of female criminality approximated that of male crime more than 50 years earlier, indicating a tremendous discrepancy in scientific knowledge. As recently as 1975, Rita Simon asserted that female criminality has been almost completely neglected as a field of study.

[4]The major premise of sexism is that women are inferior to men. The term also denotes the systematic oppression of women, economically, politically, and socially. Sexism, however, extends far beyond these more blatant forms of degradation. While much of the literature on women and crime is overtly sexist, theoretical criminology is generally guilty of a more subtle, yet nonetheless pernicious, form of sexism. Its sexist bias will be thoroughly delineated in this book's conclusion; for now the reader should simply be aware of the absence of women from the theoretical frameworks outlined in Chapters 3–7, the blindness regarding their situation and interests, and the tendency to equate male concerns with the totality of empirical reality. This, too, is sexism.

[5]It should be clear that any theory that proposes an explanation of why crime occurs also posits an explanation for any *lack* of crime. If, for example, you assume that poverty causes crime, then financial security would alleviate crime. Each theory explaining crime therefore contains within it an explanation of conformity. A theory that cannot explain both crime and conformity is inadequate and logically unsound. Thus, I will from time to time speak of a theory's treatment of female crime or the lack of female crime. These are the two sides of the coin, integrally related, and logically inseparable. A theory that fails to explain one aspect or the other is flawed.

[6]See C. Wright Mills, *The Sociological Imagination*, for a full discussion of this view of social science.

Acknowledgments

Many individuals have helped me with this book. In particular, I would like to thank a varied group of friends, relatives, and colleagues for reading parts of the manuscript at different stages in its development: Thomas J. Bresnahan, Ron Holland, Marque Miringoff, Matthew Reilly, Tara Selver, Molly Shanley, Carole Turbin, and Jeanne B. Yglesias. Robin Trainor was kind enough both to read and type various sections of the manuscript, while Mildred Tubby typed the final draft with great skill and efficiency. Special thanks must be given to Robert McAulay and Beth Weitzman who generously read and commented on the entire manuscript. All of these people were extremely helpful in offering suggestions and criticisms that substantially improved the manuscript.

I would also like to thank Peter Leonard not only for reading and rereading my work, but for his unfailing enthusiasm for the entire project. This was a constant source of encouragement for me. I owe a debt of gratitude to William B. Sanders for providing, not once but twice, the best examples I have ever seen of constructive criticism. I would also like to thank Werner Stark, who was my mentor at Fordham University. His own research and his consistent encouragement of my research have provided me with a sterling example of both friendship and scholarship.

I am very grateful to the theorists whom I criticize, at times severely. I have learned much about crime and society from their brilliant discussions, and much about women and society from their profound silences.

The author would also like to thank the following publishers for their kind permission to reprint from:

BECOMING DEVIANT by David Matza, © 1969 by Prentice-Hall, Inc. Reprinted by permission of the publisher.

SOCIAL PATHOLOGY: A SYSTEMATIC APPROACH TO THE THEORY OF SOCIOPATHIC BEHAVIOR by Edwin M. Lemert, © 1951 by McGraw-Hill Book Company. Reprinted by permission of the publisher.

"Social Problems and Sociological Theory" by Robert K. Merton, in CONTEMPORARY SOCIAL PROBLEMS, 4th ed., edited by Robert K. Merton and Robert A. Nisbet, © 1971 by Harcourt Brace Jovanovich. Reprinted by permission of the publisher.

"Social Structure and Anomie" by Robert K. Merton, including an illus-
    tration from p. 676, in *The American Sociological Review*, Vol. 3,
    October 1938. Reprinted by permission of the American Sociological
    Association.
THE SUTHERLAND PAPERS ed. by Albert Cohen, A. Lindesmith,
    and K. Schuessler, © 1956 by Indiana University Press. Reprinted
    by permission of the publisher.
WOMEN AND CRIME by Rita James Simon, © 1975 by Lexington
    Books, D.C. Heath and Company. Reprinted by permission of the
    publisher.

CHAPTER ONE

The Dismal History of Women And Crime

EARLY STUDIES

Most of the literature on women and crime, dating back to the late nineteenth and early twentieth century, is woefully inadequate. Early writers noted the lower crime rate among women and generally explained this by speaking of women as morally superior to men. Those who hesitated to accept notions of innate virtue often attributed women's lack of criminality to their biology: females were seen as more submissive, less aggressive, weaker in strength and cunning. Some research, conducted before the turn of the century, combined social and biological factors in explaining female crime. Luke Owen Pike (1876), for example, argued that women are less inclined toward criminality since lack of strength created habits that remained among women long after physical strength had lost its importance in crime due to the development of weapons. He contended that growing independence among women would increase crime, a theme frequently encountered in this literature.

Other early studies concentrated mainly on social conditions. In a two-part article written in 1876, Ely van de Warker rejected the idea of moral superiority among women and refused to believe that the causes of crime are different for men and women. Women commit fewer crimes because they face fewer temptations and have less opportunity for crime. As their opportunities become equalized, as the criminal life becomes easier to attain, we may find them equalling men in crime.

Most criminologists would probably date the beginning of the "scientific" study of female crime to 1900 with Caesar Lombroso's work, *The Female Offender*. Lombroso combined quantitative and qualitative data to understand the female criminal although his methods and results are largely unacceptable today. He saw a close connection between physical deficiencies (such as malformations of the skull, brain, or face) and crime. Female criminals are physically deformed, although they are not, according to Lombroso, as repulsive as male criminals.

Lombroso claimed that certain male criminals are "born" with an inclination toward crime. These men are moral degenerates and are physically marked by certain stigmata: squinting eyes, a twisted nose, a receding forehead, big ears, generally hairy bodies, and an instinct for tatooing. He found fewer examples of born female criminals, but those he did find he regarded as even more vicious and dangerous than their male counterparts. Lombroso explained that women are normally less sensitive to pain, less compassionate; they are usually jealous and full of revenge. These "ladylike" qualities, however, are tempered by more typical female attributes: piety, maternity, feminine weakness, and underdeveloped intelligence. Women are overgrown children, and, when bad, they are infinitely more hideous than men. Women criminals are usually devoid of maternal affection — proof of their degeneracy. They are, in fact, extremely masculine. The "shortcomings" found in normal women are untempered and extreme in women criminals.

Lombroso wrote not only of the born criminal, but also of the occasional criminal, who accounted for most of the lawless women. These women are often unstigmatized (regarding physical characteristics), and might even be drawn into crime by a man or by excessive temptation. Lombroso pointed out, for example, that shoplifting is a common female offense, due to the overwhelming temptation of the goods displayed in stores. Moreover, women do not have a very strong sense of property, and fine clothing is essential for them in attracting a man.

Although women do not always commit crimes, they frequently instigate husbands or lovers to do so. They are usually uncommonly stubborn when denying their part in a crime. Yet, at times, they confess quite readily. According to Lombroso, there are many reasons for the quick confession: "One is that need to gossip and that incapacity for keeping a secret characteristic of the female sex" (Lombroso and Ferrero, 1900: 183).

Lombroso's concept of the "born criminal" was quickly rejected by many, but his view of women has echoed in subsequent theoretical frameworks. Hargrave Adam (1914), for example, abandoned Lombroso's notion that criminality might be innate: the roots of crime lie in unfortunate social circumstances. Women, however, are almost immune to these circumstances because of "the natural and gentler characteristics of the sex" (Adam, 1914: 7). When they do turn to crime, they are incredibly cruel because their self-control and moral responsibility are underdeveloped. He, like Lombroso, noted the lack of maternal instinct in women criminals and their lust for vengeance. He believed women often instigate crime and are frequently involved in secretive crimes, such as poisoning. The law, unfortunately, encourages this by treating them leniently. Thus, Adam posited social variables as the major force behind criminality, although he also spoke of woman's nature quite apart from social circumstances.

Lombroso was not the first, nor the last, to search for the roots of crime in constitutional factors. In 1935, Sheldon and Eleanor Glueck published an enormous study entitled *Five Hundred Delinquent Women*, which typified the American effort to describe the criminal as thoroughly as possible. They analyzed 500 female offenders in terms of their family background, education, arrest record, the disposition of their case, and so on. Although they were not solely concerned with physiology, they concluded that a large portion of the delinquents were mentally defective. Most of these women came from lower-income families or were arrested mainly for illicit sexual behavior. We will soon see how these factors could have critically affected the Gluecks' findings.

POSTWAR ERA

Otto Pollak and the Criminality of Women

The Criminality of Women, published in 1950, is undoubtedly the major work on women and crime in the postwar years. Pollak's book is excellent in its organization of previous work on women and crime in the American, British, French, and German literatures. His thesis departs from most treatments of the subject by claiming that the crime rate among women probably equals that of men. Women's crime, however, has a "masked character." He states that the crimes frequently committed by women, including shoplifting, thefts by prostitutes against their clients, domestic thefts, abortions, perjury, and disturbance of the peace, are inadequately reflected in the statistics. He supports Lombroso's assertion that women are especially "addicted" to crimes that are easily concealed and seldom reported. He states, for example, that exhibitionism frequently occurs among females but is unprosecuted. (He offers no evidence for its frequent occurrence, except to say that it is easily observable by anyone.)

Pollak contends that the social roles of women are excellent covers for crime. Women are homemakers; they care for children and the sick; they are domestic workers. These roles, removed from the public sphere, are ideal for hidden crimes. One example is the opportunity a woman has to poison a sick child and the difficulty involved in detecting such an offense. Following Hargrave Adam, he also claims that women frequently instigate criminal behavior in others.

Finally, Pollak argues that policemen do not like to arrest women; judges, prosecutors, and juries do not like to assist in convicting them. This is due, in part, to their paternalistic and chivalrous attitude toward women.

Pollak assumes women's crimes are characterized by deceit and asserts that virtually all criminologists will support this. Since most criminologists are men and might be charged with bias, Pollak goes to the trouble of listing female authors who share this belief in women's deceitfulness. His reasoning is open to serious criticism. When a culture maintains a negative attitude toward women, simply being female does not prevent the acquisition of that prejudice. Both women and men can be sexists.

Pollak explains the deceitfulness of women's crimes through culture and biology. Although physical weakness can force a woman to resort to deception, he does not overestimate its importance, given the present level of technology. (Guns have a way of cancelling the value of brute strength.) So, he discusses the role of biology, in combination with social factors. He alleges that women disguise sexual response, conceal their period of menstruation, and withhold sexual information from young children. These basic facts in a woman's life, according to Pollak, give her training in deception and a different attitude toward truth. Likewise, women are expected to attract a husband indirectly, through charm and subtle pressure. Thus, society condones, even encourages, deceit among its women. All criminals wish to remain undetected, but, due to their training, women are more likely to be successful in this regard. Moreover, they concentrate on victims who are less apt to be discovered. Poisoning one's child was mentioned earlier. Sexual offenses by women against children are also easily concealed since women are expected to handle children, and a sexual attack by a woman leaves no physical evidence.

Regarding crimes against property, women are likely to play the unobtrusive role of decoy or accomplice. In addition, their roles give them opportunities to steal directly and remain unpunished: through sex, they can create situations of blackmail; as domestics, they can steal little by little from trusting employers; as prostitutes, they can steal from customers who are unlikely to report the offense.

Pollak acknowledges Edwin Sutherland's work concerning the large number of men unprosecuted for white-collar offenses. Yet he maintains that these same men are likely to employ female domestics, women whose thefts probably numerically equal those of their employers. (He admits they are not equal in terms of social harmfulness.)

Pollak maintains that greater freedom has allowed women to enter new positions and new roles, thereby giving them more opportunities for participation in crime. They still maintain their traditional roles, however, with all the criminal possibilities these afford. So, the type of involvement of women in crime has not simply changed: it has increased.

Pollak notes the social factors, including the double standard, that help create female crime. The double standard leads to frustration and envy on the part of women. It can push them toward false accusations against men (charges of rape, for example) and even result in aggressive behavior toward husbands or others. In addition, modern advertising that is aimed at women tempts them to theft. Finally, as domestics, women are in a position that fosters envy, resentment, and criminal desires.

Critical Discussion of Pollak

The most serious criticism of Pollak is that he offers no proof for his statements. It is difficult to argue the existence of undetected crime since its very nature implies that it is unknown. Such a theory cannot be based on evidence, a weakness compounded by assertions that simply defy plausibility. The likelihood that women are poisoning untold numbers of sick husbands and children is ridiculous, especially given the investigation that frequently surrounds death. How could Pollak possibly know that such crimes are taking place? Likewise, his claims of sex offenses against children and female exhibitionism are boldly stated without evidence or even reasonable explanations. Such arguments could easily be leveled against men, thereby recreating the disparity in crime rates. Pollak mentions Sutherland's study of white-collar crime among men but tries to dispel this by pointing to thefts among domestics. The contrast between Pollak's totally unfounded accusations against domestics and Sutherland's carefully documented study is striking.

Regarding underreported crimes, the trivial nature of most of these offenses should be noted. In his effort to prove that female crime equals male crime, Pollak has been forced to discuss minor domestic thefts, perjuries, and disturbances of the peace. He ignores similar, rather inconsequential, crimes by men, although he acknowledges that more serious crimes (aggravated assault, robbery, burglary) are usually committed by males.

Pollak contends that women are treated leniently throughout the criminal justice process. He ignores the possibility that women may be more severely punished for failing to meet traditional expectations.[1] His assumption that women are deceitful is supposedly based on biological and sociological arguments, yet his descriptions of the character traits of women often thinly disguise a sexist attitude. Many of Pollak's arguments are simply foolish; others focus on the deception involved in the female role (such as the traditional necessity of attracting a husband), while ignoring what deception and trickery might be learned by men in their traditional business world.

Pollak's work has some merit. The inaccuracy of official statistics deserves attention, and his claim of differential treatment for women demands further consideration. Most importantly, he recognizes that the involvement of women in crime is connected to their social positions and roles. The relationship of women to society is key in understanding their patterns of deviance. As we turn to more recent sociological studies of women and crime, it will become apparent that as deficient as this early work is, it has had a profound impact on later studies, since common themes and assumptions are found throughout.

RECENT WORKS

Much of the work on women and crime since Pollak has examined individual women criminals (Sparrow, 1970; Franklin, 1967; Parker, 1965) or women in prison (Ward and Kassebaum, 1965; Giallombardo, 1966; Burkhart, 1973). Unfortunately, these studies do not systematically examine the roots of female crime. The case studies offer insights but tend to be sensationalist. The prison studies, on the other hand, are concerned mainly with the social organization of women's prisons — their facilities and programs — but neglect the social conditions that put women there.[2]

The case studies frequently accept Pollak's assumption that female crime is more extensive than first appears. They often contend that women are not more virtuous than men but that their social roles enable them to hide their deviance. Sparrow, writing as recently as 1970, maintains that women are prone to murder by poison, and that the act is often emotionally inspired. Like Pollak, he points to women's "natural aptitude for subterfuge," which compensates for their lack of strength. His book is an account of several murder cases. Edith deRham's study (1969) has sexist implications that begin on the title page: *How Could She Do That? A Study of the Female Criminal.* Again, we find Pollak's assumptions clearly evident:

> Women possess, as most criminologists, policemen, prison authorities, and husbands would agree, an inordinate talent for concealment and deception which both characterizes the feminine style and makes the female lawbreaker harder to catch. (deRham, 1969: 5)

DeRham connects this with the subordinate role of women in society, which necessitates indirect action. She claims that like all groups in an inferior position, women use deceit to compensate for their powerless conditions, much as blacks did in the Old South. If deRham is correct in this assumption, it is difficult to explain why black males, still subordinate in society, have such high rates of reported crime. She refers to other factors mentioned by Pollak, including physical characteristics, the role of instigator or accomplice, the availability of excellent victims for women, and women's roles as cook, nurse, and shopper. She also contends in a more Freudian vein:

> There is impressive evidence that chronic shoplifting, particularly among women who can afford to buy, is sexually motivated . . . . the compulsion to steal is a form of sexual sublimation and may be minimized by psychiatric treatment of the sexual problem which causes it. (deRham, 1969: 13)

These comments and similar ones are followed by seven stories of criminal women.

The 1970s

This decade has witnessed the emergence of a literature on women and crime that substantially challenges previous work. It criticizes some of the very assumptions of earlier writings and vividly marks the impact of feminism on criminology. Although this new scholarship is not without its difficulties, it has begun to explore issues and questions that were heretofore left unexamined. Such a breakthrough is, in itself, a major contribution. I will examine some of the recent work, indicating how my study aims to fill a gap still remaining in this literature.

Rita Simon and Freda Adler

In 1975 there were two noteworthy additions to the literature: Rita Simon's *Women and Crime* and Freda Adler's *Sisters in Crime : The Rise of*

the New Female Criminal. Simon discusses the statistical picture of
women's crime over several decades. She compiles data on the extent of
female crime, the number of women involved in various types of crime,
and their treatment by courts and prison officials regarding convictions,
sentences, and parole. She also includes data on the status of women in
the labor force, marriage and fertility, income, and education. Simon
contends that certain types of female crimes, particularly white-collar
crimes, are likely to increase in the future, due largely to expanding
occupational opportunities for women. Their involvement in violence
should, however, decrease, since the frustration that leads to female violence will likely be alleviated by their widening educational and occupational opportunities. Simon's book provides excellent groundwork for
further analysis within the area of women and crime, although her own
discussion of the etiology of female crime is limited to a superficial review of the literature. She mentions that the women's movement has
probably had an important impact not only on female crime but in altering the treatment of women within the criminal justice system. While
treatment may have been more lenient in the past, it is now certain to
become increasingly egalitarian.

Adler's book presents a detailed picture of prostitution, drug addiction, and juvenile delinquency among females. She discusses startling increases in women's crime and points to the possible link between this
phenomenon and the women's liberation movement. Both of these contentions must be examined. In this chapter we will concentrate on the
latter and discuss the former in Chapter 2.

Adler connects the rise of female criminality with the rise in
women's assertiveness. Technology and the women's liberation movement have combined to equalize the ability of women to participate in
male crime. She assumes that women have the same basic motivations as
men and are entering both legitimate and illegitimate fields that were
once restricted. Adler contends, for example, that the status of women in
organized crime may change. Arguing that the mob is sensitive to competition and people of accomplishment, she writes:

> They are not likely to ignore the increasing numbers of women who are
> using guns, knives, and wits to establish themselves as full human beings, as
> capable of violence and aggression as any man. (Adler, 1975: 15)

It is extremely unlikely that women will soon obtain positions of power
in organized crime, but — much more important — note how Adler
speaks of "full human beings": women using "guns, knives, and wits,"
women proving their ability to be as "violent and aggressive as any
man." This notion of liberation must be challenged.

After discussing the physical and psychological makeup of women, Adler argues that male-female differences are much more the result of social factors. She relates the social position of females to paternalism, which, in turn, gives women an advantage with the police and decreases their likelihood of arrest. Adler points out, however, that girls are over-prosecuted for sex offences. Unlike Pollak, she contends that, at a certain point, women can be treated very harshly by the law.

Girls and women are more willing than ever to challenge traditional restrictions and social roles. Adler correctly recognizes that with the easing of restraints, females are more likely to be subject to pressures that can increase crime. She maintains that as women move into white-collar positions, most of them will perform their tasks honestly and responsibly. She feels it is unrealistic, however, to assume that women will be any more honest than men. To argue otherwise is "quixotic chivalry."

Critique of Adler: Liberation and Crime

Adler was not the first to posit a connection between the liberation of women and their increasing rates of crime. In 1931, Cecil Bishop (like Pike and Warker before him) proposed a similar thesis. The differences between their positions are instructive, and I will criticize Adler in part by reference to Bishop. Comparing the work of a contemporary woman with that written by a man in 1931, long before the reemergence of the feminist movement, is meant to be jarring.

Bishop, like Adler, argues that increasing emancipation has resulted in more female crime. He speaks of the increase in delinquency among females, the rising amount of shoplifting, and the women who have begun acting as accomplices to male criminals. Bishop differs sharply from Adler, however, in his attitude toward emancipation. He contends feminists have a misconception about the meaning of equality and are seeking what cannot be achieved. "Nature has made men and women equal in the importance of their respective functions, but neither can encroach successfully upon the other's province." (Bishop, 1931: 24) He argues that feminists are complicating a difficult situation. At the end of his book, he even questions the desirability of higher education for women since advanced education can make them view housework as a lowly occupation. Feminism has left many women discontented with their lot, but they are unfit for business life and always will be.

According to Bishop, the most pernicious claim of the feminists is the moral equality of men and women. Women have always set moral standards within the community, and while it is imperative that they continue to do so, this can only be accomplished if they stay in their proper sphere.

Thus, after initially positing a connection between freedom for women and increasing female crime, Bishop and Adler part company rather quickly. Bishop assumes that nature has destined women to the home, and any change will have negative consequences. Adler is more reserved in expressing personal opinions, but obviously favors the increasing emancipation of women. In both her work and Bishop's, the connection between crime and women's liberation is objectionable, although in different respects. Bishop's assumptions of biological imperative are unacceptable, but at least they are clear. Adler blurs the connections between crime and liberation: to be criminal is not necessarily to be liberated, although Adler frequently implies that they are one and the same. Whereas Bishop asserts that women are morally superior and should continue this tradition by remaining in their place, Adler, more current, rejects ideas of moral superiority. As women assume male roles, they will become more criminal. To expect otherwise is foolish. Adler's contention that increasing freedom might lead to greater female crime deserves consideration. Certainly the easing of restrictions on female behavior, demands for assertiveness on their part, less rigid sex-role expectations and more varied opportunities can result in increased deviant and criminal activity on the part of females by supplying the opportunity for crime while loosening social control. Innate biological conditions do not shape sex-role behavior, making it inescapable, or altered only at our peril. Social factors are crucial, and in modern society they largely determine the expected behavioral patterns of women and men. Therefore, if women and men were socially and economically equal, if they played the same roles in society, yes, their crime rates would be very similar. There are, however, two major difficulties with Adler's discussion.

First, her assumption of rapidly increasing equality among men and women is highly debatable. As Chapter 2 will reveal in great detail, women are far from equal to men in terms of occupations, income, social expectations, and so on. Adler greatly exaggerates the freedom that modern women supposedly have.

My second criticism regards her naive idea of liberation. Obviously, women's liberation is something more than women equalling men in crime, and while Adler might well agree, she does not state this explicitly. Her enthusiasm for women using "guns, knives, and wit," for women who are fully capable of violence, is unmistakable.[3] This view embodies an unreflective notion that women give evidence of liberation by undertaking any typically "male" behavior, be it violent or nonviolent. This conception of liberation is a shortsighted one, of women simply becoming more like men. It implies liberation from the *female sex role*, but not liberation in any larger sense. Much of the women's movement has a vision for women that extends far beyond that portrayed by Adler.

There are, finally, pertinent issues Adler simply does not address. Why is crime rampant among men, or increasing among women who begin to assume traditionally male roles in society? What does this imply about the traditional role of men, or about our society? By ignoring this, Adler ultimately fails to explain crime among women, since attributing it to an increase in "masculine" patterns of behavior leaves the fundamental causes of crime unexplored. The question simply becomes, why do males and women in male roles engage in crime? In addition, she concentrates solely on the rise in women's crimes and not or the overriding issue of women's tremendous conformity. Her basic assumption, that female crime is rapidly rising, will be severely criticized in the next chapter.

Role Theory

A more enlightening approach to female crime has appeared in a number of articles (Morris, 1964; Heidensohn, 1968; Hoffman-Bustamente, 1973; Klein, 1973; Rosenblum, 1975) that recognize the limitations of earlier studies and discuss female crime in terms of sex roles, not biological or psychological variables. Rather than treating women's crime as the masculinization of female behavior, as Adler did, these writers view it as the illegitimate expression of role expectations. They discuss female socialization — opportunities and lack of opportunities — and conclude that female crime is an extension of women's sex roles. For example, when women turn to crime, they shift from shoppers to shoplifters, from cashing good checks to cashing bad ones. Statistical evidence supports this, since female crime continues to be basically petty and nonviolent, with major increases only in larceny, forgery, and similar crimes.

Sex-role explanations are, however, incomplete. They offer little understanding of actual women criminals and can easily slide into discussions of inadequate female socialization, implying that individual difficulties rather than structural problems are at issue. I agree with Smart's contention (1976: 69–70) that role theory is restricted in its usefulness. It fails to discuss the structural origins of sex-role inequality or to deal with the inferior status of women in historical or cultural terms. This unfortunately enables such analyses to be interpreted as additional proof of inherent differences between men and women. What is required is a theory that delineates the structural and cultural factors that account for both sex roles and crime and does not simply view crime as the result of sex roles.

Carol Smart

Carol Smart's *Women, Crime and Criminology* (1976) is exceptional in the field of women and crime, offering a feminist critique of existing literature on female criminality. Smart is specifically interested in challenging the ideological frameworks that bolster existing theory and research on the subject. She explores classical and contemporary studies[4] and finds in both unstated and frequently sexist assumptions about female criminality. She documents the absence of a critical analysis of these assumptions and begins discussing their tacit acceptance of biological determinism and the notions of individual pathology that frequently inform this literature. Smart offers incisive criticisms of many theorists, including Lombroso and Pollak, who deal explicitly with female criminality. She also discusses prostitution and rape, contending that it is necessary to explore the ways in which women are sexually exploited. She connects such exploitation with their economic and political dependency.[5] She also discusses the treatment of female offenders and the view of mental illness as a female alternative to crime (a notion she regards as extremely simplistic).

After criticizing existing work, Smart discusses future directions for social research. She rejects the idea of treating women's crime as a separate topic within criminology and prefers that all crime be analyzed within a social and historical framework. This work, however, has yet to be accomplished, and she contends more research is needed before it is possible. She suggests specific areas for future research, including studies of the typical crimes committed by females, their treatment in the criminal justice system, and the nature of criminal laws. She concludes (1976: 185):

> Criminology and the sociology of deviance must become more than the study of men and crime if it is to play any significant part in the development of our understanding of crime, law and the criminal process and play any role in the transformation of existing social practices.

Smart's book was the first explicitly feminist attack on existing theory, and although she only examines work that deals specifically with women and crime, she provides a basis for building a new theory of crime that includes both males and females. She has been criticized by Anne Peters (1978) for not attempting to develop such a theory. She might have synthesized various insights regarding women and crime that are found throughout her book, including ideas on the political inequality of men and women, and the stabilizing function of the family in capitalist society. Peters contends Smart should have offered at least a "rough theoretical adumbration." Such sketchy attempts are, however, as unsatisfactory and as frequently criticized as the failure to provide them.

Crites, Bowker, Balkan, Berger, Schmidt

Several other books also reflect, as Carol Smart's book did, a new approach within criminology to the topic of women and crime, although these works are not as theoretically sound as Smart's contribution. Laura Crites has edited a book entitled *The Female Offender* (1976), which discusses women criminals, women and the law, women in prison, and prostitution. This work indicates the increasing interest in women and crime and also reflects the current unwillingness to accept stereotypical views of women. In addition, contentions that women are rapidly becoming involved in violent and aggressive offenses, or that the women's movement is contributing to increasing crime, are soundly rejected. The selected articles demonstrate a concern about the neglect of women in prison, their discriminatory treatment in the criminal justice system, sexist laws, and paternalism.

Lee Bowker's *Women, Crime, and the Criminal Justice System* (1978) deals extensively with statistics on women and crime, early theoretical frameworks on the subject (up to Pollak), and a variety of related topics, including female drug use, victimology, prostitution, legal inequality, and corrections.

In his introduction, Bowker sets the tone of this new literature by discussing the criminal justice system in terms of male domination. He (1978: xiv) hopes that his book will provide readers with "an increased sensitivity to the ways in which the criminal justice system systematically puts at a disadvantage the women and girls it processes." Such a statement was rarely, if ever, made about women, crime, and justice a decade or two ago. Bowker goes on to reject early explanations of female crime and to discuss male and female patterns of drug use. Discussions of female oppression surface repeatedly as he deals with male-female differences in drug use, rape, prostitution, and the legal system. He concludes that both criminological theory and sex-role theory will have to be explored in order to explain the quantitative differences in male and female crime, as well as differences in role performance within certain categories of crime. He maintains (1978: 80) that "developmental, situational, and macrostructural variables" are involved in the causes of female crime and the roles women play within crime.

Although some recent criminology textbooks include a perfunctory chapter on women and crime, many still do not even attempt a superficial review of the topic. Balkan, Berger, and Schmidt's text, *Crime and Deviance in America: A Critical Approach* (1980), is exceptional in providing a Marxist perspective on crime, which in turn reflected the book's section on "Women, Crime, and Deviance."[6] They view the types of crimes women commit as a result of their socialization under capitalism and their opportunities. They maintain that sexism underlies female criminal involvement, their treatment in the criminal justice system, and the crimes committed against women. Female offenses, which are predominantly property offenses, and the punishments women receive, are related to their roles within the political economic structure. They note that class conflict plays an important part in the criminality of women. Citing Engels, they contend that women were not always subordinate to men and argue that the roots of female oppression lie in the development of private property and class societies, not in their biological nature or their procreative functions.

Although Balkan, Berger, and Schmidt acknowledge the peculiar lack of crime among women, they believe this is due to differential socialization and social control among men and women. They choose to emphasize, instead, the crimes in which women are involved, noting for example the social control of prostitution and homosexuality. They contend that such behavior is suppressed because it threatens sex roles and family patterns, which are necessary in capitalist society.

They discuss the treatment of women in prison, as well as crimes against women, including rape, battered women, and forced sterilization. According to Balkan, Berger, and Schmidt, the sexism that bolsters capitalism in turn supports the types of crimes inflicted upon women.

In sum, this book and others cited above represent a new trend in examining women and crime. Current writings are frequently inspired by feminist understandings of the role of women in modern society and their oppression. Although the books mentioned are not exclusive in this regard, they are indicative of a new way of viewing the phenomenon.

IMAGES OF WOMEN

The image of women found in earlier studies on women and crime is dismal and simply wrong. This literature begins with naive notions of moral superiority and biological submissiveness, although a contemporary analysis provides an equally warped picture of a liberated woman carrying a revolver or involved in organized crime. These ideas should be unequivocally rejected, and yet they manage to lurk about. Cultural attitudes toward women, prejudices against them, are never far from the surface in any study concerning women. It is necessary to steer through a maze of prejudice and misinformation that is subtly woven in with the facts. In this respect, the issue of female criminality reflects basic problems confronting women and notions about them that are too frequently uncritically accepted.

The attitudes toward women in this literature are closely linked with basic assumptions about the determinants of human behavior. While these authors propose psychological and sociological explanations of behavior, they also frequently delineate differences in nature (witness Lombroso, Adam, Sparrow, deRham, Bishop). Women and men are seen as fundamentally different creatures, due to biological not cultural traits (Klein, 1973). Earlier writings stress biological differences, some in combination with sociological variables. Pollak's effort was the most sophisticated of these. In such discussions, women's nature is defined as both positive and negative. Women are purer, gentler than men, well suited to their roles as wives, mothers, and housekeepers. Yet, they are capable of engaging in criminal behavior because they are also deceptive, revengeful, greedy, and untrustworthy. They lack intelligence, moral responsibility, and courage. Only adherence to their traditional roles keeps the darker side of their nature under control (or at least hidden from the public). Women criminals lack the "maternal instinct," they are less sensitive, more vindictive and cruel. The division between good and evil in women becomes even more conspicuous when discussing and explaining crime, since here their negative side is carried to the extreme.

Female patterns of crime are generally viewed as emerging from individual female characteristics that are, unfortunately, all too familiar. Women are jealous, revengeful, and sneaky; they love to gossip, they cannot be trusted, they instigate crime. These traits might be influenced by social conditions, but the impression is unmistakable: more than social conditions are at work. Men would not act this way. Since these traits are rooted in nature, by implication, any attempt to remedy the situation must deal with individual adjustment. Questions of economic, social, or political impact are largely avoided.

Klein (1973) notes that the characteristics used to describe women are often sexual. This is vividly reflected in criminology. Female crime is seen as the inability of certain women to adhere to cultural standards. Since these standards are often sexual, deviation is typically regarded as sexual abnormality, and the crimes of women defined in such terms, even if another explanation might be more appropriate or more accurate. Prostitution, for example, could be financially motivated, linked to economic, not sexual, disturbances; but it is seldom viewed this way. DeRham's discussion of shoplifting as "a form of sexual sublimation," is even more to the point. In each case, the standards themselves are un-questioned. Discussion of the impact of social structure on female be-havior is largely ignored.

Unfortunately, such sexist and moralistic ideas are still accepted: female inferiority appears obvious and rooted in nature. Women behave in certain ways because they are women, not because of their social posi-tion, limited opportunities, and restricted roles or social expectations. The negative characteristics describing women are not, however, totally fictitious. Those who are oppressed in a society, and serve a dominant group, will show the scars of that oppression. Yet, on the one hand, we must recognize the structural roots of such difficulties (and not place the blame on the nature of women); and, on the other hand, we must realize that many of these attributes are totally undeserved, although frequently unchallenged. Women do not, for example, have a corner on greed, re-venge, or deception in modern society. Men are quite capable of muster-ing up these sentiments in full measure. Likewise, it is sheer bias to assert that women are untrustworthy and lack intelligence or moral responsi-bility; and it is most outrageous to claim they lack courage. What has been lacking, until recently, are detailed and sensitive accounts exem-plifying the admirable and courageous behavior of women. Negative attitudes toward women found in criminology, for example, have only recently begun to be closely examined and, therefore, refuted.

The literature on women and crime that developed largely during the 1970s does challenge many of the aforementioned assumptions about women. Notions that female behavior is determined by inherent female characteristics are soundly rejected. There is an explicit awareness of the role of social structure in female patterns of crime. Social, not biological, influences are seen as dominant. Gone are the more blatant sexist images of women and stereotypical notions about their untrustworthiness, their greed, or their cowardice. In their place is a vision of women as brutal-ized by society, whether as conformists, criminals, or victims of crime. Women are neither purer nor more manipulative than man. They are, very simply, creatures of their social system.

Despite this new literature, competent studies on women and crime are still lacking, in part because women are readily deterred from crime and, thus, cause less concern. "As a result of this lack of official concern, orthodox, control-oriented criminology, which has been in-volved in serving the needs of administrators and policymakers, has virtually ignored the existence of female offenders" (Smart, 1976: 3). Such deficiencies are being corrected, albeit slowly.

A sexist image of women is tremendously effective in terms of social control. It reinforces social relationships by warning of the danger in challenging existing frameworks. Even Adler is guilty in this regard. Her book questions some traditional assumptions about women and, unlike many, assumes a basic likeness in the nature of men and women, thus inferring that, as part of similar social structures, they will behave in similar ways. Given that women are entering male roles, their crime is rising. Adler's claim of rapid increases in female crime is, however, doubtful. Moreover, she never asks whether becoming more "masculine" (hence, more criminal) is truly liberating. Thus, this image of women, although not explicitly sexist and certainly more immediately acceptable, still poses difficulties for anyone defining liberation as more than the ability or opportunity to succeed in a man's world. Adler's image of the female criminal stirs up memories of Lombroso's assertion that female criminals are masculine and implies that the traditional place of women (the home) is the safest. Further, it discredits the women's movement by publicizing mistaken notions of "liberation."

The dual image of women, extreme in its praise and its condemnation, can be understood in terms of existing power relationships. Women are rewarded with all the superlatives when they remain in accepted roles. Yet, in spite of their goodness, piety, and virtue (characteristics that would suggest they play a pivotal role in governing society), we are reminded of their dark side. To contain this, women must be controlled and protected, which is most effectively accomplished when they remain wives and mothers. Increasing female crime is often mistakenly regarded as a necessary result of women attempting to surmount traditional roles and expectations.

The literature on women and crime leaves fundamental issues to discuss. The earlier writings are horrifying in their intellectual inadequacy and in their portrayal of women. Although the more recent literature tends to be much more satisfactory in its analysis of the social roots of female behavior and its examination of previously ignored issues, it is still only developing. It has accomplished a great deal with its discussion of, for example, women and the criminal justice system, law, prostitution, drugs, prison, and so on. It has not, however, provided an adequate theoretical understanding of women and crime. Carol Smart's book, with its critique of earlier theory, was an important step in this direction. No one, however, has systematically examined current theories of crime in light of women. An established discipline like criminology can and must do better.

After ascertaining, as far as possible, the actual involvement of women in crime, I will analyze contemporary theoretical criminology to determine if it is adequate to the task of explaining female patterns of crime.

NOTES

[1] We will discuss the treatment of women within the criminal justice system more thoroughly in Chapter 2. This will substantiate the notion that, at best, Pollak's claims should be viewed skeptically.

[2] Burkhart's book, *Women in Prison*, significantly differs from other prison studies in its more contemporary, feminist outlook. Burkhart is consciously aware of the exploitation of women in modern society and uses an informal style to report on women in the prisons of the United States. The stories of these women, frequently told in their own words, elicit a more compassionate understanding of their plight.

[3] There is a literature that discusses the liberating role violence can play in the lives of oppressed people (see, for example, Frantz Fanon's *The Wretched of the Earth*). Alder's arguments do not, however, approach this level of sophistication.

[4] Smart's careful criticisms of contemporary role theory have been discussed above in my treatment of this theoretical framework.

[5] In this regard, Smart recognizes the importance of the position of women in contemporary society. She also comments on cultural attitudes toward both sexuality and women.

[6] This text was preceded by an article by Balkan and Berger (1979) on female delinquency and the women's movement. They relate female crime to sex-role expectations an socioeconomic conditions, contending that female property offenses reflect female roles in the marketplace, increased opportunities, the current economic crisis, and increased economic goals among women. They argue that rising juvenile violence among females is due to the economic climate, not to the women's liberation movement.

CHAPTER TWO

Female Crime: The Statistical Picture

INTRODUCTION

Although the number of women involved in crime is debated in the literature, we must attempt to estimate female participation as accurately as possible, since our theoretical analysis necessarily depends on this. Therefore, this chapter summarizes recent statistics regarding women and crime and, in addition, explores the difficulties surrounding criminal statistics in general and those relating to women in particular.

I begin by examining the position of women in American society and the changes that have occurred regarding them. This will include an analysis of women's fertility, employment, education, and income over the past 25 years, roughly 1955–1980. I will focus in particular on the decade of the 1970s, the time period most profoundly affected by changes in the roles of women and the women's liberation movement. This discussion will enhance our understanding of women and crime, since criminal patterns are closely associated with structural conditions.[1]

WOMEN IN AMERICA: FERTILITY, EMPLOYMENT, EDUCATION, INCOME

Although the role of women in American society has obviously changed since the turn of the century, in certain respects it has not changed very dramatically since the early 1950s. Birth rates have been dropping, and from the mid-1960s onward, a larger proportion of women, particularly white women, have been postponing marriage until at least age 25. The median age at first marriage increased a full year for women between 1970 and 1978, but most women still marry, and in fact the number of unmarried women over 35 years of age has not changed significantly in this decade, declining slightly from 5.5 percent in 1970 to 4.9 percent in 1978. Moreover, few women remain childless or even bear only one child. The fertility of American women declined during the 1970s, since women 35–39 years old had borne approximately 3 children per woman in 1970, while this figure dropped to about 2.7 children per woman in 1978. The trend is toward smaller families, but as Simon (1975: 20) points out, "smaller families do not imply that female socialization is undergoing a basic departure from the traditional pattern."

Women's representation in the labor force increased by 40 percent between 1948 and 1971. This trend continued during the 1970s, giving women an increasing share in the work force (from about 37 percent in 1970 to about 41 percent in 1978). Women have not, however, achieved positions of prestige and authority in similar proportions. In fact, there have been no substantial changes in the types of employment obtained by men and women over the last 25 years. Women remain concentrated in servicelike roles, with less responsibility and lower income. Table 1 demonstrates this distribution regarding white-collar employment in 1978. Although women occupy more than half of all white-collar positions, most of them are employed in clerical types of work (54.8 percent), where they outnumber men nearly 4 to 1. Moreover, they are also concentrated in very specific jobs within the larger occupational groupings. Among professional workers, for example, women are mainly registered nurses, dieticians, therapists, and teachers (except college and university). Men, however, vastly outnumber women among engineers, lawyers and judges, life and physical scientists, physicians, dentists, and so forth.

In terms of education, women have been as likely as men to graduate from high school for at least the last 25 years. Substantial differences existed regarding college education, but this has begun to change. Between 1950 and 1970, the proportion of women college graduates increased by 70 percent (Simon, 1975: 26). This expansion continued through the 1970s. In 1970, women had received 43 percent of the

TABLE 1. OCCUPATION OF EMPLOYED PERSONS, BY SEX: ANNUAL AVERAGES FOR 1978 (Numbers in thousands. Civilian noninstitutional population 16 years and over.)

Occupation 1978	Women	Women (percent)	Men	Men (percent)
Total employed	38,882		55,491	
White-Collar Workers				
Total	24,572	100	22,634	100
Professional, technical, and kindred workers	6,082	24.7	8,163	36.1
Accountants	293		682	
Computer specialists	99		329	
Engineers	35		1,231	
Lawyers and judges	47		452	
Librarians, archivists, and curators	163		38	
Life and physical scientists	49		224	
Personnel and labor relations workers	177		228	
Physicians, dentists, and related practitioners	79		677	
Registered nurses, dietitians, and therapists	1,255		96	
Health technologists and technicians	353		145	
Religious workers	48		277	
Social scientists	86		169	
Social and recreation workers	308		197	
Teachers, college and university	190		372	
Teachers, except college and university	2,124		868	
Engineering and science technicians	132		853	
Writers, artists, and entertainers	424		768	
All other professional, technical, and kindred workers	220		557	
Managers and administrators, except farm	2,361	9.6	7,744	34.2
Bank officers and financial managers	174		399	
Health administrators	85		99	
Office managers	241		130	
Officials and administrators, public administration	104		316	
Restaurant, cafeteria, and bar managers	199		390	
Sales managers and department heads, retail trade	128		215	
Sales managers, except retail trade	23		307	
All other managers and administrators	1,407		5,888	
Sales workers	2,666	10.8	3,285	14.5
Demonstrators, hucksters, and peddlers	255		45	
Insurance agents, brokers, and underwriters	111		437	
Real estate agents and brokers	250		304	
Sales clerks, retail trade	1,671		667	
All other sales workers	379		1,832	
Clerical and kindred workers	13,463	54.8	3,442	15.2
Bank tellers	411		38	
Bookkeepers	1,659		171	
Cashiers	1,222		180	
Estimators and investigators	241		209	
Mail carriers, post office	30		226	
Office machine operators	614		213	
Receptionists	570		18	
Secretaries, stenographers, and typists	4,654		74	
Shipping and receiving clerks	105		355	
Stock clerks and storekeepers	158		349	
Teachers aides, except school monitors	315		27	
Telephone operators	293		19	
All other clerical and kindred workers	3,191		1,563	

Source: Adapted from *A Statistical Portrait of Women in the United States: 1978* (Washington, D.C.: U.S. Dept. of Commerce, Bureau of the Census, 1980), Table 8–1.

TABLE 2. DEGREES CONFERRED BY INSTITUTIONS OF HIGHER
EDUCATION IN THE UNITED STATES, BY SELECTED FIELDS OF
STUDY: ACADEMIC YEAR 1976–1977

	Bachelor's degree		Master's degree		Doctoral degree	
Year and field of study	Number of women receiving degree	Percent of degrees received by women	Number of women receiving degree	Percent of degrees received by women	Number of women receiving degree	Percent of degrees received by women
All fields	424,004	46.1	149,381	47.1	8,090	24.3
Biological sciences ..	19,387	36.2	2,396	33.7	726	21.4
Business and management	35,583	23.4	6,664	14.3	55	6.3
Education	103,740	72.2	83,201	65.8	2,769	34.8
Engineering	2,218	4.5	720	4.4	73	2.8
Fine and applied arts	25,627	61.3	4,425	51.2	215	32.5
Foreign languages ..	10,573	75.8	2,182	69.3	387	51.5
Health professions ..	45,381	79.2	8,788	67.9	172	32.0
Physical sciences	4,501	20.0	· 881	16.5	319	9.5
Social sciences	46,131	39.3	5,089	32.9	835	22.1

Source: Adapted from *A Statistical Portrait of Women in the United States: 1978*
(Washington, D.C.: U.S. Dept. of Commerce, Bureau of the Census, 1980). Table 5–3.

bachelor's degrees awarded. By 1977 this increased to 46 percent (Table
2). These are substantial gains from 1950, when women received less
than one quarter of college degrees. Women concentrate in certain fields
— education, foreign languages, and health professions — and they still
receive less than 25 percent of doctoral degrees, but their educational
achievements are among the brightest changes in their social position.

The discrimination faced by women is most evident in terms of income. Figure 1 indicates that working women, black and white, continue to receive substantially lower earnings than their male counterparts.
The gap between men's and women's salaries has not narrowed over the
past 25 years (Simon, 1975: 29) nor, in particular, has it narrowed
through the 1970s. In 1970 women working year round and full-time
earned 59 percent of what comparably employed men earned; in 1977
this figure remained unchanged. Even when we control for the type of
employment (Table 3) or level of education (Table 4), women's salaries
remain substantially lower than those of men. Thus, as ·of 1977, women
professional and technical workers earned 66 percent of what comparably employed men earned; the ratio is 42 percent among sales workers,
and even among clericals, women earn only 62 percent of what similarly
employed men earn. Likewise, regarding education, in 1977 female college graduates had a median income not quite two-thirds that of their
male counterparts. In fact, such women had incomes generally lower

Figure I. Median Earnings of Year-Round, Full-Time Workers with Income, by Race and Sex: 1970–1977 (Persons 14 years and over).

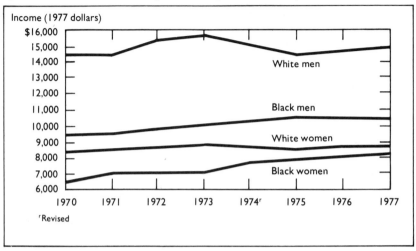

Source: *A Statistical Portrait of Women in the United States: 1978* **(Washington, D.C.: U.S. Dept. of Commerce, Bureau of the Census, 1980), Figure 12–2.**

than males with only a high school education (*Statistical Portrait*, 1980: 70).

Minority women have been hardest hit. In 1978, their unemployment rate (13.1 percent) was more than double that of white women. This is particularly significant since many of them support their families (39 percent of black families were headed by a woman in 1978, compared with 12 percent of white families). Among these women, 51 percent were below the poverty level in 1977 compared to 24 percent of similar white families. These figures continue to support Crites's (1976: 37) assertion that, "in spite of the women's rights movement, unemployment, underemployment, and poverty are visited mostly on women and disproportionately on minority women."

These statistics indicate that in many respects the status of American women has not radically changed over the last 10 or 20 years. Certainly, more women are delaying marriage, more are attending college, they are having fewer children, and are more likely to join the labor force once their children begin school; but little change has occurred in the types of jobs they are holding or the amount of compensation they are receiving relative to men. The overwhelming majority still marry and have children. The recent women's movement successfully increased the legal rights of women and made Americans more aware of women's inferior position in our society, but crucial alterations in terms of occupation and

TABLE 3. MEDIAN EARNINGS OF YEAR-ROUND, FULL-TIME CIVILIAN WORKERS WITH EARNINGS, BY OCCUPATION OF LONGEST JOB AND SEX: 1977 and 1970 (In 1977 dollars. Numbers in thousands. Persons as of the following year. Civilian noninstitutional population 14 years and over.)

Occupation of longest job	1977		Ratio Women/ Men	1970		Ratio Women/ Men
	Median earnings Women	Men		Median earnings Women	Men	
Total	$8,618	$14,626	0.59	$8,307	$13,993	0.59
Professional, technical, and kindred workers	11,995	18,224	0.66	12,251	19,125	0.64
Salaried	12,026	17,810	0.68	12,260	18,629	0.66
Self-employed	(B)	26,946	(X)	(B)	31,261	(X)
Managers and administrators, except farm	9,799	18,086	0.54	9,940	18,205	0.55
Salaried	10,272	19,023	0.54	10,745	19,659	0.55
Self-employed	4,258	12,428	0.34	5,635	12,121	0.46
Sales workers	6,825	16,067	0.42	6,514	15,239	0.43
Clerical and kindred workers	8,601	13,966	0.62	8,644	13,502	0.64
Craft and kindred workers.	8,902	14,517	0.61	7,733	14,440	0.54
Operatives, including transport	7,350	12,612	0.58	6,968	11,929	0.58
Laborers, except farm	7,441	10,824	0.69	6,828	10,085	0.68
Service workers except private household	6,330	10,338	0.61	6,047	10,868	0.56
Private household workers	2,714	(B)	(X)	3,106	(B)	(X)
Farmers and farm managers	(B)	5,601	(X)	(B)	6,057	(X)
Farm laborers and supervisors	(B)	7,278	(X)	(B)	5,236	(X)

Source: Adapted from *A Statistical Picture of Women in the United States: 1978* (Washington, D.C.: U.S. Dept. of Commerce, Bureau of the Census, 1980), Table 9–4.

income simply have not occurred. I am *not* arguing that women are the same as they were at the turn of the century, 25 years ago, or even a decade ago. Profound differences exist in the way women view themselves and in their values and expectations. Moreover, these changes could become much greater as the ramifications of the women's movement, and legal and cultural change, are experienced by new generations of women. But anyone who feels that the battle has been won and that women have attained an equal if not privileged position in our society is incorrect. The "hard data" substantiate the vast inequality that continues to exist. Although changing values, opinions, and attitudes should not be dismissed — indeed they crucially affect the way we choose to live our lives — neither should we assume that traditional expectations (marriage, family, et cetera) or traditional barriers (types of employment, wages, and so forth) have been discarded or surmounted. Structural changes in women's education and labor force participation, as well as exposure to the women's movement, have changed women and undermined, but not

TABLE 4. MEDIAN INCOME OF YEAR-ROUND, FULL-TIME CIVILIAN WORKERS 25 YEARS OLD AND OVER WITH INCOME, BY YEARS OF SCHOOL COMPLETED AND SEX: 1977 and 1970 (In 1977 dollars. Numbers in thousands. Persons as of the following year. Civilian noninstitutional population.)

Age and years of school completed	1977 Median income		Ratio	1970 Median income		Ratio
	Women	Men	Women/ Men	Women	Men	Women/ Men
Total	$ 9,257	$15,726	0.59	$ 8,764	$14,859	0.59
Elementary: 0 to 7 years	6,074	9,419	0.64	5,927	9,431	0.63
8 years	6,564	12,083	0.54	6,525	11,759	0.55
High school: 1 to 3 years	7,387	13,120	0.56	7,265	13,287	0.55
4 years	8,894	15,434	0.58	8,708	14,930	0.58
College: 1 to 3 years	10,157	16,235	0.63	10,306	17,452	0.59
4 or more years	12,656	20,625	0.61	13,607	21,647	0.63

Source: Adapted from *A Statistical Portrait of Women in the United States: 1978* (Washington, D.C.: U.S. Dept. of Commerce, Bureau of the Census, 1980), Table 9–3.

replaced, traditional expectations.

Bearing this information in mind, we will examine the statistics on women and crime to see what changes have occurred in female criminality and how this relates to the status of women.

STATISTICS ON CRIME

Since 1930, the Federal Bureau of Investigation has published an annual report on crime in the United States: the *Uniform Crime Reports*. This document tabulates crimes *reported* to the police[2] and also records the number of people *arrested* and their crimes, as well as their age, sex, and racial background. In addition, changes over time are noted.

Offenses are divided into two categories: Type I and Type II. Type I offences (deemed more serious) are subdivided into (1) violent crimes (criminal homicide, forcible rape, aggravated assault, and robbery) and (2) property crimes (burglary, larceny, and auto theft).[3] Arson is also included as a Type I offense, as of 1979. Type II offenses include a variety of less serious offenses: forgery and counterfeiting, drug law violations, gambling, vandalism, fraud, embezzlement, et cetera.[4]

Tabulations of crimes reported to the police are the most comprehensive statistics available and cover the widest field. They have drawbacks, however. Their accuracy necessarily depends on the competency of different police departments throughout the nation, in terms of collecting and recording information about crime. In addition, many crimes are simply unknown, and cannot be recorded by the police.[5] Finally, many *known* crimes go unreported by the public for various reasons.[6] Thus, the "actual crime rate" is undoubtedly much higher than the statistics indicate. This assumption is supported by research estimating crime unofficially, including surveys of victims and anonymous self-report measures.[7]

Although the statistics on crime are far from precise, they are still valuable, since they reduce the amount of unknown information, and are at least useful in speculating on the amount of criminal involvement.[8] But the most important drawback of police statistics, for our purposes, is that they rarely describe the offender. They cover a wider range of crime, but they cannot tell us if those involved were young, old, white, black, male, or female. To examine the issue of women and crime, we are forced to use *arrest* statistics since they alone indicate personal characteristics, such as age, race, and sex. They depend, however, upon the discretion of arresting officers and, unfortunately, are another step removed from the volume of crime actually taking place.[9] I will discuss the problems associated with arrest statistics more closely later. First, let us examine the available data on women and crime.

WOMEN CRIMINALS: THE STATISTICS

Uniform Crime Reports

Many more men are arrested than women. In 1979, for example, arrests of males outnumbered those of females, five to one, and even this represented a narrowing of the gap between male and female arrests. The percentage of women arrested has increased, however, for crime in general, as well as serious offenses in particular (Type I offenses, excluding rape). Still, as of 1979, women represented only 15.7 percent of arrests for all crimes, and 19.5 percent of arrests for serious crimes. This is considerably less than their proportion of the population, even though it marks a rise over the past 25 years and, more particularly, an increase from 1970.

I will begin by briefly examining Rita Simon's analysis of *Uniform Crime Reports* data on female crime trends from 1955 to 1970. Then I will analyze more closely changes that have occurred during the 1970s since this supposedly represents a time of great change in women's social position and their criminal involvement.

As shown in Table 5, the percentage of arrests for serious crimes among all female arrests has generally increased. It was 8.5 percent in 1955, 18.9 percent in 1965, and 23.8 percent by 1970. Among males, this percentage has also increased, but not as rapidly. In addition, a smaller proportion of males are arrested for serious crimes (18.4 percent in 1970), yet numerically these arrests are much higher than among females.

TABLE 5. MALES AND FEMALES ARRESTED FOR SERIOUS CRIMES AS PERCENTAGES OF THEIR RESPECTIVE SEX COHORTS ARRESTED FOR ALL CRIMES FOR SELECTED YEARS: 1955–1970

Year	Females arrested for serious crimes as percent of all females arrested	Males arrested for serious crimes as percent of all males arrested
1955	8.5	10.4
1960	12.4	12.6
1965	18.9	15.5
1970	23.8	18.4

Source: Adapted from Rita Simon, *Women and Crime* (Lexington, Mass.: Lexington Books, 1975) p. 37.

This increase in the percentage of females arrested for serious crimes has, however, been confined to serious *property* crimes. The percentage of females arrested for violent crimes has, however, fluctuated very little (see Table 6). Thus, the increasing proportion of women arrested for serious crimes is due almost entirely to changes in their rate of property offenses.

TABLE 6. BREAKDOWN OF SERIOUS CRIMES: PERCENTAGE OF FEMALES ARRESTED AMONG ALL ARRESTS FOR VIOLENT AND PROPERTY CRIMES FOR SELECTED YEARS: 1955–1970

Year	Violent crimes	Property crimes	Serious crimes
1955	12.03	8.36	9.12
1960	11.77	10.76	10.95
1965	11.41	14.99	14.37
1970	10.50	19.71	18.04

Source: Adapted from Rita Simon, *Women and Crime* (Lexington, Mass.: Lexington Books, 1975) p. 38.

Table 7 gives much the same information but allows us to compare the changes among arrested females and males separately. Obviously, the percentage of females arrested for violent crimes (among all females arrested) barely changed from 1955 through 1970. The proportion of men arrested for violent crimes increased much more than that of women whereas, in regard to property crimes, the reverse applies.

TABLE 7. FEMALES AND MALES ARRESTED FOR CRIMES OF VIOLENCE
AND PROPERTY AS PERCENTAGE OF ALL ARRESTS IN THEIR
RESPECTIVE SEX COHORTS FOR SELECTED YEARS: 1955–1970

Year	Violent crimes		Property crimes	
	Female	Male	Female	Male
1955	2.3	2.1	6.2	8.3
1960	2.5	2.4	9.9	10.2
1965	2.6	2.7	16.3	12.8
1970	2.5	3.6	21.3	14.8

Source: Adapted from Rita Simon, *Women and Crime* (Lexington, Mass.: Lexington
Books, 1975) p. 39.

The arrest figures for women among Type I offenses are significant.
Table 8 indicates that among the six serious offenses (rape has been omitted), only *one* shows a marked increase for women over time: larceny-
theft. Until 1960, the proportions of women arrested for homicide and
aggravated assault were similar to that of larceny-theft. Since 1960,
however, larceny-theft has almost doubled while homicide and aggravated assault decreased slightly. Although the percentage of females
arrested for robbery, burglary, and auto theft increased somewhat, their
participation is minor compared to the total arrests for these crimes. By
1970, only larceny-theft showed a significant female involvement — this
was double the percentage of women involved in any other type of serious crime, yet still *less than one-third* the percentage of males arrested for
that crime.

The percentages of women involved in certain Type II offenses have
also changed. As indicated in Table 9, the percentage of females arrested
for embezzlement and fraud, forgery and counterfeiting, and offenses
against family and children have all increased. The first two increased

TABLE 8. FEMALES ARRESTED AS PERCENTAGE OF ALL ARRESTS FOR TYPE
I OFFENSES FOR SELECTED YEARS: 1955–1970.[a]

Year	Criminal homicide	Robbery	Aggravated assault	Burglary	Larceny-theft	Auto theft
1955	14.2	4.2	16.0	2.3	13.3	2.6
1960	16.1	4.6	15.3	2.8	16.8	3.6
1965	16.3	5.3	14.4	3.8	23.2	4.2
1970	14.8	6.2	13.3	4.6	29.0	5.0

[a]Rape has been omitted.
Source: Adapted from Rita Simon, *Women and Crime* (Lexington, Mass.: Lexington
Books, 1975), p. 40.

TABLE 9. OTHER CRIMES: FEMALES ARRESTED AS PERCENTAGE OF ALL
PEOPLE ARRESTED FOR VARIOUS CRIMES FOR SELECTED YEARS:
1955–1970

Year	Embezzlement and fraud	Forgery and counterfeiting	Offenses against family and children	Narcotic drug laws	Prostitution and commercialized vice
1955	15.6	15.2	9.8	17.1	68.8
1960	15.7	16.8	9.7	14.6	73.5
1965	20.7	19.2	11.0	13.4	77.6
1970	27.8	24.4	11.3	15.7	79.1

Source: Adapted from Rita Simon, *Women and Crime* (Lexington, Mass.: Lexington Books, 1975) p. 43.

most dramatically and could be compared to female involvement in larceny-theft. In 1970, women accounted for 27.8 percent of those arrested for embezzlement and fraud; 24.4 percent of those arrested for forgery and counterfeiting. Their percentage of arrests for narcotic drug laws had declined slightly to 15.7 percent. Their involvement in commercialized vice and prostitution seemed to increase through the 1960s to 79.1 percent in 1970.[10] Significantly, this crime category and runaways are the only ones in which the participation of women officially surpasses that of men. Rita Simon (1975: 42) observes that if present trends continue, "approximately equal numbers of men and women will be arrested for larceny and for fraud and embezzlement by the 1990s; and for forgery and counterfeiting the proportions should be equal by the 2010s." Present trends also indicate a decreasing percentage of female involvement in homicide and aggravated assault.

The 1970s

Data from the *Uniform Crime Reports* indicate that women's crime generally increased from 1955 through 1970, particularly property offenses, and mainly larceny-theft. What has happened during the 1970s to women's participation in crime? Many observers predicted and publicized vast increases in female crime in the wake of increasing freedom for women. Do the arrest statistics of the F.B.I. support this? We will look first at 1979 F.B.I. figures, then at changes over the decade. Table 10 examines the distribution of arrests by sex for all offenses in 1979. Here we see that women are still vastly underrepresented in official statistics. They account for only 15.7 percent of all arrests (bear in mind they are more than half our population) and 19.5 percent of serious arrests. Similar to earlier patterns, their involvement in serious crime was still largely con-

TABLE 10. TOTAL ARRESTS, DISTRIBUTION BY SEX: 1979 (11,758 agencies, 1979 estimated population 204,622,000)

Offense charged	Number of persons arrested			Male percent	Female percent
	Total	Male	Female		
TOTAL	9,506,347	8,011,417	1,494,930	84.3	15.7
Murder and nonnegligent					
manslaughter	18,264	15,761	2,503	86.3	13.7
Forcible rape	29,164	28,945	219	99.2	8
Robbery	130,753	121,107	9,646	92.6	7.4
Aggravated assault	256,597	224,753	31,844	87.6	12.4
Burglary	468,085	438,411	29,674	93.7	6.3
Larceny-theft	1,098,398	765,862	332,536	69.7	30.3
Motor vehicle theft	143,654	130,840	12,814	91.1	8.9
Arson	18,387	16,303	2,084	88.7	11.3
Violent crime[1]	434,778	390,566	44,212	89.8	10.2
Property crime[2]	1,728,524	1,351,416	377,108	78.2	21.8
Crime Index total[3]	2,163,302	1,741,982	421,320	80.5	19.5
Other assaults	451,475	390,055	61,420	86.4	13.6
Forgery and counterfeiting	70,977	49,016	21,961	69.1	30.9
Fraud	243,461	145,185	98,276	59.6	40.4
Embezzlement	7,882	5,884	1,998	74.7	25.3
Stolen property; buying,					
receiving, possessing	107,621	96,107	11,514	89.3	10.7
Vandalism	239,246	219,118	20,128	91.6	8.4
Weapons; carrying,					
possessing, etc.	152,731	141,496	11,235	92.6	7.4
Prostitution and					
commercialized vice ..	83,088	26,992	56,096	32.5	67.5
Sex offenses (except					
forcible rape and					
prostitution)	62,633	57,764	4,869	92.2	7.8
Drug abuse violations ...	519,377	449,137	70,240	86.5	13.5
Gambling	50,974	46,151	4,823	90.5	9.5
Offenses against family					
and children	53,321	48,031	5,290	90.1	9.9
Driving under the					
influence	1,231,665	1,124,798	106,867	91.3	8.7
Liquor laws	386,957	330,180	56,777	85.3	14.7
Drunkenness	1,090,233	1,010,569	79,664	92.7	7.3
Disorderly conduct	711,730	602,336	109,394	84.6	15.4
Vagrancy	34,662	26,851	7,811	77.5	22.5
All other offenses					
(except traffic)	1,595,864	1,359,734	236,130	85.2	14.8
Suspicion	18,135	15,502	2,633	85.5	14.5
Curfew and loitering					
law violations	78,147	60,923	17,224	78.0	22.0
Runaways	152,866	63,606	89,260	41.6	58.4

[1] Violent crimes include murder, forcible rape, robbery, and aggravated assault.
[2] Property crimes include burglary, larceny-theft, motor vehicle theft, and arson.
[3] Includes arson, a newly established Index offense in 1979.
Source: Adapted from *Uniform Crime Reports* (Washington, D.C.: Federal Bureau of Investigation, U.S. Dept. of Justice, 1979). Table 34.

fined to property offenses in 1979. They account for 21.8 percent of serious property crimes and only 10.2 percent of violent crimes.

Scanning Type II offenses, we see that even here, most of those arrested are male. Female arrests exceed those of males only in two categories: prostitution and runaways. Female arrests for forgery and counterfeiting, fraud, and embezzlement are somewhat high, although male arrests are higher. In every other crime category females represent less than one quarter of those arrested, and sometimes much less than this.

Examining Table 11, we can see that the percentage of arrests among females increased during the 1970s, although their volume of crime is still extremely limited compared to that of males. For example, their arrests for auto theft increased 54 percent over the decade (while male arrests for auto theft declined); but looked at another way, roughly 8,000 women were arrested for auto theft in 1979 compared to 80,000 men. Their arrests also declined in certain categories throughout this decade (murder, embezzlement, sex offenses, gambling, offenses against the family and children, drunkenness, and so on).

Table 12 examines female arrest trends for the latter part of the 1970s. Although female arrests for many crimes increased over the entire decade, decreases are frequently noted in the latter part of the 1970s. Between 1975 and 1979, for example, female arrests for murder, robbery, stolen property, weapons charges, drug abuse violations, gambling, embezzlement, and even larceny-theft decreased. A similar pattern of decreasing arrests occurred in many categories between 1978 and 1979. These figures do not seem to verify the gloomy predictions about vastly increasing crime among newly "liberated" women.

Finally, Table 13 indicates the crimes for which men and women are most likely to be arrested. These crimes are crucial since they account for 69 percent of the men and fully 71 percent of the women arrested in 1979. For women, larceny-theft represents, by far, the largest category. Arrests for driving under the influence rank first among men. The comparatively minor offenses for which most men and particularly women are arrested should be noted.

Conclusion

Important changes have occurred in women's participation in crime (insofar, at least, as arrest rates indicate). Females represent a greater proportion of arrests in 1979 than they did 25 years before. This increase is mainly in "serious" offenses, and almost entirely within serious property crimes, particularly larceny-theft. Violent crime among females, however, has barely changed. Within Type II offenses, fraud and forgery-

TABLE 11. TOTAL ARREST TRENDS BY SEX: 1970–1979 (3,943 agencies; 1979 estimated population 114,952,000)

Offense charged	Males			Females		
	Total			Total		
	1970	1979	Percent change	1970	1979	Percent change
TOTAL	4,440,899	4,590,254	+3.4	743,226	923,363	+24.2
Murder and nonnegligent manslaughter	8,247	9,530	+15.6	1,524	1,497	−1.8
Forcible rape	11,754	17,904	+52.3	3	136	+4,433.3
Robbery	56,651	77,032	+36.0	3,580	6,241	+74.3
Aggravated assault	82,221	129,499	+57.5	11,906	18,934	+59.0
Burglary	212,245	267,226	+25.9	10,737	18,430	+71.6
Larceny-theft	350,992	493,752	+40.7	138,826	224,769	+61.9
Motor vehicle theft	95,284	80,169	−15.9	5,329	8,207	+54.0
Arson	6,454	9,491	+47.1	611	1,232	+101.6
Violent crime[1]	158,873	233,965	+47.3	17,013	26,808	+57.6
Property crime[2]	664,975	850,638	+27.9	155,503	252,638	+62.5
Crime Index total[3]	823,848	1,084,603	+31.7	172,516	279,446	+62.0

Other assaults	196,384	240,377	+22.4	29,220	39,410	+34.9
Forgery and counterfeiting	25,077	28,959	+15.5	8,366	13,590	+62.4
Fraud	44,423	73,076	+64.5	16,673	51,041	+206.1
Embezzlement	4,610	3,065	-33.5	1,704	1,059	-37.9
Stolen property; buying, receiving, possessing	34,794	56,755	+63.2	3,600	6,865	+90.7
Vandalism	79,543	134,131	+68.6	6,759	12,616	+86.7
Weapons; carrying, possessing, etc.	73,520	90,206	+22.7	5,321	7,504	+41.0
Prostitution and commercialized vice	7,662	19,288	+151.7	26,771	36,847	+37.6
Sex offenses (except forcible rape and prostitution)	34,707	38,494	+10.9	5,427	3,645	-32.8
Drug abuse violations	211,824	273,117	+28.9	42,329	44,786	+5.8
Gambling	56,992	32,875	-42.3	4,981	3,497	-29.8
Offenses against family and children	39,108	21,385	-45.3	4,095	3,108	-24.1
Driving under the influence	337,786	540,905	+60.1	24,558	55,219	+124.9
Liquor laws	151,899	187,616	+23.5	22,408	33,324	+48.7
Drunkenness	1,195,079	641,367	-46.3	91,143	51,745	-43.2
Disorderly conduct	428,046	401,003	-6.3	73,481	78,386	+6.7
Vagrancy	46,452	15,737	-66.1	6,847	2,487	-63.7
All other offenses (except traffic)	508,542	622,746	+22.5	103,245	127,961	+23.9
Suspicion (not included in totals)	49,617	9,190	-81.5	7,995	1,632	-79.6
Curfew and loitering law violations	70,169	43,649	-37.8	18,286	11,583	-36.6
Runaways	70,434	40,880	-42.0	75,496	59,242	-21.5

[1] Violent crimes are offenses of murder, forcible rape, robbery, and aggravated assault.

[2] Property crimes are offenses of burglary, larceny-theft, motor vehicle theft, and arson.

[3] Includes arson, a newly established Index offense in 1979.

Source: Adapted from *Uniform Crime Reports* (Washington, D.C.: Federal Bureau of Investigation, U.S. Dept. of Justice, 1979), Table 27.

TABLE 12. TOTAL ARREST TRENDS FOR FEMALES: 1975–1978, 1978–1979

Offense charged	Percentage change 1978–1979	Offense charged	Percentage change 1975–1979
Murder and nonnegligent manslaughter	−1.9	Murder and nonnegligent manslaughter	−19.1
Forcible rape	−1.9	Forcible rape	−10.2
Robbery	+6.0	Robbery	−8.6
Aggravated assault	+3.1	Aggravated assault	+4.3
Burglary	+1.8	Burglary	+4.6
Larceny-theft	−1.2	Larceny-theft	−1.2
Motor vehicle theft	+3.3	Motor vehicle theft	+30.7
Arson	−1.0	Arson	+8.8
Violent crime[1]	+3.4	Violent crime[1]	−.4
Property crime[2]	−.8	Property crime[2]	+.1
Other assaults	+3.4	Other assault	+6.6
Forgery and counterfeiting	+2.6	Forgery and counterfeiting	+12.7
Fraud	+11.0	Fraud	+48.8
Embezzlement	+6.4	Embezzlement	−46.1
Stolen property; buying, receiving, possessing	−4.8	Stolen property; buying, receiving, possessing	−7.6
Vandalism	+10.1	Vandalism	+21.6
Weapons; carrying, possessing, etc.	+.9	Weapons; carrying, possessing, etc.	−12.2
Prostitution and commercialized vice	−3.7	Prostitution and commercialized vice	+20.1
Sex offenses (except forcible rape and prostitution)	−3.7	Sex offenses (except forcible rape and prostitution)	+16.4
Drug abuse violations	−12.3	Drug abuse violations	−16.1
Gambling	+5.4	Gambling	−15.4
Offenses against family and children	−5.5	Offenses against family and children	−25.8
Driving under the influence	+5.7	Driving under the influence	+25.7
Liquor laws	+11.5	Liquor laws	+35.1
Drunkenness	−4.2	Drunkenness	−18.5
Disorderly conduct	+.7	Disorderly conduct	−35.2
Vagrancy	−40.8	Vagrancy	+21.9
All other offenses (except traffic)	−2.1	All other offenses (except traffic)	+26.6
Suspicion (not included in totals)	+3.4	Suspicion (not included in totals)	−48.2
Curfew and loitering law violations	+.4	Curfew and loitering law violations	−33.6
Runaways	−8.5	Runaways	−29.5

[1]Violent crimes are offenses of murder, forcible rape, robbery, and aggravated assault.
[2]Property crimes include burglary, larceny-theft, motor vehicle theft, and arson.
Source: Adapted from *Uniform Crime Reports* (Washington, D.C.: Federal Bureau of Investigation, U.S. Dept, of Justice, 1979), Tables 29, 31.

TABLE 13. RANK ORDER OF OFFENSES FOR WHICH FEMALES AND MALES
ARE MOST LIKELY TO BE ARRESTED: 1979

Rank	Offense	Percentage arrested out of all female arrests	Offense	Percentage arrested out of all male arrests
1	Larceny-theft	22.2	Driving under the influence	14.0
2	Disorderly conduct	7.3	Drunkenness	12.6
3	Driving under the influence	7.1	Larceny-theft	9.6
4	Fraud	6.6	Disorderly conduct	7.5
5	Runaways	6.0	Drug abuse violations	5.6
6	Drunkenness	5.3	Burglary	5.5
7	Drug abuse violations	4.7	Other assaults	4.9
8	Other assaults	4.1	Liquor laws	4.1
9	Prostitution	3.8	Aggravated assault	2.8
10	Liquor laws	3.8	Vandalism	2.7

Source: Adapted from *Uniform Crime Reports* (Washington, D.C.: Federal Bureau of Investigation, U.S. Dept. of Justice, 1979), Table 34.

counterfeiting show significant increases. Except for prostitution and runaways, there are no other offenses in which women are so strongly represented as larceny-theft, fraud, and forgery-counterfeiting.

The data presented earlier on the status of American women indicated limited changes, in many respects, over the past 25 years. Similarly, the criminality of women is still very low, as it was 25 years ago. There have been, however, important changes in female crime, although this is insignificant compared to potential changes in women's role and their crime.

A Note on Race and Social Class

Amid all these statistics, I have not mentioned the race or social class of women criminals. Incredibly, the F.B.I. does not record this information. Such omissions are telling, since they accurately, if unintentionally, mirror assumptions and concerns underlying official reactions to crime.

While national statistics on the racial breakdown of women offenders are lacking, individual studies (Wolfgang, 1966; Winick and Kinsie, 1971) reveal that black female criminality more closely approaches that of black men than white female criminality does that of white men and, moreover, that "the black female's criminality exceeds that of the white female by a much greater margin than black males over white males" (Adler, 1975: 139). As usual, it is difficult to say whether the crime rate of black females exceeds that of white females because of actual differences in criminal participation or whether, and to what extent, differential law enforcement distorts these figures.

Although the official crime rate for males always exceeds that of females, perhaps the smaller differential among American blacks occurs because black males and females more closely approach each other in social standing compared to their white counterparts. This should alert us to the fact that inherent sexual differences do not explain varying rates of crime. Social variables are crucial.[11]

There is a tremendous discrepancy between the number of offenses committed by women and the number of women who find themselves in prison. Simon's data (1975) indicate that in 1971, 18 out of every 100 people arrested for serious crimes were women, while only 3 out of 100 sentenced to federal or state prison were women. Figure 2 indicates that the vast majority of inmates in state and federal prisons throughout the 1970s were men. This reflects, in part, the minor offenses in which women are involved. The particular women who are arrested are mainly poor, frequently responsible for supporting themselves and others, and, in addition, uneducated (Crites, 1976; Simon, 1975).[12] A recent study by Glick (1974–1976) reported that 64 percent of institutionalized women are from racial minorities.

PROBLEMS WITH STATISTICS

Statistics are open to interpretation and, as we shall see, can be manipulated. I would like to discuss some of the difficulties associated with statistics on female crime, in order to allow the reader a more reasonable and informed assessment of them.

Arrest Statistics

While arrest statistics in general are fraught with difficulties,[13] the statistics on women are particularly problematic. Criminologists frequently argue that female offenders are the beneficiaries of lenient treatment throughout the criminal justice system. As the argument goes, the public perceives women as less threatening — so they do not demand official intervention for female misbehavior, male criminals often protect their female partners, and even police officers are less likely to detain or arrest a woman. This necessarily shrinks female arrest statistics.[14]

Figure 2. Sentenced Prisoners in State and Federal Institutions on December 31, by Sex, United States: 1971–1977.

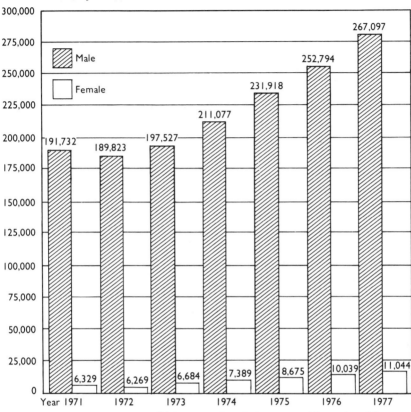

Source: *Sourcebook of Criminal Statistics* (Washington, D.C.: U.S. Department of Justice, Law Enforcement Assistance Administration, 1979, Figure 6.6.

These arguments have found a warm reception among the public and, to some extent, appeal to common sense. Yet, common sense is often an unreliable index of reality, and, in this case, empirical evidence fails to support these notions of chivalry. The data are inconclusive but suggest that the treatment of women is often much harsher than that of men. Moreover, if chivalry is at work, its benefits are not likely to be equally distributed. Middle-class offenders and white offenders can expect more consideration. Dorie Klein (1973: 23) notes this succinctly:

> Chivalry is a racist and classist concept founded on the notion of women as "ladies" which applies to wealthy white women. . . . These "ladies," however, are the least likely ever to come in contact with the criminal justice system in the first place.

When people nod their heads and agree that the police undoubtedly are chivalrous with females, the offender they visualize more likely resembles a white, middle-class college student than a poor black prostitute. Preferential treatment can be accorded both males and females, but leniency is frequently drawn along class and racial lines. Lower-class black women are unlikely to be treated with unbounded chivalry, yet they are still underrepresented in crime compared to males. Admittedly, few women go the complete route of the criminal justice system and find themselves in prison. But as Babcock (1973: 292) has shown, those who do are "almost all poor, almost all from racial minorities, and almost all accused or convicted of non-violent crimes."

The issue of chivalry is frequently used to challenge the reliability of female arrest statistics, and therefore it merits further consideration. I will briefly examine the treatment of women in other areas of our criminal justice system to see if this can throw some light on the reliability of the statistics.

Chivalry Revisited

Women in court.   Nagel and Weitzman (1971) argue that women receive favorable treatment in court due to paternalism. Women are less likely to be convicted, detained before trial, or punished as severely as men. Yet, they also lack protection since they are less likely to have an attorney, a preliminary hearing, or a jury trial. Nagel and Weitzman found paternalism operating in both assault and larceny cases, but less evident with assault, which is, presumably, more unacceptable for a women. Other evidence (Temin, 1973) disputes these findings on paternalism and documents more punitive treatment of women, particularly young females. Girls are more likely than boys to be incarcerated for minor offenses, despite less extensive records. Furthermore, they spend more time in facilities that are stricter and less adequate than those for males (Singer, 1973).

Convictions and sentencing.   Unfortunately, there are no comprehensive judicial statistics for the United States. Among the states, however, California has the best and most complete data. Crites (1976) found that an examination of the 1972 court statistics in California generally indicated an even-handed treatment of men and women. Simon (1975) also analyzed California data and found, for 1969–1972, a similar proportion of men and women convicted in court. For violent offenses, the proportion of men convicted was slightly higher; for property offenses, conviction rates were equal. But Simon also found that women pleading not guilty are more likely to be acquitted for robbery and burglary as well as larceny. She concludes that this indicates some preferential treatment for women.

Women also seem to get some preferential treatment at sentencing. Crites (1976) maintains, for example, that convicted men are twice as likely to be sent to prison. However, women's crimes are typically nonviolent and, thus, less threatening to the community. The violence they engage in is usually unplanned, and frequently directed against family members or lovers who have been abusive. Moreover, women often play a secondary role in serious crime, and judges might be inclined to consider the impact of imprisonment on a woman's family. Babcock (1973), on the other hand, asserts that women are given indeterminant sentences for potentially longer periods of time than men convicted of the same offenses. Additional evidence of harsh treatment for women is easy to find, particularly when we direct our attention toward the statutes themselves and the treatment of juveniles.

Juvenile justice. Evidence of discrimination against female delinquents is readily available. Terry (1970) and Cohn (1970) found that girls are more likely to be sentenced to institutions. Rogers' study (1972) of juvenile institutions in Connecticut noted that 31 percent of the girls and *none* of the boys were institutionalized for sexual behavior. In addition, 30 percent of the girls were institutionalized for noncriminal offenses (such as being incorrigible), while only 0.05 percent of the boys were incarcerated for such offenses. The vast majority of female offenders were charged with status violations (Sarri, 1976), offenses which are not illegal for adults (such as truancy, promiscuity, curfew violations). Many states permit only females to be arrested for such offenses (Chesney-Lind, 1973). In addition, juvenile courts give severe dispositions to females, although males are more frequently involved in serious offenses. Likewise, females are more likely to get a physical examination. (In the Honolulu juvenile court, 1925–1955, 70–80 percent of the females received examinations; 12–28 percent of the males). Gynecological examinations were ordered for burglary and larceny offenses, reflecting society's unrelenting concern with controlling the sexual activities of minor females as opposed to males.

Self-Report Studies

Official data on women and crime have been interpreted in various ways (Simon, 1975; Adler, 1975; Steffensmeier, Steffensmeier, and Rosenthal, 1979; Noblit and Burcart, 1976, etc.) but overall concerns about the

validity of these data has led to alternative sources of information, including self-report studies. While it may be problematic to use official
arrest statistics as a basis for drawing inferences about trends in female
crime, self-report studies are certainly not unproblematic. They contain
difficulties regarding sampling (most are local, not national, samples),
the honesty of the respondents, and problems of measurement, but they
are well worth examining for a potentially more accurate estimation of
female crime. Here is a sampling of such studies.

Gold and Reimer (1975) examined self-report data on delinquency
among 13-to-16-year-old Americans in 1967 and 1972. This information
was part of a National Survey of Youth. They concluded that offenses
among girls increased during this time period, but mainly offenses such
as drinking and marijuana and drug use. According to Gold and Reimer
(1975: 495), if these offenses are excluded, "we find no change over the 5
years in per capita frequency of offenses among girls." Thus, serious
crime among females had not, in their estimation, become more severe.

Jensen and Eve (1976) distributed questionnaires to 4,000 black and
white adolescents in the Richmond, California, vicinity in 1964–1965.
Examining the results of their study, and other sources of alternative data
(Gold, 1970; Wise, 1967; Hindelang, 1971) led them to conclude that
girls are less delinquent than boys. They assert that precisely why girls
are less criminal is a key issue.

Cernkovich and Giordano (1979) studied the results of questionnaires
they had administered to 822 adolescents in 1977. These boys and girls
were urban high school students in a large midwestern state. Their major
findings were that males are more likely to be involved in delinquent
acts, with the exception of a few minor offenses, although the gap between male and female delinquency is not as great as official data indicate.

Bowker (1978) reviewed various self-report studies on female delinquency (Gold, 1970; Gold and Reimer, 1975; Jensen and Eve, 1976; Kratcoski, and Kratcoski, 1975, etc.) and claims that such studies probably
give a more accurate picture of female delinquency than official statistics.
The lack of studies on adult females, however, is a difficulty. He indicates that self-report studies show smaller differentials between male and
female crime than official data, but that males still greatly outnumber
females. Female property offenses are much more likely to be underreported than serious violent offenses. Female offenses are also more likely
to be inappropriately sexualized, as we have discussed previously. Bowker notes that both official and self-report data confirm that female crime
had been increasing until about 1975, when a decline began. Male-female
differentials in crime have also been decreasing, although this is due
mainly to changes in property offenses. Much of the apparent rise in

female crime is the result of the exceedingly small base statistics from which increases occurred.

Smith and Visher (1980) have cited the inadequacy of official indicators of female crime. They note, however, that no attempt has been made to examine the overall evidence on female crime in various studies completed over the last 25 years. While no general agreement exists regarding female patterns of crime and how they are changing, Smith and Visher summarize the available information, reducing the data on sex and deviance or criminality to a single data base. They include studies on both self-report and official data (44 studies in all during 1940–1975. See Smith and Visher, 1980: 693, for the complete listing).

The findings of Smith and Visher (necessarily based on the studies they examine) indicate that the association between sex and deviance is smaller among the young and among nonwhites than among adults and whites. They contend that official data indicate a greater disparity between the sexes than alternative data, but that the type of offense is a crucial variable. Males are more likely to exceed females regarding more serious offenses. Smith and Visher (1980: 695) also indicate that the gap between male and female deviance is shrinking, but more so for personal offenses (drug and alcohol offenses), youth offenses (truancy, school problems), and even property offenses (theft, fraud) than for violent crimes. Self-report studies indicate a more rapid decline in male-female differentials than do official statistics, although both sets of data support this. Smith and Visher (1980: 697–698) conclude: "Indeed, it appears that women *are* closing the gap in terms of involvement in minor deviant acts, but that equal gender representation in the area of serious criminal behaviour has not yet occurred."

Conclusion

Self-report studies and our discussion of the criminal justice system both reflect legitimate concerns regarding official statistics. However, the notion of a chivalrous criminal justice system should not be accepted at face value. Women are occasionally treated differently from men in our criminal justice system, at times to their disadvantage. Female adolescents are particularly discriminated against. The belief that women receive preferential treatment is frequently based on unreflective assumptions. The double standard is a double-edged sword and can operate to the detriment, as much as to the benefit, of women.

In light of this discussion and self-report studies, I believe it is reasonable to accept the discrepancy between male and female crime rates as generally accurate. Gender differentials appear so consistently that it can be concluded that at least a gross relationship exists in fact. Women may, at times, escape arrest because they are female, but they are also, at times, more apt to be arrested than a male, especially when they fail to meet certain expectations for women in a male-dominated society.

THE "NEW FEMALE CRIMINAL"

Where in all of this is the much heralded "new female criminal"? Freda Adler's treatment (1975) of rising female crime must be discussed in this regard.

Adler argues in rather sensationalist terms that crime among women is rapidly increasing. She states that between 1960 and 1972, the arrest rate for robbery increased 277 percent for females, 169 percent for males. Likewise, embezzlement arrests were up 280 percent for females, 50 percent for males; larceny up 303 percent for females, 82 percent for males; and, finally, burglary was up 168 percent for females, 63 percent for males. This sounds astounding and would lead anyone to imagine that female crime is becoming a phenomenal problem. I will not dispute these figures, but they are only part of the picture and give a totally inaccurate impression. Unless schooled in criminology, or a regular reader of the *Uniform Crime Reports*, one could easily be misled by such statistics. Yes, it is true that female burglary rates are up 168 percent, but, as of 1972, men were still responsible for 94.9 percent of the arrests for burglary, women for only 5.1 percent. Similarly, in 1972 males accounted for 93.4 percent of robbery arrests, 70.3 percent of arrests for embezzlement and fraud, and 69.2 percent of larceny-theft arrests. Adler never gives these statistics. Female arrests are rising, but they are still a minor part of the total crime picture. When presented in this fashion, a much more interesting question surfaces: Why is official crime among women so low? Despite what seems to be astronomical increases in women's crime, they are still extremely underrepresented.

Adler mentions in passing that men are still arrested for the majority of crimes but statements of this sort fail to rectify the distorted impression she has conveyed. She comments that female arests for murder and aggravated assault have not increased. Yet her dramatic discussion of violent crime among women again belies this statement. Her perverse association of female crime and women's liberation, criticized earlier, reappears in her treatment of violent crime. Discussing violence among women, she (1975: 16) comments:

> Since these are primarily offenses of passion in which well over half of the
> victim-offender relationships are interpersonal, as opposed to the econom-

ically motivated offenses, it would appear that the liberated [sic!] female criminals, like their male counterparts, are chiefly interested in improving their financial circumstances and only secondarily in committing violence.

Adler's new woman criminal is more a myth than a reality. As Crites (1976: 38) astutely notes, female crimes are indicative of women's roles in society: "They are predominantly small-scale property and victimless offenses reflecting both the female status as a minor consumer and her tendency to inflict self-directed rather than outward-directed injury." The increases in female crime occur mainly in larceny-theft, which probably indicates greater participation in shoplifting.[15] Here, certainly, is a type of behavior more closely associated with traditional female roles than anything "new."

In addition, increases in fraud and embezzlement arrests among women have been linked to expanding opportunities for white-collar employment and white-collar crime (Adler, 1975; Simon, 1975). Yet, as my examination of female employment demonstrates, women are basically absent from lucrative corporate positions. Increases in female arrests for fraud most likely reflect increases in passing bad checks and welfare fraud and nothing more glamorous, unconventional, or untraditional than this. Indeed, embezzlement, which involves the misuse of entrusted money and implies employment, actually *declined* among women during the 1970s (down 37.9 percent during 1970–1979).

Adler's discussion indicates how statistics can be interpreted — or better, manipulated. The media have focused on rising female criminality, exaggerated it tremendously, and in the process disparaged the women's movement by hinting at connections between liberation and criminal activity. I would argue, on the contrary, that an accurate analysis of these statistics indicates that although female crime is rising somewhat, it is basically limited to a few nonviolent crimes, and that the most challenging and unexplained issue is the astonishing absence of criminality within the female population. I say this bearing in mind the problematic aspects of available statistics, indicating I am willing to believe they are at least generally accurate in portraying the limited involvement in crime of women as compared to men.[16] I find the discussion of hidden crime among women unconvincing, to say the least.

LEGAL INEQUALITY

In order to fully appreciate the statistics on female crime, it is imperative to deal with criminal law. Criminologists have frequently been negligent in this regard, simply accepting the law as given. Yet, law is not distinct from society nor untouched by social influences. Rather, it reflects and bolsters social opinions and values. It mirrors, for example, a dual morality regarding men and women, which, in turn, effects what is defined as criminal behavior and who gets arrested for what. In *Women and the Law*, Leo Kanowitz (1969) argues convincingly that legal discrimination is not a thing of the past, rather "sex-based inequality continues to be a fact of life both here and abroad" (1969: 1). This is due, in part, to the tremendous predominance of men in legislative and judicial capacities. Yet, some observers quickly give this male dominance a sexist cast and make it seem as though women are the villains, not the victims, in this scenario. Take, for example, as prominent a criminologist as Hermann Mannheim (1965: 691):

> The legislators, being male, may have unwittingly moulded the whole system of criminal law in such a way as to turn a blind eye to some of those anti-social actions most frequently committed by women, such as prostitution — which unless accompanied by certain other activities, is not an offense in most countries — or lesbianism, lying or quarrelling.

Note the offenses Mannheim feels men have graciously (if naively) overlooked — like quarrelling and lying — and the explicit assumption that women (not men) frequently engage in this behavior. But men have indeed moulded our legal system, which echoes the contradictions felt toward women: at times regarding them as evil and deceptive, at times treating them as childlike and defenseless. I will briefly examine certain laws, mainly to demonstrate that law must be examined in any thorough treatment of crime.

Criminal Law

To a large extent, criminal law measures the inequality of men and women in our society. For example, laws on prostitution and their enforcement indicate that illicit sexual behavior is more unacceptable in women than men. Illegal in every part of the United States (except Nevada where local counties can choose to legalize it), prostitution nevertheless flourishes. Estimates of the number of full-time prostitutes range from 250,000 to 500,000 (Winick and Kinsie, 1971). Although the customers are typically white, middle-class, middle-aged men, those penalized for this crime are women, frequently black and poor. The double standard and discrimination operate, once again, along class, race, and sexist lines. In certain jurisdictions, only the conduct of the woman is illegal. In others, it is theoretically possible to punish the male customer, but this rarely occurs. Haft (1976: 215), for example, observes that in New York State it is illegal to patronize a prostitute (thus the male is criminally liable), but in 1968 only 112 customers were arrested in New York City as opposed to 8,000 arrests of prostitutes.

Prostitution laws aim to protect the traditional family, but only the woman is punished for such behavior. Many rationalizations are used to explain why the prostitute should be punished and not her customer but, as Kanowitz (1969) points out, female prostitutes could not exist without male customers.

Rape Laws

Rape laws are frequently sexist. There are indications that their purpose is to protect the woman as male property, not to protect her from rape itself. For example, the law has traditionally held that it is not rape if a husband forces his wife to submit to sexual intercourse. Further, the treatment accorded rape victims at times borders on persecution. According to Karen DeCrow (1974: 235), "The criminal code sections on rape are as sexist as those on prostitution. Rape is the only violent crime in which a victim is required to convince the jury that she vigorously tried to fight off her attacker."

Another type of discrimination occurs in cases of statutory rape. In most states, it is criminal for a man to have sexual intercourse with a female, not his wife, who is below a certain age, usually 14–21 years. Although the female is voluntarily cooperating, this is still a crime and the punishment for the male is often severe. It is, however, rare for similar behavior on the part of an older woman toward a younger man to be considered criminal. According to Kanowitz, the courts maintain that a young woman is incapable of consenting to intercourse. Since the reverse situation is not illegal, "lawmakers presumably believe that, unlike girls, boys of that age are capable of meaningfully consenting to sexual intercourse" (Kanowitz, 1969: 19). This can be viewed as discrimination against the male, who risks being severely punished, but in fact the double standard is at work again, since society exhibits a more punitive and a more protective attitude toward its young females. Penalties for rape, statutory or not, are often harsh, indicating the desire to protect the female, but the ambivalence toward women shines through in the actual treatment of rape victims.

These laws and others (earlier abortion laws, contraception laws, family law) reflect the concerns of society and its traditional values. American society exerts greater control over females (who are not supposed to be sexually active) than males, (who prove themselves in this way). This explains the great concern and severe penalties in juvenile court for female (not male) sexual behavior. "Males are expected to be aggressive and tough; females are supposed to be sweet and nice. And so, the criminal law chauvinistically protects nice sweet girls from bad aggressive boys, while punishing the naughty and sinful women who fail to conform to a sugary image" (Frankel, 1973: 469).

Laws, Theories, and Their Effects

Both our laws and our theories reflect dominant views toward women, but that is not all: they perpetuate such opinions. When Pollak advises us to beware of deceptive women and false accusations of rape, or when Kingsley Davis (1971) states that social disruption would occur if the clients of prostitutes were arrested (whereas the prostitute is apparently expendable), these notions do not lie stillborn in criminology texts. "Davis and Pollak may be merely reflecting cultural attitudes toward women and sexual behavior; nevertheless their work provides a scientific gloss for discriminatory practices against women" (Smart, 1976: 131). Theories of crime, like laws, have practical and political consequences. For this reason, criminologists concerned with the equality of men and women have a responsibility regarding their analyses and their recommendations for change. Theories of criminal law and crime can and do effect the reality that they initially describe.

CONCLUSION

Female crime continues to lag far behind that of males. Indeed, female violence is as limited as it was, perhaps even more limited than, 25 years ago. Substantial increases have occurred in property crime, particularly larceny-theft. Fraud has also risen noticeably.

These increases might be due to changes in the role of women in our society. But perhaps the limited amount of increased crime reflects, in part, the limited changes in the structural position of women. (Although the changes in education and labor force participation are crucial.) These issues will be discussed as I examine various theories of crime and relate them to female patterns of crime. It should be mentioned, however, that connections between rising crime and the women's liberation movement are unsound not only because of senseless notions of liberation but also because changes in female crime began before the women's movement had an impact.[17] As Steffensmeier (1978: 579) observes:

Female increases occurred uniformly during the 1960–1975 time period, suggesting that other forces in socialization already were providing an impetus for changing patterns of female crime well before the initial rise of the women's movement.

In line with Steffensmeier's thinking, it is infinitely more plausible to argue that structural changes were occurring that effected both women's crime and the women's movement.

I will now analyze theoretical criminology, to determine if it can explain female patterns of crime, including women's generally low participation and current (if slight) increases.

NOTES

[1]This chapter relies heavily on Rita Simon's very helpful book, *Women and Crime*, which assembles vital data regarding women's crime and the role of women in American society, particularly during 1953–1972. Information on the decade of the 1970s is mainly found in a 1980 Bureau of the Census publication, *A Statistical Portrait of Women in the United States: 1978*.

[2]These figures cover approximately 91 percent of the total population and have already deleted those complaints, about 4 percent, found to be without basis through subsequent police investigation.

[3]Statutory rape is not included as a Type I offense. Robbery is defined by the F.B.I. as theft or attempted theft from a person by the use or threat of violence, whereas burglary involves the unlawful entry of a structure with the intent to commit a felony or a theft. Larceny-theft is stealing the property of others and includes thefts of bicycles, automobile accessories, pickpocketing, shoplifting, and so forth. Burglary and larceny-theft (unlike robbery) are *not* violent crimes. For complete definitions of all index crimes, see the *Uniform Crime Reports*.

[4]Although embezzlement, forgery, or confidence games can involve tremendous financial losses, they are not treated as major crimes since they involve fraud. The arbitrariness of this is obvious, since larceny includes crimes that are not unanimously viewed as serious: pickpocketing, thefts from cars, and purse-snatching.

[5]Certain crimes are unnoticed (the theft of an item), or unrecognized as a crime (although aware an item is missing, one might assume it was misplaced).

[6]Crimes are often unreported because people wish to remain uninvolved; they believe the police will be ineffective; or they might be protecting friends or relatives involved in the crime.

[7]We will examine these types of data shortly.

[8]Some crimes are more reliably recorded than others: murder is more accurately tabulated than rape, for obvious reasons.

[9]The percentage of arrest varies within each crime category. For example, in 1972, 82 percent of murders resulted in arrests, 57 percent of rapes, 60 percent of aggravated assaults, 30 percent of robberies, 19 percent of burglaries, 20 percent of larcenies, and 17 percent of auto thefts (Simon, 1975: 34). Obviously, we can be more certain about the number of men and women involved in violent, as opposed to property, crime since greater proportions of those committing violent offenses are arrested.

[10]The fluctuations seen in this crime category can probably be attributed to varying law enforcement practices.

[11]It would be extremely helpful to have solid comparative data on women and crime, but unfortunately, the statistics from other societies are frequently unavailable, unreliable, and subject to difficulties in terms of defining and then comparing similar offenses.

[12]In view of these data, the operation of women's prisons is ironic, although not unexpected. They typically support the traditional female role. Most of the opportunities for women involve domestic tasks; they are seldom involved in any training programs. Thus, their secondary role is reinforced — they are simply not expected to have to support themselves. Smart (1976) suggests that this might be based on the assumption that women who accept their traditional role are more likely to be conforming and noncriminal.

[13]The decision to arrest, particularly for minor offenses, can be influenced by many factors: race, social class, personal demeanor, and age.

[14]Even if arrested, women are supposedly subject to preferential treatment since judges and juries are reluctant to punish them, especially since they are regarded as harmless.

[15]Shoplifting is often a strictly amateur affair, with most of the stolen items having little value. Although women are overinvolved in this crime, an estimated 25 women enter department stores for every man, and arrests roughly reflect this same proportion (Peyster, 1960). As Cameron (1967: 114) notes, "There are no data yet established to support the belief that shoplifting is particularly characteristic of women beyond the expected numbers implied in their presence as shoppers in places where shoplifting arrests are made."

[16]The accuracy of crime statistics regarding other population groups would have to be addressed separately. I do not accept the statistics comprehensively.

[17]Changes in women's sex-role attitudes also began before the rise of the women's movement. See, for example, Oppenheim and Czajka, 1976.

CHAPTER THREE

Anomie Theory

INTRODUCTION

Many sociologists view Robert Merton's anomie theory as the most influential approach to crime and deviance. His formulation first appeared in 1938 in a frequently cited article entitled "Social Structure and Anomie." My discussion will be based on this article, although I will consider the revisions, clarifications, and additions Merton offered in later years.

Merton's explanation of crime stems from the classic work of Emile Durkheim whose concept of anomie attempted to describe situations of normlessness: when the collective order has been disrupted and aspirations are unregulated and unattainable. Durkheim, however, referred to human aspirations as "natural," whereas Merton speaks of socially learned needs and restricted structural access to their attainment. Merton intended to offer a comprehensive explanation for crime and deviance; his success is still debated.

"SOCIAL STRUCTURE AND ANOMIE"

Merton (1938: 672) immediately dismisses biological explanations of deviant behavior and focuses instead on the role of social structure: "Our primary aim lies in discovering how some social structures *exert a definite pressure* upon certain persons in the society to engage in nonconformist rather than conformist conduct." He analytically distinguishes between cultural goals, those aspirations or objectives that are socially learned; and institutionalized means, the distribution of opportunities to achieve these goals in normatively acceptable ways. Merton contends that it is possible for societies to overemphasize either the goals or the means. Overemphasis of the means implies an obsessive concern with correct conduct. (He refers to the "occupational psychosis" of the bureaucrat as an illustration. This is the employee who has long forgotten the ultimate objectives of the organization, but fanatically adheres to all its rules.) Merton argues, however, that in America the tendency is to overemphasize the *goals*, without sufficient attention to institutional means. He accurately specifies the overwhelming desire for monetary success and material goods in our society and contends this extreme emphasis on financial success leads to a willingness to use *any* means (regardless of legality) to see that the goal is attained. "The technically most feasible procedure, whether legitimate or not, is preferred to the institutionally prescribed conduct. As this process continues, the integration of society becomes tenuous and anomie ensues" (Merton, 1938: 674). The ideal situation, according to Merton, would be one of balance between the goals and means; conforming individuals would feel they were justly rewarded. Deviant behavior, however, results when cultural goals are accepted (people would like to be financially successful), but access to these goals is structurally limited (a lucrative job is unavailable).

Merton outlines the possible reactions or adaptations that can occur when the goals have been internalized but cannot be legitimately attained. His approach is explicitly sociological since he focuses on one's position within the social system, not one's personality characteristics. The following table summarizes these adaptations (Merton, 1938: 676). Within this table, (+) refers to acceptance, (−) refers to elimination, and (±) is the "rejection and substitution of new goals and standards."

		Culture goals	Institutionalized means
I.	Conformity	+	+
II.	Innovation	+	−
III.	Ritualism	−	+
IV.	Retreatism	−	−
V.	Rebellion	±	±

Merton recognizes that the responses of individuals can change, but reactions are not random. He claims that conformity is the most common response, otherwise society would be unstable. Likewise, retreatism is least common. Merton refers to retreatists, who reject both the goals and means, as true "aliens"; they are "in the society but not *of* it" (Merton, 1938: 677). This includes psychotics, vagrants, tramps, drug addicts, and chronic alcoholics. This adaptation occurs when individuals have accepted both the goals and means and yet do not have access to legitimate and effective means. Illegitimate means are unacceptable to them, and yet they still desire the goals. Retreatism is their response: they give up on both the goals and the means. The ritualist has lost all hope of attaining the goals, but conforms rigorously to the accepted means; the rebel attempts to bring about a new social order.

Merton's major concern, however, is with the innovator: the person who uses illegitimate, but nonetheless effective, means to cultural goals. For example, the person who achieves financial success by robbing a bank, rather than by starting a savings account, is an innovator. Merton describes how the social structure encourages criminality, by pointing to specific population groups who find it extremely difficult to succeed in traditional ways. These people are asked to strive for financial success, and want to achieve it, but are denied the structural opportunities to be successful within the law. Merton notes the problem is not simply a lack of opportunity:

> It is only when the system of cultural values extols, virtually above all else, certain *common* symbols of success *for the population at large* while its social structure rigorously restricts or completely eliminates access to approved modes of acquiring these symbols *for a considerable part of the same population*, that anti-social behavior ensues on a considerable scale (Merton, 1938: 680).

Merton implies that the problem of crime might be corrected if everyone had equal opportunities, or, if those denied opportunities had different expectations in life (as in some cultures where the poor are simply not expected to achieve in the same way the rich are). In America, however, virtually everyone (rich and poor) aims for financial success, although not everyone has the structural opportunities to succeed. These people are then subject to enormous strain, which can result in deviant behavior. It is noteworthy that Merton maintains a value-free approach: "Whatever the sentiments of the writer or the reader concerning the ethical desirability of coordinating the means-and-goals phases of the social structure, one must agree that lack of such coordination leads to anomie" (Merton, 1938: 682). Although he notes that the American emphasis on financial success for everyone encourages "exaggerated anxieties, hostilities, neuroses and anti-social behaviour," he denies he is making a moral point (Merton, 1938: 680). Moreover, he speaks only of coordinating the system; more fundamental alternatives are ignored.

DEVELOPMENTS IN THE THEORY

Merton concludes his article by claiming that although his discussion is incomplete, his framework can be used to explore various issues in more depth. In revisions and elaborations made in later years, he acknowledged that wealth is not the only symbol of success in American society, but he continued to stress its critical importance (1957). He also noted the absence of a stopping point in the American dream — no matter how wealthy, one can always make more money. Alternative goals (Merton mentions, for example, intellectual and artistic goals) can be actively pursued and can benefit society, particularly from a functionalist point of view, which concerns the maintenance of social order: "To the extent that the cultural structure attaches prestige to these alternatives and the social structure permits access to them, the system is somewhat stabilized" (Merton, 1957: 157). Yet the pressure toward anomie continues since the goal of monetary success is excessively extolled in America, while lack of opportunity produces strain. In addition, failure is viewed as the responsibility of the individual, not as rooted in social sources. Extreme pressure can thus push individuals in the direction of illegitimate behavior: they decide to use *any* means to gain what they and their society values. Although Merton recognizes that changes have occurred in American society and notions of equal opportunity have been qualified in light of the actual situation, he contends that the success theme still dominates.

In subsequent work, Merton admitted that all crime and delinquency are not explained in terms of anomie. However, he never specifies what is and is not explicated. He notes that social groups do not accept the success goal in precisely the same way, nor is everyone in the lower classes pushed toward deviant behavior. But he argues that some people in the lower classes *do* accept society's success goal, and they are subject to more strain than people in the upper classes. Thus, he contends subgroups suffer varying amounts of strain, but those at the bottom are most severely pressed. "Recourse to legitimate channels for 'getting in the money' is limited by a class structure which is not fully open at each level to men of good capacity" (Merton, 1957: 145). Merton admits that upper-class people can experience pressure to "innovate" and can engage in illegal business practices, but he still emphasizes that the greatest pressure (and, hence, crime) is found among the lower strata. Although opportunity can be much more rigidly restricted than it is in the United States, other systems (caste systems, for example) do not advance the same success goals for everyone and, thus, do not put as much pressure on the lower classes.

Merton (1957) expanded his thoughts on ritualism, which he sees as a private escape from cultural demands to continuously seek higher rewards. He claims this adaptation is most often found within the lower middle class, where children are strictly socialized to adhere to social rules but, at the same time, opportunities for success are extremely limited. Merton asserts that deviant behaviour is not necessarily disfunctional for the values of the group since some "innovation" can initiate patterns of behavior that succeed in goal attainment. Anomie may also result in the development of new norms, which Merton has categorized as "rebellion."

In an essay in *Contemporary Social Problems* (1966), Merton sharpened his concept of deviant behavior by distinguishing between nonconforming and aberrant behavior. This is essentially a recognition that rebellion differs from the other adaptations. For purposes of illustration, think of the behavior of a rebel such as a Black Panther, as opposed to that of a bank robber. According to Merton, nonconforming (or revolutionary) behavior involves *public* dissent (Black Panthers) whereas aberrant behavior is hidden (bank robbers). The nonconformist directly challenges the legitimacy of the social norms, which the aberrant acknowledges even as he or she violates them. Moreover, the nonconformist attempts to change the norms of society and appeals to a higher morality in the process. The aberrant simply acts in his or her own interest and wishes to avoid punishment. Finally, the nonconformist can claim to be seeking the ultimate (although unpracticed) values of society, while the aberrant is only interested in his or her private concerns (Merton, 1966: 808–810).

In this essay, Merton also discusses responses to deviant behavior. He acknowledges that people of power and authority exercise a crucial role in determining what is judged a serious violation of social standards. In a complex society, social norms are not uniformly accepted and thus opinions differ as to what constitutes a social problem. Merton (1966: 788) shuns the relativism this implies by arguing that sociologists

...need not become separated from good sense by imprisoning themselves in the situation of logically impregnable premises that only those situations constitute social problems which are so defined by the people involved in them. For social problems are not only subjective states of mind; they are also and equally, objective states of affairs.

Yet he agrees that the powerful set the norms, and violations are certainly not equally punished in terms of class, race, or age. Merton recognizes that deviant behavior not only involves what a person actually does, but importantly, how this behavior is perceived by those in authority.

In further clarifying anomie theory (1964), Merton maintains that continuous deviant behavior is exceptional, and conformity the modal response. He acknowledges the importance of associates in terms of innovation, rebellion, and the like: "Whether these [deviant acts] will find open expression and then become recurrent depends, in the aggregate of cases, at least as much on the responses of associates as on our own character and personality" (Merton, 1964: 219). He calls for more research on how social strains are mediated through interpersonal groups.

CRITICISMS OF ANOMIE THEORY

Merton's anomie theory is an outstanding attempt to explain deviant behavior. The vast amount of critical discussion it has elicited is, perhaps, a measure of its value and substance. It delineates the relationship between one's social position, the strain which accompanies that position, and the resulting deviant and nondeviant adaptations. Estimates of Merton's success have varied, but in examining the literature, five important criticisms emerge.

Scope and Specifics

Anomie theory is not as all-embracing as Merton first hoped it would be. It cannot, for example, explain certain behavior commonly held to be deviant, such as homosexuality, or marijuana smoking among people who accept both the goals and means in society. It certainly does not adequately explain mental illness or sexual deviance. The theory is also incomplete in other respects: Cohen (1966) points out that it does not demonstrate why certain adaptations are chosen, nor does it associate different types of strain with different outcomes. Merton anticipated such criticism in his 1938 article, and although he made some improvements along these lines, the criticisms are still appropriate. Gibbons and Jones (1975) maintain that the incomplete nature of anomie theory has prevented its application to various forms of deviance, in spite of the fact that it is so popular.

The particular adaptations themselves have been criticized for their lack of specificity. Taylor, Walton, and Young (1973), for example,

point out that Merton does not adequately discuss his notion of conformity, making it difficult to distinguish between conformity and ritualism, categories that should be fundamentally distinct. Clinard (1964) has
commented that the concept of retreatism is imprecise and oversimplified. It is also unclear why certain people choose the adaptations they
do, while others subject to strain do not succumb.

Cultural Assumptions

A second cluster of arguments propose a more serious criticism of anomie theory. They maintain that the theory disregards interaction with
others, which is crucially involved in deviant behavior. According to
Cohen (1965), Merton overemphasizes the individual actor and does not
recognize the impact of others in determining an individual's response to
a situation. Cohen feels that, for this reason, anomie theory is extremely
limited in explaining delinquent subcultures, particularly the nonutilitarian forms. Merton has acknowledged Cohen's criticism and argues it is
justified regarding earlier versions of anomie theory. In later versions of
the theory, however, he did mention that patterns of interaction should
be considered. Merely dealing with this issue in passing, however, is not
the same as addressing oneself to all the implications involved.

Thus, a major problem with anomie theory is its failure to explicate
the intervening variables of the interactive situation. The deviant is
viewed, more or less, as acted upon, rather than engaging in any type of
personally meaningful behavior. Merton's lack of interest in the role of
group or collective adaptations is further evidence of this difficulty.

Closely related is the criticism that Merton's entire scheme is invalid
because of its basic assumptions about society, particularly the notion that
universally accepted values and goals can be pinpointed in a complex
modern society. Many people, like Taylor (1971), argue that goals develop within the demands of reference groups. Rather than developing the
possibility that very different and even conflicting subgroups make up
the whole, Merton assumes shared values throughout society. Lemert
(1972) also criticizes Merton by arguing that value pluralism is an infinitely more accurate view of America than the notion of patterned
values. If Lemert is correct, Merton's means-ends paradigm becomes
problematic and generally insufficient in explaining deviance. Merton
can be defended since he did state that different goals are possible within
his scheme, but he does not consider different groups and different
values; generally he posits a single source of deviance. This is unacceptable to Lemert and other critics.

Lower-Class Crime

Merton has been challenged for assuming that deviance is most wide-spread among the lower classes. He explained that the lower classes are subject to strain since they lack structural opportunities even though equality of opportunity is proclaimed. Evidence suggests, however, that deviant behavior is much more common throughout society than Merton's formula indicates. Part of the difficulty is that his theory is based on official statistics, which do indeed suggest that the bulk of deviance occurs among the lower echelons of society. But these statistics cannot be accepted at face value. They can and do reflect public concern with particular types of crime, police practices, class bias, labeling effects, and so on. Anomie theory, however, is hard pressed to explain deviance among those who are well placed in society in terms of advantage and opportunity. Why does a successful business executive, who obviously has access to legitimate means, embezzle? To discuss this would have involved Merton in a more fundamental criticism of American society since not only unsuccessful but also successful people turn to crime, indicating more serious problems within the system. Merton also has difficulty explaining why so many people in the lower classes *do* conform. Thus, anomie theory predicts both too little deviance (among the upper classes) and too much (among the lower classes).

Reaction to Deviance

Another difficulty limiting the usefulness of anomie theory is its failure to deal with reactions to deviant behavior. This has been touched upon in those remarks criticizing Merton for ignoring the responses of a deviant's reference group or subculture. Along the same lines, Merton has not dealt with the results of official reaction toward the deviant. Lemert (1972) criticizes him for ignoring the role social control agencies play, particularly in the continuation of deviant behavior. The labeling perspective will be analyzed in detail later, but now it is simply observed that official reaction to deviance is largely overlooked in Merton's analysis. More informal elements, such as the stereotypes of deviants portrayed in the mass media, are also left untouched, indicating Merton's lack of interest in societal reactions and their ramifications.

Critique of Society and Beyond

Merton explicitly criticizes modern society, particularly American society. He disapproves of the widespread strain resulting from existing social arrangements. He sees the suffering that occurs when a society, which is, in fact, unequally structured, claims to offer equality of opportunity. Further, Merton is critical of the overemphasis placed on money, and the never-ending drive to gain more and more wealth. He sees the ritualist as an object of pity. Thus, he recognizes basic problems within our social order, and his solution is to realign our goals and means and ensure that merit meets with success.

Although Merton rejects the present system, his criticisms are not basic; they are neither as fundamental nor as extensive as they might be. For example, he does not explain the initial existence of inequality, nor the exaggerated emphasis on money making. Taylor, Walton, and Young (1973) contend that if Merton's arguments were followed through logically, they would point toward radical social change. But Merton avoids this route. He believes beneficial changes can occur within the present system. Taylor et al. retort that Merton's hopes for reforming the present system are in vain. The very reasons for inequality are rooted within the system, and serve the interests of the few. The talent and potential of the lower classes will not be salvaged through piecemeal reform:

> That the provision of sufficient jobs, of an instrumentally and expressively satisfying nature, is beyond the possibilities of the social system as we now know it, is the bitter reality of the matter. The liberal plans of sociologists such as Merton serve merely to attempt to contain and obscure this reality (Taylor, Walton, and Young, 1973: 104).

Thus, Merton is criticized for neglecting the cause of the dysfunction that exists between the goals and the means in our society. Instead of questioning our political economy, as Taylor et al. would have him do, he settles for supporting meritocracy. He seems confident that social problems can be alleviated within the existing system. The possibility of this will be more fully explored as we examine the explanations of crime offered by the Marxists.

ANOMIE AND WOMEN

Merton made no attempt to apply his typology to women, and initially it seems inapplicable to them. He argues vigorously that the dominant goal in American society is monetary success, and yet he has forgotten at least half the population with this formulation. Ruth Morris (1964) accurately contends that the goals of women and girls are relational goals (successful relationships with others) rather than the financial goals sought by men. More specifically: the goal women have traditionally been taught to seek is marriage and children. A woman might legitimately achieve tremendous financial success in the business world and still find people curious to know if she is married and has a family. If the answer is no, her success is tainted. At the opposite extreme is the financially poor woman, married and raising three children. She, unlike her husband, has not completely failed in the eyes of our culture.

Although anomie theory seems inappropriate regarding women, Merton claims different goals can be considered within his framework. I will make the necessary alterations in his scheme to see if the resulting information explains the traditionally low crime rate among women and the increases presently occurring.

Women: Goals and Means

I accept Merton's argument that one's aspirations are socially learned, not biologically conditioned. This is accurate regarding the goals of women, in spite of any vociferous arguments to the contrary. The goal that women are traditionally socialized to desire, above all else, is marriage and a family; the accepted means is to secure the romantic love of a man through courtship. Despite the much discussed emancipation of women, the great majority of them are still taught to find primary fulfillment through marriage and children. Their main concerns revolve around family, husband, children, and home. Money and financial success are simply not as vital. This, of course, contrasts with Merton's analysis of economic success as paramount. Women are certainly interested in financial status, but this is largely seen as the responsibility of their husbands.

Low Crime Rate Among Women

Given the above revisions in terms of goals and means, Merton's anomie theory can be used, in general terms, to explain the low rate of criminal involvement among women. According to anomie theory, deviant behavior occurs when common goals are extolled for the population at large, but legitimate access is restricted. Those who lack access are under tremendous strain, and may seek alternative (and illegal) means to their objectives. This formulation assumes a very different cast when the goals of women are substituted. It becomes obvious that most women are able to marry and have a family. What is problematic is that simply *being* married and *having* children, not necessarily rewarding relationships or a skillful handling of responsibility, are expected. Seen in this light, the difficulty is that such an easily attainable goal is all that is expected of women. But given that they can usually achieve socially approved ends in a legitimate way, they avoid the types of strain Merton discussed regarding men. Therefore, the low rate of crime among women exists because they are not pressured toward deviant behavior. Women have very low aspirations and their goals are extremely accessible.

A revised anomie theory highlights the relationship between the subordinate position of women and their crime patterns. It indicates women are protected from involvement in the criminal world since they are not subject to the types of pressure and frustration men experience. On the other hand, the social expectations for women in our society (marriage and family) explain why they are severely punished for prostitution and, until recently, abortion. Why certain women initially become involved in prostitution and shoplifting is not clarified by anomie theory.

Ironically, the low crime rate among women may indicate their lack of success, in the crudest of terms, in altering their aspirations. Their limited desires in the economic realm might shield them from both financial pressures (Merton's main concern) and situational pressures (to be expanded later). Merton realized the problem he was addressing only exists when common success goals are held by the population at large. What he neglected to mention is that possibly half our population does not primarily strive directly for financial success. Such an oversight on Merton's part is appalling; but for those who have reviewed the field of women and crime, it is not unexpected.

Increases in Women's Crime

Just as Merton's theory can be used, to some extent, to explain the lack of crime among women, it can, likewise, elucidate the increases that are occurring. Merton recognized (although not specifically in regard to women) that as changes occur in the social structure or goals, we can expect similar changes regarding those most severely subject to strain. If the goals of women shift, for example, toward male success goals, their rate of crime might increase, since access to such goals is typically closed to women in an unequally structured society, such as ours. Emancipation has increased somewhat, and certain women are now aiming to achieve financial success. These changes are not momentous, but they can result in disruption. Challenging traditional restrictions and expectations can lead to anomie and, hence, to an increase in female crime. It is noteworthy that the increases in women's crime have been in property offenses, mainly larceny-theft. Likewise, fraud and counterfeiting and forgery are up. Violent crime has not increased among women. In terms of anomie theory, changing expectations can bring strain, yet any new pressure on women seems to be manifest in property, not personal, crimes. This might indicate escalating financial pressure on women, but little modification in the expectations that they be nonviolent, cooperative, and even docile.

The very fact, however, that the crime rate among women has not changed drastically in the last 25 years indicates that the position of women in our society might not be radically different. The most outstanding fact about women and crime is still their limited involvement. Anomie theory explains this to a certain extent, yet there are difficulties in applying this perspective.

Problematic Aspects

Anomie theory is useful in advancing the possibility that women are freer from certain strains in our society and, hence, less likely to engage in deviant behavior. Yet in applying this theory, I have posited a common goal for all women, a position that was criticized in regard to men. Anomie theory simply does not lend itself to the careful consideration of subcultures or patterns of interaction existing between the deviant and her reference group. With the existing framework, one's thinking is directed toward considering the major goal or goals in society, not toward examining subtle, although important, variations. The claim that marriage and a family is the objective of American women is accurate to a certain extent, but there are many differences among these women that should be taken into account. Furthermore, a study of the reactions (official and unofficial) to crime is not suggested by this theory, although it might be particularly important regarding women.

Anomie theory is generally helpful in explaining the low criminality among women, but when it comes to analyzing the crime that actually occurs, serious problems arise. First of all, the scheme of adaptations becomes problematic. Regarding the category of innovation, which is of major concern to Merton, it is difficult to think of illegal means to achieve the goal of marriage and family. Less than fully acceptable means can certainly be utilized (consider how our culture criticizes those who marry for money rather than love); but this is hardly illegal. Means that are illegal (purchasing a husband, marriage through force) occur seldom, if ever. Prostitution and shoplifting are certainly not alternative means to the goal. Thus, when specifically using this framework to analyze women and crime, it simply does not work. The criticisms of the theory discussed earlier become more obvious with an application to women and crime.

The imprecise nature of Merton's categories becomes clear. Prostitutes might be considered retreatists since they reject both the accepted goals and means for women. Yet, it is also possible to think of them as rebels if their primary goal is seen as financial success rather than marriage, particularly when they belong to groups that are vocal about the rights of prostitutes. Women alcoholics and drug addicts can also be called retreatists, but Merton's explanation of this category is often inapplicable. Escapism supposedly characterizes those who have given up on both the goals and means, yet many female drug addicts and alcoholics have followed the normatively accepted patterns for women and are married and have children. In addition, it is difficult to distinguish between women who are ritualists and play all the feminine games, although they have lost hope of securing a husband and family, and conformists who are still striving for this goal but are as yet unsuccessful. It is impossible to locate shoplifters anywhere within this scheme since their behavior is criminal, but they are often conformists regarding marriage and a family. Moreover, nothing helps us explain why women deviate in the way they do, nor what type of strain leads to each specific outcome.

Official statistics indicate that crime is more common among women of the lower classes, although, as mentioned above, it is difficult to relate this directly to the category of innovation. Furthermore, it is particularly troublesome to explain shoplifting among married, middle-class women in Merton's terms. Finally, a ritualistic adaptation is not more likely among lower-middle-class women, since they are not particularly restricted from the means to the accepted goal for women.

CONCLUSION

The application of anomie theory to women and crime has important implications regarding the theory itself, as well as crime among women and men. It clearly illustrates this theory only applies to men and mainly to the goal of financial success. This has value within limits, but it highlights the criticism that anomie theory ignores subgroups within society. When these subgroups (such as women) are examined, it is not a matter of making minor revisions; in fact the theory fails in important respects. Obviously, anomie theory must precisely categorize what it claims to explain.

Although anomie theory is deficient in analyzing the criminality of women, it is helpful in emphasizing the absence of certain types of strain experienced by women in our society, and how this relates to their low rate of crime. Merton recognized the structural inequalities that exist regarding social class, but he neglected to note similar inequalities regarding sex. Importantly, however, while women are denied lucrative careers, they are also carefully taught not to seek them (unlike lower-class males). The common symbols of success Merton discusses are not so common after all. Women are, in fact, free from certain pressures toward crime that men do not escape quite so easily. For a man, tremendous pressure typically exists to find an occupation that offers substantial rewards. Many men are broken under these demands. While they bear this burden, an analysis of anomie theory highlights a very different although equally disturbing situation for women. When revised to apply to women, the theory illuminates the astonishingly low expectations we have had for females in our society. The goal of marriage and a family is available to virtually all women, and achieving such a goal demands little talent. Merton contends that having accessible alternative goals helps stabilize the social system. Undoubtedly this is the case regarding women, but the price paid is unacceptable since it means curbing the energy and resources of fully half the population.

This does not denigrate the role of homemaker and mother, which can be a demanding and fulfilling occupation when utilized to its fullest, and certainly more challenging and rewarding than many business occupations. But being a successful homemaker or the mother of three happy, well-adjusted children is not necessarily expected. It is better to be unhappily married or even divorced than never to have married at all; better to have two neurotic children than to be childless. Just as with men, the goal is not personal satisfaction or the successful completion of any task — it is the trappings of success we seek. For men, that is money; for women, marriage and a family.

This situation ensures that we will lose a great deal of the skill and talent of the women in our society by expecting little of them and by only rewarding them for very specific and confined behavior.[1] More choice should be available,[2] but the solution does not lie in substituting traditional male success goals and increasing our crime rate. The over-emphasis on financial success for males is as problematic as the lack of challenge for females.

The application of anomie theory to women and crime has resulted in two important considerations: the lack of financial strain experienced by women and their uninspiring cultural goals.

NOTES

[1]The limited expectations for women are problematic in many ways. I am concentrating on the impact this has in confining women to certain roles and preventing them from exploring others. Equally dismal, however, is the situation of women who do not achieve these goals. When social expectations are so specific, those who do not fall into the conventional mold can expect to experience difficulties in our society. We refuse women socially approved alternatives. To those who do not bear children, or have not married, for any of a variety of reasons, we generally extend our pity. What is infinitely more desirable are viable alternatives (in terms of careers, living situations, varied expectations, etc.) Fortunately, the women's movement has increased our awareness that there are other goals — that we can live outside the mold with support from others and creative thinking. But I do not believe this is widely accepted in our society, as yet. And so, aside from the few strong and individualistic women (and men) who can flout social expectations at little personal expense, this situation means, very simply, that many women will suffer, and suffer unnecessarily.

[2]This should include the choice of being a wife and mother, having a career, or whatever combination one prefers. Women are frequently scorned, at the present time,unless they do it all. We are beginning to mock the woman who stays home to care for children as readily as the successful business-woman who is unmarried. What we frequently ignore is the quality of a person's life. Poorer women, of course, are locked into their class, without the luxury of discussing career options.

CHAPTER FOUR

Labeling Theory

INTRODUCTION

Anomie theory views deviant or criminal behavior as a violation of accepted norms in society, as behavior that disturbs the social equilibrium. Merton ignored the reactions such behavior elicits, implying that societal response is not a crucial element in the behavior under study. The structural-functionalist perspective (which Merton represents) assumes deviant behavior occurs in a world that is basically stable and culturally homogeneous. Such formulations, often referred to as the "Eastern" school of thought, have been challenged by a new perspective offering a sharp alternative to conventional views of deviance. This orientation claims that the very meaning of deviance is problematic, that the social world is diverse and conflict laden, that official information regarding deviance is severely limited at best, and that attempts to control deviance may in fact increase it. Developed by American sociologists, this analysis is sometimes identified as the "Western" or "Pacific Coast" school. The perspective itself is commonly called the "social reactions approach," "labeling theory," or the "social interactional" view. It is not a unitary perspective, containing a single theoretical position, but it has distinctive qualities and a relatively coherent collection of themes or viewpoints.

The precedents for labeling theory (as we shall call it) are found in the writings of Frank Tannenbaum (1938) and, more importantly, Edwin Lemert (1951). It gained widespread popularity in studies of crime and deviance during the 1960s, through the work of sociologists like Becker, Erikson, Kitsuse, Matza, and Schur. Today, it assumes a position of major importance in sociology and has been the focus of much discussion, critical and otherwise.

Previously theoretical criminology basically sought to explain why certain people or groups of people engage in crime, but labeling assumes that most people have committed deviant acts and examines why society officially brands some people, and not others, criminal. For example, many citizens steal, but lower-class males who steal cars are more likely to be labeled criminals than upper-class executives who embezzle corporate funds. Labeling shifts the focus to the audience, to those who label, and the effects of this (the process of rule making and rule enforcement). Sociologists have long recognized that behavior defined as deviant varies over time and culture. They also realize that a person's self-image and behavior is intimately connected with the responses of others. Until recently, however, these insights were overlooked in criminology. Labeling theory resurrected them by claiming that nothing intrinsic in behavior makes it deviant. On the contrary, deviance is "created" by those with the power to make rules about certain forms of behavior. Furthermore, the reaction of enforcers crucially affects one's self-concept, life chances, and future behavior. (Being officially labeled a juvenile delinquent can encourage one to act that way.)

Labeling theorists (unlike Merton) regard official data on crime and deviance (such as the *Uniform Crime Reports*) as extremely suspect, since it is the product of social interactions and is influenced by class, racial, age, and sexual biases (Kitsuse and Cicourel, 1963; Douglas, 1970). The only utility of these statistics is what they tell us about agencies of social control. Case studies and participant observations, on the other hand, are recommended as the best sources of data since they allow a first-hand understanding of the deviant, free from the more obvious limitations of conventional data.

These central themes are emphasized and elaborated in various ways by different theorists, as will be seen below, beginning with the pioneering work of Frank Tannenbaum.

THEORETICAL DEVELOPMENTS

Frank Tannenbaum

Modern labeling theory began in 1938 with the publication of *Crime and the Community* by Frank Tannenbaum. He noted that the community first defines the actions of an individual as evil, but eventually defines the individual himself as evil, thus casting suspicion on all his actions. Importantly, the person's self-image changes in a similar direction. The crucial element, for Tannenbaum, was the "dramatization of evil," that is, the process of public labeling. He felt that this experience perhaps plays a "greater role" than any other in making a criminal. Since Tannenbaum, labeling theorists have stressed the way social reaction encourages individuals to redefine themselves[1] and actually become the criminals the community describes them as being. To alleviate these problems, Tannenbaum suggests avoiding official labeling, an idea Edwin Schur (1973) later explored in more detail.

Edwin Lemert

After Tannenbaum, labeling theory was largely undeveloped until Edwin Lemert's publication of *Social Pathology* in 1951. Lemert is the major architect of labeling, offering the first sophisticated version of the theory. He noted that a new emphasis was emerging in deviance, recognizing reform movements as a necessary focus of research, since they often create more problems than they alleviate.

Lemert's concern, like Tannenbaum's, is with the social reaction deviance elicits and the subsequent processes that take place. Earlier models focused on deviance as a simple stimulus-response situation, discussing the variables present before the occurrence of the deviant behavior, but exhibiting little interest in anything that took place afterwards. Lemert shows that critical elements have been ignored as a result. Early acts of deviant behavior may be extremely tentative and barely significant until developed into an organized way of life. Initial behavior can be rationalized by individuals, enabling them to maintain a socially acceptable view of themselves. However, according to Lemert (1951: 76):

> If the deviant acts are repetitive and have a high visibility, and if there is a severe societal reaction, which, through a process of identification is incorporated as part of the "me" of the individual, the probability is greatly increased that the integration of existing roles will be disrupted and that reorganization based upon a new role or roles will occur.

Thus, individuals do not view initial or "primary" deviance as central to themselves, but if these activities are subject to societal reaction, a crisis may occur as formal stigmatization takes place, and the individual might be driven deeper into a deviant life. For example, a person who steals a car and is not caught may be less likely to continue stealing than those who are arrested, defined as criminal, and begin thinking of themselves that way.[2] Consequently, societal reaction may be more important than anything that occurred before a person's involvement in rule breaking. At this point, the individual reorganizes his view of himself around a deviant role, and he is now what Lemert calls a "secondary" deviant.

Deviance, then, is not static, but should be explained in terms of constantly changing situations, due to human interaction. Primary deviance may or may not develop into secondary deviance, depending in part on the number of violations and the intensity of social reaction. According to Lemert, primary deviance has many causes, but secondary deviance results from being labeled and relabeled until one accepts a deviant role. These concepts reflect his concern with process and the impact of societal reaction. As the following statement indicates, Lemert (1951: 77) recognized the extremely complex and progressive nature of these developments:

> The sequence of interaction leading to secondary deviation is roughly as follows: (1) primary deviation; (2) social penalties; (3) further primary deviation; (4) stronger penalties and rejections; (5) further deviation, perhaps with hostilities and resentments beginning to focus on those who are doing the penalizing; (6) crisis reached in the tolerance quotient, expressed in formal action by the community stigmatizing the deviant; (7) strengthening of the deviant conduct as a reaction to the stigmatizing and penalties; (8) ultimate acceptance of deviant social status and efforts at adjustment on the basis of the associated role.

The deviant makes choices, but within certain frameworks that are more or less restricted.

Twenty years later, Lemert published the second edition of *Human Deviance, Social Problems, and Social Control*. He could now point to the tremendous growth of a perspective which he largely founded, and which focuses on social interaction and social control, rather than structural sources of deviance. The rejection of anomie, and the new emphasis on value pluralism, reflected the rapid social change occurring since the 1950s. At a time when authority was challenged, labeling theory presented social control as arbitrary and deemphasized the initial causes of deviance over and against this arbitrary control. Lemert, however, regards much of the development of labeling theory as a vulgarization that leaves important aspects of deviance unexplained. He contends, for example, that interaction is not unilinear or unidirectional, as certain labeling theorists seem to believe. "Others" do not always begin the process; deviants are not "empty organisms" who simply react to a label.

Closely related is Lemert's quarrel with the "underdog ideology," which has evolved within labeling, arguing that it distorts reality by sympathizing with the deviant, while overemphasizing the oppressive and discretionary nature of social control agencies. More importantly, he rejects the notion of the individual deviant this implies — a person without choices, one who merely reacts. According to Lemert (1972: 19), labeling theory must recognize that "individuals define themselves as deviant on their own terms and independent of specific societal reactions . . . the interaction process seen in full organic reciprocity allows that individuals court, risk, even create conditions of their own deviance."

Much of labeling theory also implies a consensus on the part of the powerful vis-à-vis the deviant, while conflict within the dominant group is ignored. (Lemert specifically criticized Becker in this regard.) The great variety of rules, and how agents of control must choose among them, is ignored. Lemert (1974: 460) complains: "There is little that I can find in labeling theory which deals with this kind of conflict and choice making in the context of a pluralism of groups so conspicuous in modern society."

Lemert agrees with both the phenomenologists, who criticize labeling for failing to recognize the tentative and uncertain nature of social situations, and the radicals, who criticize certain aspects as superficial and blind to the subtleties of power. What is needed is a model of interaction that encompasses the role of a variety of groups in the development of moral and legal control.[3] Lemert maintains that this must sort out the shifting concerns that operate in the development of patterns of social control. "The chief gain is a method for specifying the way in which human choices affect the societal reaction without generalizing the claims of others or reducing them to reified ideas of culture, class, or power" (Lemert, 1974: 466). Lemert concludes that sociologists cannot return to the old structural explanations of deviance, but the new work is incomplete.

John Kitsuse

Labeling theory was greatly advanced throughout the 1960s, although I have stepped ahead of myself by mentioning Lemert's criticisms of these efforts. Nonetheless, vital developments took place, and, in fact, labeling was not accepted until the work of Kitsuse, Erikson, and Becker was published in the early 1960s. In 1962, John Kitsuse discussed the theoretical and methodological issues involved in explaining societal reaction. His aim was clear: "I propose to shift the focus of theory and research from the forms of deviant behavior to the *processes by which persons come to be defined as deviant by others*" (Kitsuse, 1962: 248). He accurately notes that this involves questioning what is usually taken for granted: the very definition of deviance. For Kitsuse, a major concern is understanding why behavior is considered deviant (since this varies) and when such behavior will elicit reactions that lead to labeling (which also varies). Thus deviance, is, once again, viewed as a process involving: first, a judgment that a particular behavior is deviant; second, defining people who behave in such a fashion as deviants; and third, treating them differentially as a result.

Kitsuse applies these considerations to homosexuality, but broader implications are evident. Sociological theory must deal with the tremendous variety of behavioral expectations among different population groups. In a modern (diverse) society, it is difficult if not impossible to locate behavioral rules uniformly accepted and enforced. Consequently, behavior that differs from expectations or even behavior defined as deviant is not the central issue. Instead, the interactional process leading to such definitions and initiating sanctions must be the focus. According to Kitsuse, if a person's behavior is observed and defined as deviant, but that individual is not treated differently as a result, he or she is not sociologically deviant. Distinguishing deviants from nondeviants is not primarily a matter of behavior but, rather, depends upon "circumstances of situation, social and personal biography, and the bureaucratically organized activities of agencies of control" (Kitsuse, 1962: 256).

Kai Erikson

Later in 1962, Kai Erikson published an article criticizing the conventional treatment of deviance for its extremely limited scope. Initial acts of deviance may indeed result from anomie, but Erikson (like Lemert) recognizes that stable deviant patterns are still unexplained, as is the way deviance changes, develops, or persists over time. To remedy this, Erikson turns to the social *audience*, which he sees as the crucial variable, since deviance is not inherent in an act but, rather, a judgment conferred on that behavior by society. He is interested in understanding why certain people are selected for labeling, and why only certain social actions are sanctioned. (Why, for example, is homosexual behavior outlawed in this society and not others; and why, within this society, are certain homosexuals harassed and prosecuted while many engaging in similar behavior are overlooked?) Erikson maintains that this selection process operates on the basis of factors unrelated to the deviant act itself, such as social class, previous record, and even demonstrations of remorse.

Erikson believes that deviants provide a valuable service by helping reaffirm the boundaries of society through public censure of their activities. He notes that organizations aiming to limit or prevent deviance actually maintain it, and he wonders if this might be the "real" function of these agencies, given the importance of boundary maintenance. He suggests examining societies that welcome deviants back into routine social life, to see if deviance functions in the same way in these societies and, if possible, to learn ways of avoiding the more detrimental effects of labeling.

Thus, Erikson agrees that social structures may play a part in inclining some people toward deviant or criminal behavior, but we must understand why a certain portion of people engage in extended patterns of deviance, which necessarily involves examining the reaction of social audiences.

Howard Becker

Howard Becker is another early and extremely influential contributor to labeling theory. His major work, *Outsiders*, published in 1963, added substantially to the study of deviance and labeling. The title refers to those who supposedly broke a rule and are subject to enforcement policies. People are curious as to why the outsider broke the rule, and social science tries to supply the answer. But Becker observes that this implies that certain behavior is inherently deviant and the only significant issue is why a person acts that way, whereas, in fact, groups disagree about what behavior is deviant. "This should alert us to the possibility that the person making the judgement of deviance, the process by which that judgment is arrived at, and the situation in which it is made may all be intimately involved in the phenomenon of deviance" (Becker, 1963: 4). According to Becker, many definitions of deviance ignore the fact that it is created by society, not simply in the sense that social factors elicit such behavior, but rather, "that *social groups create deviance by making the rules whose infraction constitutes deviance*, and by applying those rules to particular people and labeling them as outsiders." Becker continues, "deviance is *not* a quality of the act the person commits, but rather a consequence of the application by others of rules and sanctions to an 'offender.' The deviant is one to whom that label has successfully been applied; deviant behavior is behavior that people so label" (Becker, 1963: 9).[4]

Here Becker is positing a central argument of labeling theory: that deviance is problematic and a matter of social judgment. He claims that the only characteristic deviants share is the experience of being labeled, and he begins his analysis with this, viewing deviance as resulting from interaction between a social group and the individual they regard as a rule breaker. Becker is less concerned with the social or personal characteristics of individual deviants than with the process they experience. Becker elaborates on Lemert's analysis of this process of social differentiation, emphasizing the deviant label. Social response to a particular action varies (in terms of time, consequences, and the identity of the perpetrator and victim), bolstering the claim that the activity itself is not crucial, but rather the responses of others. "In short, whether a given act is deviant or not depends in part on the nature of the act (that is, whether or not it violates some rule) and in part on what other people do about it" (Becker, 1963: 14).

Labeling theory asserts that reactions to rule breaking are not indiscriminate, partly because only certain people are sufficiently powerful to make rules and enforce them. Becker contends that differences of race, age, sex, and social class are influential in determining whose rules are operating. These variables represent power differentials.

Becker introduces the category of "secret deviant" (one who breaks a rule but is not noticed or labeled) to emphasize that more than publicly sanctioned actions are deviant. But public deviance is most critical, and its *development* needs explaining. One of Becker's major contributions was his insistence that sociologists treat the dynamics of deviance. He proposed certain concepts to do this: the notion of "deviant careers" emphasizes process, the movement from one position to another within a system. This involves "career contingencies," factors responsible for mobility, or its absence. Becker suggests concentrating on those variables that help sustain patterns of deviance, and contends that official labeling is a decisive step in building a deviant career since it limits contact with nondeviants and alters one's self-image in a deviant direction. Finally, membership in a deviant group results in, and further stabilizes, a "deviant career."

Another major insight is Becker's realization that a deviant label is a "master status." Once labeled deviant, this identification outweighs any other, coloring all social relationships. Being known as an "ex-convict," for example, is the central fact of your social existence as far as others are concerned — not your occupation, marital status, number of children, and so on. Such a designation can increasingly sever a person from conventional social groups.

Becker claims that rules result from the initiative of *moral entre-*

preneurs, his term for those who create new rules and the agencies that enforce them. He notes that deviance research emphasizes the rule breakers, not rule makers. "If we are to achieve a full understanding of deviant behavior, we must get these two possible foci of inquiry into balance" (Becker, 1963: 163).

Current examinations of deviance, according to Becker, neglect the lives of deviant individuals, and result in inadequate explanations of their behavior; but the concerns of rule enforcers must also be extensively analyzed.

Other theorists have been influential in advancing labeling theory (Schur, Cicourel, Lofland, Matza, Goffman, Scheff, and so on), but those discussed above are most significant. Their work, however, has not been spared serious criticism, which I will now discuss.

CRITICISMS OF LABELING THEORY

The Definition and Explanation of Deviance

Labeling has been accused (Gibbs, 1966; Taylor, Walton, and Young, 1973; etc.) of being a vague perspective, not a fully developed theory containing consistent and interrelated concepts. It describes aspects of social reality that have been neglected and thus aids in theoretical development, but it fails to crisply distinguish between mere description and causal statements (Taylor, Walton, and Young, 1973). The processual discussion of deviance is too ambiguous to be referred to as causal analysis. Schur (1971) and others correctly note that labeling's insights offer directives for research, but current formulations lack testable propositions.

Closely connected is the criticism that labeling does not clearly define deviance. Gibbs claims it never precisely explains what kind of behavior or what kind of reaction identifies deviant acts, or if reaction is the only way deviance is identified.

According to Jack Gibbs, Kitsuse, Becker, and Erikson assert that an act is deviant only if a certain reaction follows. This troubles Gibbs (1966: 11) since, "the essential feature of a deviant or a deviant act is *external* to the actor and the act." He contends that this conception of deviance is extremely relativistic. Schur (1971) disputes this, stating that such features illustrate the strengths of labeling. The perspective does not deny the reality of deviance or pretend that crimes such as murder would cease if they were not labeled deviant; but reactions do affect future behavior, no matter what initially evoked it. According to Schur, there is no unequivocal basis for deciding what is or is not deviant. Moreover, a processual approach indicates that such precision is impossible, at least in terms of defining an individual deviant, since so-called deviant acts represent only part of an individual's behavior, and the degree of deviance or conformity is constantly changing.

Gibbs also contends that labeling never clarifies whether it aims to explain deviant behavior or the reactions to it. According to Ronald Akers (1968), the goal is to do both, to give structural as well as processual explanations of deviance. Previously, the emphasis has been on structure, but labeling theory helps balance the picture by concentrating on who applies the labels, to whom, under what circumstances, and to what effect. The emphasis on social reaction has been understood to mean that only those labeled are truly deviants. But labeling theorists themselves are not unanimous on this point, since such concepts as secret deviants (Becker) and primary deviants (Lemert) are discussed. However, the stress on social reactions is undoubtedly at the heart of labeling since everyone contends that it matters greatly whether an act is known or not.

Initial Causes of Deviance

A major criticism of labeling theory is its neglect of the initial causes of deviant behavior. It offers little to explain the factors or processes that lead some people, and not others, to first engage in rule breaking. Certainly labeling reminds us of facts that are often overlooked: rules are socially produced and enforced by those who have power; not all rule breaking results in labeling — this depends on an often arbitrary social process; finally (and most significant), social reaction can actually produce further deviance. But these momentous contributions do not eliminate the need for a thorough treatment of initial entrance into rule breaking. Why do some people first get involved in activities that ultimately lead to labeling? Labeling theorists disagree on the necessity of explaining this. Some simply argue that it is impossible to specify all the elements involved. Lemert claims that primary deviance is "polygenic"; Scheff sees it as evolving from "diverse sources." Structural explanations are disregarded.

The use of statistics among labeling theorists highlights the criticism that this perspective has a narrow focus and neglects the systemic causes of deviance. Kitsuse and Cicourel (1963), for example, suggest that shifting one's concern from the origins of deviance to societal reactions enables statistics to have a new utility. They now represent "cultural definitions" of behavior deemed undesirable, not cross-cultural absolutes. They are measurements of official reaction processes, not simply deviant behavior. As such, they are valuable social facts — but not as Merton used them, to measure class differences in the volume of deviance. Instead, they are viewed in terms of interest-centered laws and differential law enforcement. Rates of deviance reflect official reaction processes, not necessarily anything else.

Gibbs (1966) is frequently cited for observing that labeling ignores the variations in the occurrence of deviance, and etiological factors in general. Schur (1971, 1969) acknowledges Gibb's concerns that labeling focuses on social reaction rather than precipitating "causes." He asserts, however, that this complements and rounds out a structural approach: the two are not necessarily exclusive. Schur admits that a labeling theorist like Erikson implies all deviance is the result of social reaction.[5] "Yet in general it is more characteristic of the reactions perspective merely to emphasize the relative importance of processing, and perhaps to view labeling as a necessary feature of the sequence leading to at least some kinds of deviance rather than as a necessary and sufficient condition" (Schur, 1969: 135).

Schur (1971) also contends that labeling theory is concerned with rule making and interpersonal reactions. The focus has been on agents of control, but other research possibilities are obvious and would ultimately increase the substantive contribution of labeling theory. This does not, however, invalidate the criticism that labeling is incomplete, since it omits structural considerations.

Minimizing the importance of initial deviance has raised other concerns that disturb critics. If the primary causes of deviance are not explored, the implication is that this behavior has little meaning or importance. Labeling theorists discuss the thief who has been officially sanctioned and the ramifications of this. Whether the theft initially occurred because of need, or for the thrill of stealing, is disregarded. Taylor, Walton, and Young (1973) argue that primary and secondary deviance are not so easily separated. Ignoring the initial causes of deviance is ultimately to ignore the conditions that give deviant behavior its very meaning. They view deviance as rooted in the inequalities of larger society and contend that without examining these inequities a full understanding of deviant behavior is lost. Whether or not you accept this analysis, the point remains: if labeling avoids discussing the causes of initial deviance, it implies that this is not essential.

Results of Labeling

Closely related to the above argument, and another major criticism of this perspective, concerns the results of labeling. First of all, in spite of much speculation, little empirical evidence exists regarding the effects of labeling. Cross-cultural data are lacking, as well as detailed information on informal reaction. Even empirical evidence concerning the effects of control agencies is not as substantial as labeling implies, calling into question its central argument: the negative impact of official reaction.

Labeling theory gives the impression that official attempts at punishment or rehabilitation are worse than useless, they are harmful. Gibbs (1966) notes, however, that labeling theorists have not systematically examined the *deterrent* effects official reaction can elicit. Bordua (1967: 161) agrees that labeling rarely discusses the positive effects of social control and contends that, "The processes which produce stabilized deviants may be precisely the ones which reduce deviance in the population as a whole." By focusing on negative cases, we may be ignoring the benefits of labeling.[6]

Becker (1963) did mention that if apprehension for a deviant act occurs when other choices of action are still available, further deviance might be avoided. Neither he nor Lemert argue that labeling always results in an increasing commitment to deviance, but that it can do so. Precisely how important social reaction is has not, however, been demonstrated empirically. Studies that exist indicate that labeling can have more diverse effects than these theorists generally acknowledge or systematically discuss. At times, labeling certainly creates more deviance, as illustrated in Schur's work *Crimes Without Victims* (1965). But it has also been known to prevent further deviance, as Cameron's study of shoplifting indicates; and to have no lasting effect, as in the case of doctors who are narcotic addicts (Winick, 1961), and those sued for malpractice (Schwartz and Skolnick, 1962). Schur (1969b) contends that this perspective could examine "positive" labeling; but in fact, it does not. More research is needed to explain systematically which conditions lead to what results.

Thorsell and Klemke (1972) argue that the positive or negative effects of labeling depend on many circumstances, and they make several observations that future research might explore. They claim, for example, that the process is likely to be positive when a person is sensitive to the evaluation of the labeler. Labeling has little deterrent effect on professional shoplifters, for instance, since the subcultural support they receive is significant. They also maintain that the more easily a label is removed, the less its negative effect, and that positive labeling has received little attention, although it might increase acceptable behavior.[7]

In general, then, the effects of labeling must be elaborated and refined, but emphasizing the negative aspects of this process has led to a further criticism. Just as labeling theory's reluctance to discuss initial deviance implies the meaninglessness of such actions, likewise, the emphasis on the negative repercussions of labeling implies an actor totally at the mercy of official labelers,[8] not an independent or responsible person. The individual is always forced into future deviance, and this assumes, according to David Bordua (1967), that people have little ability to determine their own conduct. Societal reaction is overemphasized at the expense of individual choice regarding one's response to labeling, or one's initial reasons for rule breaking. Ronald Akers contends that labeling comes too close to arguing that actual behavior is not essential, although the contribution of this perspective lies in discussing the very impact of official processing. Much of the literature admittedly gives the impression of innocent actors who are suddenly stuck with a label and pushed into future deviance. "However, it is exactly this image, toned down and made reasonable, which is the central contribution of the labeling school to the sociology of deviance" (Akers, 1968: 463).

Robert Broadhead (1974) presents an excellent critique of labeling when he contends that it views the development of a deviant self-image and a deviant career strictly in terms of the negative results of official processes. This conjures up images of "oversocialization" — people are viewed as totally shaped by social forces, unable to defy, resist, or even contribute to such processes. Broadhead argues that this image contrasts with, even contradicts, another notion of the deviant, which labeling fosters, that of the "drifter" who slips into primary deviance, with structural factors unexplored. Neither of these images gives a well-rounded treatment of deviants, nor do they combine to do so.

Taylor, Walton, and Young (1973) put this in a wider framework by contesting labeling's definition of deviance. Although they agree that deviance is not simply an inherent property of an act, neither is it as arbitrary as labeling implies. Our world is not free of social meaning: most people are readily aware of whether behavior is deviant or not. "In contrast to these theorists, we would assert that *most deviant behavior is a quality of the act*, since the way in which we distinguish between *behavior* and *action* is that behavior is merely physical and action has meaning that is socially given" (Taylor, Walton, and Young, 1973: 147). Taylor, Walton, and Young feel that recognizing certain actions as deviant shifts the focus from the passive actor to a decision maker, who chooses to break rules. This suggests that while deviance is sometimes explained in terms of official reaction, in other cases it reflects initial motives and choices. By deemphasizing such choice, and by concentrating on secondary deviance, the original causes of action are avoided, and the psychological effects of social reaction are emphasized. This is unacceptable for a complete explanation of deviance.

Locating the fate of deviants in the hands of reactors, and concentrating on the negative effects of official action, has generated an "underdog ideology." This encourages labeling theorists to take the side of the deviant. Some contend that this balances out a criminology literature severely biased against the deviant; others argue that it is distorted, leads to an overly critical attitude toward decision makers, and is naive in terms of the very complicated problem of balancing order and justice.

Power

One final criticism raises issues closely connected with the failure of labeling to explain adequately initial deviance. This concerns labeling theory's neglect of the power structures that ultimately underlie the production of deviance.

Howard Becker (1963) began to discuss *whose* rules are being enacted and enforced. He recognized and plainly stated (1963: 17–18) that differences in the ability to make and enforce rules essentially boil down to a question of power; and that age, sex, ethnic, and class differences are intimately related to this. Labeling theory held out the promise of focusing on conflict and power in understanding deviance, yet Akers (1968), among others, complains that it reneged on this promise and instead concentrated on those who violate rules. Although aware of the centrality of power, they do not examine it.

Laurie Taylor (1971) agrees that labeling stopped short of offering a sophisticated analysis of the rule maker:

> For labeling theory only nods toward the labelers, admits their presence, documents their effects, but then fails to demonstrate the social processes which allow them to indulge in such labeling, which have allowed one group not simply to have the right to make rules, but also to sit in judgment over those who flout them" (Taylor, 1971: 195).

The penetrating insights of labeling enabled theoretical criminology to shift its emphasis from the deviant act to the reaction it triggers (with the resulting stigmatization and changes in self-image). But without a fundamental consideration of power relations, this insight becomes too individualistic and limits potential questions. Alexander Liazos (1972) explains this quite convincingly. He contends labeling theorists attempted to "normalize" the deviant, to show she or he is one of us, but the opposite effect has occurred. By concentrating on the more dramatic forms of deviance (prostitution, delinquency, homosexuality), and neglecting the deviance of the powerful, they necessarily imply an acceptance of current conceptions of deviance, and unfortunately perpetuate the very ideas they aim to dispel. By omitting a detailed structural analysis, labeling forces us back to uneasy considerations that inherent individual or class differences must be fundamental. We are left believing that deviance is more widespread among the powerless. By neglecting the structures of power, violence, for example, is viewed as lower-class behavior. We avoid any discussion of a political and economic system that, as Liazos points out, denies job opportunities, traps people in poverty and slums, and manipulates them through the media. Many suffer from the anguish and violence this causes, but criminology research (even by labeling theorists) concentrates elsewhere.[9]

This neglect of power, social structure, and ultimately primary deviance, can be understood through the underlying assumptions of labeling theory. Alex Thio (1973) persuasively argues that labeling assumes rules are made against those who commit deviant acts. (Whereas, according to Thio, rules are also made against potential deviants, especially the powerless, leading others to view them as needing control. This also prevents the powerful from viewing their own illegitimate actions as truly deviant.) Second, labeling implies that official processing only affects actual deviants. (Whereas, it encourages larger society to view the powerless, in general, as potential deviants. This, in turn, fosters primary deviance among the powerless by its effects on their self-conceptions.) Third, labeling presumes that only the powerless are secondary deviants, ignoring the fact that the powerful may also engage in deviance, and can even be encouraged to do so since they are unlikely to be punished.

These assumptions have prevented the systematic exploration of the deviance of the powerful, as well as the structures which cause deviance in general. Thio feels this reflects a class bias which labeling theory, for all its talk about rule-makers, has not escaped. He contends that until the deviance of the powerful is explained, any general theory remains in dispute.

To summarize this criticism, the promise of an analysis of power, offered by Becker and others, is unfulfilled. Labeling theorists have, to the detriment of their work, overlooked the element of power.

Conclusion

Labeling theory has given criminology an opportunity to re-emphasize that crime and deviance are socially defined, and that certain groups and individuals, especially those lacking wealth, power, and status, are more likely to be officially stigmatized as deviants. This should remind us that deviance is closely connected with larger society, and to understand it, we must go beyond an attempt to analyze the law breaker, and scrutinize the law maker as well.

Following Mead, labeling theory recognizes the impact social definitions and official processing have on an individual and focuses on the importance of social control mechanisms in the development of deviance. It is also invaluable in taking the vantage point of the "underdog" and fostering a new appreciation for methods like participant observation.

Labeling theory tries to correct the limitations of structural theory, but fails to explicate the larger causes of deviance. Its focus on social reactions is crucial and could be extended to a structural analysis, but it neglects to do this. It also neglects to explore adequately the results (positive and negative) of labeling.

Although the promise of labeling theory remains unfulfilled, its impact on our understanding of deviance and social control has been profound. It has redirected analysis to areas to concern commonly overlooked. Rooted in traditional sociological theory (like symbolic interactionism, functionalism, and conflict theory), it could be extremely useful in integrating our thinking on crime and deviance. A structural explanation, however, must be combined with a processual one.

LABELING AND WOMEN

No one, to my knowledge, has presented a systematic analysis of women and crime from the labeling perspective. Frances Heidensohn (1968) contends that the few available discussions of female deviance and labeling are deficient in various respects. She mentions, for example, Lemert's chapter on prostitution (1951), which ironically is more concerned with structural elements than social reaction. Heidensohn observes that Lemert's own attitudes are apparent and reflect those of his society, since he treats prostitution as sexual deviation, although the prostitute herself frequently views it as economic. (This is clearly at odds with the stated intentions of labeling theory: to understand the deviant's perspective.)

Howard Becker, among others, remarks that the response to rule breaking depends on many variables, including *who* violates the rule. Sex could easily be considered here. He explicitly states, in reference to rule makers, that men typically make the rules for women (1963: 17). Thus, there are conspicuous entry points where labeling might have begun a thorough analysis of women and crime, but once again this analysis was not forthcoming. I will begin to explore how the insights of labeling theory might apply to this issue.

LOW CRIME RATE AMONG WOMEN

Labeling recognizes that behavior defined as deviant or criminal varies, depending on the time, cultural, and even subcultural elements involved. This certainly applies to activities involving women. Prostitution and extensive sexual activity among young girls, for example, have been viewed as legitimate at other times, in other cultures. Labeling theory enables us to recognize the cultural relativity of these definitions, and the unreliability of official crime statistics, which are riddled with sexual bias, indicating more about what society views as unacceptable for women, and official reactions to this, than actual behavior. As noted in Chapter 2, our laws mirror contradictory images of women and simultaneously reflect and support a dual morality for males and females. Laws regarding statutory rape, contraception, abortion, and prostitution, as well as family law and juvenile law are particularly apt here. Equally essential is the application of these statutes, which varies in terms of males and females (see Chapter 2).

Beyond this, labeling suggests focusing on the social reaction to deviance, on the audience, rather than the criminal. It is aware that certain groups, usually middle- and upper-class people, are not associated with criminal status and, hence, are less likely to be labeled. Women certainly do not fit the stereotype of a criminal. Such preconceptions might enable the criminal justice system to take their crimes less seriously, helping them avoid arrest and severe punishment. These attitudes (social in nature) are likely to receive support from the wider public, who are less fearful of women criminals. Moreover, due to their traditional roles as wives and mothers, the "weaker sex" might not only evoke the sympathy of officials but avoid suspicion altogether. This could explain the lack of secondary deviance among women, since they are less likely to be labeled and punished by informal groups and official organizations. Reflecting their role in society and our perception of it, both interpersonal and official reaction steer women away from crime. Note that labeling theory is not particularly concerned with how traditional structures prevent individuals from initial involvement in crime, but rather how they effect social reaction.

Females are generally subject to more rigorous social control than males. This enables interpersonal groups to thoroughly dominate those who initially deviate and quickly terminate further involvement in unacceptable behavior. Restricting male behavior, early and effectively, is not an available alternative, since society has different expectations for males and infinitely more tolerance for their misbehavior.

Women are socialized to be particularly sensitive to the opinions of others, especially those in authority. Thorsell and Klemke (1972) suggest that when a deviant exhibits concern with the labeler's evaluation, the process will more likely draw that person away from deviant involvement. Thus, the social reaction to female crime or deviance might not be the same, nor have the same effects it would with men. A real audience might even be unnecessary: due to stricter socialization, women could avoid deviant behavior because of *potential* social reaction.

Labeling theory not only discusses social reaction, but the stigmatizing effects of public labeling. By avoiding official (and interpersonal) labeling, however, women maintain low levels of criminal involvement, and even return to nondeviant lives more easily. In addition, because of the patronizing attitude toward women, they may have their deviant actions treated as "sickness" rather than criminality. The view that women are helpless and require treatment could enable them to avoid the negative effects of criminal labeling.[10] While Pollak argues that much hidden crime exists among women, labeling extends this to the general public. They both would agree that women are often spared the disgrace of public sanction: Pollak concentrates on the reasons for this (attributes of women, their social roles and opportunities); while labeling simply emphasizes the detrimental effects of negative labeling and the benefits of avoiding it. (Both approaches suffer from unproven assumptions and statements about initial deviance, as we shall see.)

Becker (1963) argues a deviant label is a master status, which isolates individuals from conventional groups. Given that women are still deeply involved in traditional roles as wives and mothers (see Chapter 2), this "master status" is less applicable to them, even if they are officially labeled. Most of their activities take place in a private, not a public world, thus blunting any rejection from conventional groups. They are already isolated from larger society. Moreover, many opportunities like career alternatives, which are blocked for labeled males, are frequently absent for females, criminal or not. Thus, women feel less pressured to conform to a deviant label that, in turn, is more easily discarded, since it clashes with the accepted image of women, and is limited in its harmful effects. Thus, it might be easier for women to reenter their conventional society.

Elaborating on the stigmatizing effects of official labeling, these theorists point to changes in self-perception, and the development of career deviance. Women, however, seem protected from these developments to some extent. Schur (1969b) observes that the labeling orientation at least implies notions of positive labeling. Women certainly benefit from this. We can reasonably assume that the "positive" labeling of women as nonviolent, passive, conformist, law abiding, et cetera, maintains and even increases this behavior (although labeling has not concentrated on this).

Cameron's study of shoplifting (1964) supports this idea. She asserts that amateur thieves caught by store detectives do not consider themselves criminals. Indeed, it is often difficult even to convince them that they have been arrested. Store personnel attempted to teach the shoplifters (many of them women) that their behavior was wrong and that they should think of themselves as thieves. Such treatment, and the possibility of being brought to court, often resulted in changes of attitude and behavior. Thus, social reaction can steer individuals away from crime, especially if a person's self-image is at odds with a criminal label, as a woman's is likely to be.

Thus, women are more likely to reject a deviant label and the resultant changes in self-concept since this contrasts with their images of themselves and women in general, fostered through long years of socialization.

Labeling theory reminds criminologists that rule making is an important consideration, and rules typically reflect the interests of the powerful. Certain forms of behavior considered unacceptable for women are proscribed. Yet, women have also been labeled as noncriminal. This reflects traditional views of women and reinforces social relationships, which is advantageous for the powerful segments of society. To a large degree, this might stem the criminal activity of women (by protecting them from negative labeling and secondary deviance) and explain, in part, the limited official involvement of women in crime.

INCREASES IN WOMEN'S CRIME

Assuming that the traditional view of women has protected them from official labeling, changes in this view can result in declining protection. Earlier I argued that radical change in women's status (as measured by employment, marriage, number of children, and other statistics) has not occurred in the last 25 years. This is not to say, however, that everything is static; changed perceptions of women might lurk behind the current (although limited) increases in their crime rates. With the reemergence of a women's movement in the United States, and conscious efforts to change their image as passive, dependent, nonassertive beings, public attitudes toward women have been affected. Consequently, both informal and official social reaction can be expected to change, with women becoming more likely candidates for labeling.

Social change necessarily affects those with the power to label. If sympathetic attitudes toward women, and the belief that they are typically noncriminal, have previously given them lenient treatment, a decline in public support for such attitudes — and indeed mass media sensationalizes female crime — could make the public increasingly fearful, police officers more inclined to arrest, and courts stricter.

Informal reaction would also be affected and subtly connected with changes in the socialization of women. It is less acceptable to teach female children to be as docile and submissive regarding authority as in the past. Thus, their behavior is not as thoroughly controlled by primary groups as it has been traditionally. This implies a decline in "positive" labeling, which previously enabled women to resist more deviant roles and commitment. Such resistance is socially rooted and subject to change. It might now be more difficult for women to avoid negative (deviant or criminal) labels and their effect on self-image.

In addition, to the extent that women desire entry to the male occupational world, criminal labels are exceedingly harmful and, in fact, have the repercussions described by Becker in terms of a "master status."

Attitudes toward women, however, have not changed drastically; nor have their crime rates. In fact, as discussed earlier, the largest criminal increases have been in larceny, fraud, and counterfeiting and forgery. These types of crimes readily fit traditional images of female crime (petty, nonviolent). This might further facilitate official labeling, since it does not depend on drastic changes in the image of women as entailed in a crime like armed robbery.

In summary, then, conditions that previously protected women from the pernicious effects of labeling have declined. With this, women are more likely to be subject to the stigma of official labeling. The result, according to labeling theory, is an increased likelihood that their criminal involvement will become deeper and more intractable.

PROBLEMATIC ASPECTS

Although much of the above analysis is plausible, obvious difficulties exist in applying this model to women and crime. First of all, even in this application, it was necessary to extend the usual boundaries of labeling theory by seriously considering, for example, positive labeling as well as informal reaction. But other, more serious issues require discussion and relate, to some extent, to the criticisms of labeling theory mentioned earlier.

Volume of Female Crime

I noted the possibility that women have lower crime rates because they are less likely to be officially labeled and driven into criminal careers. It is equally plausible, however, that very few women are labeled because very few of them are involved in crime. If this is so, labeling is powerless to explain the phenomenon. By concentrating on social reactions, and ignoring initial causes of crime, labeling is unable to discuss women and crime.

Similarly, rising crime rates among women may reflect an increased readiness to label them — but it may simply reflect more deviance on their part. These questions cannot be definitively resolved without more empirical evidence on female participation in crime (labeling theory is quite correct to be skeptical about official statistics). But even lacking conclusive data, informed judgments can be made regarding the varying criminal involvement of different population groups, based on an assessment (albeit skeptical) of official data. There is good reason to assume (from official reports and careful thought) that white middle-class females are less criminal than young black lower-class males. These differences require explanation. Thus, structural considerations must be combined with discussions of social reaction.

Frances Heidensohn (1968) observes that the increasing participation of women in social and business activities could have triggered a rapid increase in female crime. "That this does not appear to be the case reflects significantly upon the deviant behavior of women and, perhaps more importantly, upon the societal reactions to it" (Heidensohn, 1968: 162). Heidensohn blurs any distinction between the occurrence of deviance and the social reaction to it. These are two very different things: if deviance does not occur, it cannot elicit a reaction. I am convinced the official crime rate among women represents much more than labeling activity, especially since there presently appears to be an increased willingness to label women, and yet their crime rate is persistently low.

Structural Concerns

Social perceptions of women have changed, and this could result in mounting female crime and increased official labeling. Changes in self-perception and socialization can precipitate crime among women, given structural preconditions. But to explain these changes by focusing on the audience and not structural change, labeling has to argue (as I did earlier) that women were previously treated more leniently by official agencies. The difficulty is that "the development of a deviant self-image and deviant career is not looked upon by the societal reaction approach as a result of anything *other than* the consequences of labeling and successful degradation ceremonies" (Broadhead, 1974: 295). This is a consequence of inadequate structural explanations and an overly critical attitude toward official statistics (paralleling Merton's insufficient criticisms of them). The lenient treatment women supposedly received in the past is debatable. Minority and lower-class women are not protected from official reaction, nor is any women whose behavior fails to meet institutionalized expectations.

Kai Erikson admits social structure plays a part in deviance but claims social reaction explains the extensive involvement of particular groups, especially the young and lower class. This defense seems acceptable, until one thinks of another population group (women) and recognizes that social structure is not pushed aside quite so easily. Erikson would have difficulty explaining why young and lower-class males — but not females — are subject to negative social reaction, if the variables of age and class are so crucial. No, a discussion of initial deviance is simply unavoidable if a well-rounded theory is to evolve, as is a consideration of women.

Effects of Labeling and Initial Motivation

Labeling theory has also been criticized for overemphasizing the negative effects of social reaction and failing to discuss the positive aspects of deterrence. Empirical evidence is lacking, once again, but this criticism is pertinent when applying the theory to women and crime. Official reaction may have a different impact on women: it may reduce their deviance because of their preoccupation with the unpleasant consequences of crime. Furthermore, women are typically labeled noncriminals, thus discouraging initial and future deviant activities.

A deepening commitment to deviance can frequently be explained in terms of social reaction, but at times understanding initial motivation is essential. By ignoring this, labeling theory is necessarily one-sided and incomplete. It implies that initial behavior is meaningless and certainly not crucial in forging a commitment to deviance — only official reaction is vital. By examining two crimes in which women are particularly involved, I can further illustrate these difficulties.

A career in prostitution seems easily explained by labeling. This behavior violates the rules of society, and powerless women are arrested and subjected to the detrimental effects of official labeling, which encourages them to view themselves as prostitutes and pushes them further into a criminal career. How does this differ from shoplifting? We have evidence that once officially reprimanded for this offense, women are often deterred from further involvement. The discrepancies are difficult to explain solely in terms of official reaction. Labeling theory is simply too deterministic. Behavior is meaningful, and understanding the initial reasons why people engage in deviant behavior is crucial in explaining its future development. Lemert (1951: 267), discussing prostitution, claims: "The paths leading to the commercialization of sex are numerous and diverse. Generalizations as to why women engage in primary sex deviation become so broad as to be practically without value." The reasons for engaging in shoplifting are also diverse and likely to be quite different from those resulting in prostitution. But perhaps it is precisely because the initial reasons for involvement are so different that official reaction can bring such different results. Labeling theory disregards this and thus *not only* avoids explaining initial deviance but fails to explain secondary deviance as well, if the relationship between official reaction and secondary deviance depends, to any appreciable extent, on the motives behind initial deviance (a point most critics overlook).

Power

Labeling theory also neglects expanding its insight about the role of power in the production of deviance.[11] This closely relates to the absence of structural explanations, which might have encouraged a full discussion of social inequalities. Consequently, labeling is limited and individualistic, focusing on the deviant, rather than on the connections between that person and broader structures. Thio (1973) complains about the class bias evident in labeling, which studiously ignores the crimes of the powerful (similar omissions are found in deviance and criminology in general). I will add that labeling (and other theories) do not simply suffer from a class bias, but also from a problem of sexism. A sophisticated analysis of the role of power is required to understand deviance in general and to answer questions regarding women and crime that challenge labeling theory. For example, labeling contends that the powerless are not necessarily more criminal but, rather, suffer the detrimental effects of official labeling due to biased laws and differential law enforcement. Many critics agree and want this insight explored. This, however, ignores crime among women and any explanation as to why, although certainly powerless, their involvement is so different from that of (lower-class) males. Women are infrequently labeled, and when labeled, the effects seem less pernicious. Why is this so? Without a detailed discussion of power relations and structural factors, this cannot be explained. Surprisingly, few criminologists are even asking these questions. Although we have been alerted to the class bias found in our theories, most criminologists are still afflicted by a similar blindness regarding women.

Thio (1973), concerned about class bias, claims that the powerful do not view themselves as potential deviants, while the powerless do see themselves this way. Does this apply to women? He claims that sociology has seriously studied the powerless, but not the powerful. Is this true regarding women? He concludes that until the behavior of the powerful is explored (an immense omission), any general theory of deviance will remain "suspect." The same should be said regarding women. The failure to examine their behavior confounds any theory that purports to explain human behavior in general terms.

Liazos (1972) briefly mentions that the stigma of prostitution and abortion are carried by women due to their powerlessness. Statements of this sort must be extended to a full analysis of power interests in dictating the very conditions of women in this society. Labeling theory generally argues that those who lack wealth, status, and power are more likely to be officially labeled. This might be correct, and the limited official labeling of women (who typically lack the above) might indicate they seldom deviate (although labeling also assumes everyone deviates). What is required is an understanding of initial deviance and the impact of labeling (positive and negative) as well as a thorough analysis of the structures of power and how they impinge on women. Labeling theory lacks all of the above and, thus, fails to explain the phenomena of women and crime.

CONCLUSION

Labeling theory offers valuable and very welcome insights pertaining to women and crime. It suggests a deeper understanding of the role of women in society and their crime patterns will emerge through an examination of the laws dealing with their behavior, bearing in mind that these laws are socially defined and greatly influenced by the powerful. Secondly, it emphasizes the impact social reaction has on the development of the self. Some groups (the powerless) are more likely to experience the negative effects of official reaction, but beyond this (by extending labeling theory), we can examine both the harsh treatment, and the "positive" labeling of women, through informal groups and official procedures. Being labeled obedient, passive, nonviolent, et cetera, will, as the social interaction theorists suggest, be incorporated into the self-image of women and, perhaps, decrease their very involvement in crime.

Labeling theory advises that official reaction can (often) push a person further into crime. By and large I agree and have severe reservations about people-changing institutions. The processes of social control, however, are not limited to explicit official reaction. Socialization and primary groups are potent means of social control and seem to operate particularly effectively in regard to women.

Thus, labeling is helpful but incomplete. It lacks structural explanations, a clear discussion of the impact of labeling, and a full treatment of power in society.

NOTES

[1] See Harold Garfinkel's article, "Conditions of Successful Degradation Ceremonies," *American Journal of Sociology* 61 (March 1956), for an ethnomethodological treatment of the redefinition of the self, which is akin to labeling theory.

[2] This is ironic, given the commonsense assumption that criminal behavior is best controlled and even thwarted by punishment, or the threat of punishment.

[3] Lemert claims that labeling theory's dependence on the symbolic interactionism of George Herbert Mead has been a hindrance since the ambiguities in Mead's work are a poor foundation for theoretical development. But neither is Lemert enchanted with the work of the conflict theorists.

[4] In *Wayward Puritans*, Erikson (1966: 6) makes a similar statement: "Deviance is not a property *inherent in* any particular kind of behavior; it is a property conferred upon that behavior by the people who come into direct or indirect contact with it."

[5] In *Wayward Puritans*, Erikson deals with witchcraft and religious heresies in seventeenth-century New England, which labeling might explain more suitably than other phenomena.

[6] Labeling is certainly not irreversible. Many forms of deviance decline as a person ages, although additional official labeling should have an increasingly powerful negative impact.

[7] Thorsell and Klemke (1972) also claim that labeling seems to have fewer effects, positive or negative, once the stage of secondary deviance has been reached; that additional rule breaking is more apt to be avoided when labeling is confidential, with the threat of exposure for future deviance; and that the societal reaction which accompanies labeling is crucial: if the reaction is helpful, supportive, and aimed at reintegrating the deviant, labeling will be less harmful.

[8] Of course, the more sophisticated versions of labeling theory would not defend this position, even though it might be implicit to some extent.

[9] Understandably, many of these criticisms originate with Marxists or neo-

Marxists. Writers such as Taylor, Walton, and Young, Quinney, et cetera, reject labeling's focus on the individual offender, rather than on social structures. Moreover, they reject its tolerance of our economic system and the idea that capitalism is a minor detail, not an essential variable, in the production of crime and crime control. See Peter Manning (1975) for further discussion of this.

[10]Being labeled mentally ill can be as harmful and as painful as any other deviant label, but mental illness is not my main concern. Those interested should see Phyllis Chesler, *Women and Madness*, 1972; Thomas Scheff, *Labeling Madness*, 1975; Irving Goffman, *Asylums*, 1961.

[11]Although certain labeling theorists (Becker, Erikson) mention power, this cannot substitute for a sophisticated discussion of the issue.

CHAPTER FIVE

Differential Association

INTRODUCTION: SUTHERLAND AND HIS WORK

Edwin Sutherland (1883–1950) is a major figure in criminology, and his theoretical explanation of crime (differential association) has continuously inspired discussion and stimulated empirical research. Differential association describes crime as similar to any other learned behavior. Individuals learn to rob a bank in much the same way they learn to fix a car — they simply are taught by others. This sharply departs from theories that assume crime is rooted in biological or psychological disorders. If criminal activity is learned in a "normal" fashion, individual abnormality is not a necessary or even a noteworthy precondition of crime.

Sutherland, like the labeling theorists, stressed the significance of understanding the social processes by which individuals become criminals. He maintained criminal patterns are transmitted within a cultural world, and that individuals are affected by group associations, which support either adherence to the law or its violation. (Here Sutherland's work is akin to that of subcultural theory, which will be discussed later.)

Differential association has, in many respects, dominated criminology, perhaps for two reasons (Gibbons, 1977: 244). First, it represents an outstanding attempt to postulate a general theory explaining all types of crime. Its scope is broad, its propositions are closely linked with one another, and it explains individual participation and nonparticipation in crime. Although Sutherland thought of his propositions more as hypotheses than theoretical laws, he was convinced that a general theory of crime is desirable. Second, Sutherland was consistently sociological. Differential association demonstrates the impact of social experiences and primary groups. It is untainted by subtle psychological assumptions.

In addition to his discussion of differential association, Sutherland was also concerned with a structural analysis of "differential social organization." Furthermore, his thoughtful studies of professional theft and white-collar crime challenged unspoken assumptions about criminality and had a lasting (and beneficial) effect on criminology. For these reasons, and more, he deserves his title as the "dean" of American criminology (Reid, 1976: 211).

DIFFERENTIAL ASSOCIATION: THE STATEMENT, ITS DEVELOPMENT, AND APPLICATION

Statement of Differential Association

Differential association is a thoughtful description of social (associational) influence on individuals. It systematically describes and connects the variables involved in learning criminal behavior, concentrating on social relations. Sutherland attempted to be as "scientific" as possible by specifying those aspects of association that could be quantified (Vold, 1958: 193). The first formal statement of differential association appeared in the 1939 (third) edition of his well-known text, *Principles of Criminology*. At that time, the theory contained seven propositions, accounting for all "systematic criminal behavior." A revised version was published in the 1947 text, with the now familiar nine propositions Sutherland claimed would explain *all* criminal behavior.[1]

These two statements are the only published accounts of differential association, and unfortunately they are not systematically incorporated throughout his text. Sutherland did not regard his theory as definitive, but rather as subject to whatever revisions future empirical evidence might dictate. The nine propositions are best quoted directly, with some commentary (Sutherland and Cressey, 1960: 77–79):

1. Criminal behavior is learned. It is not inherited or invented by particular individuals, nor is it the result of physical deficiencies such as low intelligence or brain damage.

2. Criminal behavior is learned in interaction with others in a process of communication. Sutherland is concerned with both verbal communication and gestures.

3. The principal part of the learning of criminal behavior occurs within intimate personal groups. The focus is on primary groups; impersonal agents like television, newspapers, and magazines play, at best, a secondary role in the criminal process.

4. When criminal behavior is learned, the learning includes (a) techniques of committing the crime, which are sometimes very complicated, sometimes very simple; (b) the specific direction of motives, drives, rationalizations, and attitudes. The criminal must learn, for example, how to pass a bad check, how to illegally enter an apartment, as well as the reasons, justifications, etc., for doing so.

5. The specific direction of motives and drives is learned from definitions of the legal codes as favorable or unfavorable. Sutherland contends that in a complex modern society like the United States, reasons for obeying and violating the law are simultaneously expounded, and cultural conflict regarding the law results. Individuals may learn reasons for both maintaining and violating a particular law. We can be taught, for example, that it is wrong to steal — but that large stores will hardly miss stolen merchandise.

6. A person becomes delinquent because of an excess of definitions favorable to violation of law over definitions unfavorable to violation of law. This is the central proposition. It refers to both criminal and noncriminal associations and claims that a predominance of contact with criminal patterns (not necessarily persons) will result in criminal behavior. The element of conflict is vital; without it Sutherland believes a person will simply assimilate the given culture.

7. Differential associations may vary in frequency, duration, priority, and intensity. These variables pertain to both criminal and noncriminal associations. According to Sutherland, the meaning of frequency and duration are "obvious." Priority refers to the time (childhood or later) of exposure to different patterns. Intensity, by Sutherland's admission, is not precisely defined, but relates to the prestige or emotional content of differential associations. He (1960: 79) claims that: "In a precise description of the criminal behavior of a person these modalities would be stated in quantitative form and a mathematical ratio be reached." He recognizes, however, that this task is incomplete and extremely difficult.

8. *The process of learning criminal behavior by association with criminal and noncriminal patterns involves all the mechanisms that are involved in any other learning.* Sutherland is not speaking merely of imitation, but he claims that no special learning process is involved: one learns crime through one's associations.

9. *While criminal behavior is an expression of general needs and values, it is not explained by those general needs and values since noncriminal behavior is an expression of the same needs and values.* The desire for happiness, social status, money, and so on is not an acceptable explanation of criminal behavior, since it can also be used to explain lawful behavior. For example, the desire for money can motivate a person either to seek a job or to rob a bank.

After stating his nine principles, Sutherland (1960: 79) adds that it "is not necessary, at this level of explanation, to explain why a person has the associations which he has; this certainly involves a complex of many things." Differential association focuses on the criminal behavior of individual people, unlike theories that specifically explain the crime rates of nations or groups. Sutherland (1960: 80) claims, however, that these two levels of analysis should be consistent, "since the crime rate is a summary statement of the number of persons in the group who commit crimes and the frequency with which they commit crimes."

The essence of differential association, then, is that crime (techniques, motives, etc.) is learned through interaction with others who define law violation as acceptable, while relatively isolated from anticriminal definitions. According to Donald Cressey (a student of Sutherland, and a strong proponent of his theory), when the theory is applied to a group or nation, it becomes a strictly sociological theory, studying rates of crime, as opposed to a sociopsychological theory dealing with individuals.

DIFFERENTIAL SOCIAL ORGANIZATION

Although chiefly concerned with the processes by which individuals become criminal, Sutherland noted the larger picture. Dissatisfied with the term *social disorganization*, he began to discuss "differential social organization,"[2] in order to explain the reasons for varying *rates* of crime. In other words, it is necessary to understand why one person rather than another becomes criminal (John as opposed to Mary), but it is equally imperative to understand why one group is more criminal than another (males as opposed to females). Sutherland recognized that this demands a concern with social conditions and social change. He tried to demonstrate how conflict between subcultures affects crime rates, and he discussed crime within various immigrant communities and during war (Cohen et al., 1956, Part 3). Cressey (1960b: 3) states that the essence of differential social organization is that:

> in a multi-group type of social organization, alternative and inconsistent standards of conduct are possessed by various groups, so that individuals who are members of one group have a higher probability of learning to use legal means for achieving success, or of learning to deny the importance of success, while individuals in other groups learn to accept the importance of success and to achieve it by illegal means.

Most unfortunately, Sutherland did not systematically elaborate this aspect of his work.

In an address given in 1942 (Cohen et al., 1956: 13–29), Sutherland discussed the development of his theory. His reflections are noteworthy for several reasons: first, they indicate the depth of his thinking and his openness to the criticism and reformulation of his theory in light of criticism. In addition, his comments enable us to delve more deeply into issues pertinent to understanding differential association. Finally, they give a refreshingly candid picture of a thoughtful scholar at work. In this address, Sutherland reaffirms his commitment to a general theory of crime causation, which explains empirical data, "either by organizing the multiple factors in relation to each other or by abstracting from them certain common elements" (Cohen et al., 1956: 18). Sutherland notes that "hundreds" of things are associated with criminal behavior, including being a male, but these factors, in and of themselves, do not account for crime: "I reached the general conclusion that a concrete condition cannot be a cause of crime, and that the only way to get a causal explanation of criminal behavior is by abstracting from the varying concrete conditions things that are universally associated with crime" (Cohen et al., 1956: 19). Thus, Sutherland began to examine the role of learning, interaction, and communication in the development of criminal behavior. His principle of differential association seemed to explain the basic empirical data on criminality (including the higher crime rate among males).

In the same address, Sutherland discusses certain difficulties surrounding differential association. He mentions, for example, the connections among the concepts of differential association, social disorganization, and culture conflict. He admits that his writing on this is "very far from clear" (Cohen et al., 1956: 20). He explains that culture conflict is a basic principle in understanding crime and that differential association treats culture conflict from the standpoint of an individual person who has different cultures influencing him or associations that reflect different cultures. Social disorganization (preferably referred to as differential social organization) explains crime rates, rather than the criminal behavior of an individual.

Critics have complained that differential association disregards how crime first originated, but Sutherland contends such behavior probably existed before the law prohibited it, and thus is available to be learned after it is criminalized.

Sutherland also raises the issue of the relationship between personal traits and cultural patterns regarding the causes of crime. He views this as a central question in criminology but contends that "Personal traits have a causal relation to criminal behavior only as they affect the person's associations" (Cohen et al., 1956: 25). Sutherland notes that this formulation has elicited much disagreement and concedes it must be wrong but frankly admits he does not know precisely how to change it. He believes that his theory is basically correct, and that modification is the best solution.

White Collar Crime

To many, Sutherland is best known for his treatment of white-collar crime. His interest in this began shortly after the publication of the first edition of *Criminology* in 1924. Later editions contained references to this kind of crime, and in 1939, his presidential address before the American Sociological Society took white-collar crime as its theme. His 1945 article, "Is 'White Collar Crime' Crime?" replied to criticisms of his work; and finally, in 1949, he published a detailed study of 70 corporations, entitled *White Collar Crime*. Cohen, Lindesmith, and Schuessler (1956: 45) argue that Sutherland's interest in this topic is intimately connected with his dissatisfaction with criminological theories that discuss crime in terms of poverty and social disorganization. It reflects his persistent search for a general theory of crime, and, in fact, he explains white-collar crime through differential association.

Sutherland (1961: xiii) referred to *White Collar Crime* as "an attempt to reform the theory of criminal behavior." He claims that poverty is an inadequate explanation of crime, since it does not fit the empirical data. For example, approximately equal numbers of boys and girls are poor, but male delinquency greatly overshadows female delinquency; some groups are extremely poor and have low rates of crime; moreover, only a slight relationship exists between economic depressions and crime. Sutherland realized that the statistics used to connect crime and poverty are badly distorted, since upper-class individuals are often able to avoid arrest and conviction. He reasons that if white-collar crime is common, it invalidates theories relating crime and poverty and can help in the search for a theory adequate to explain the crime of both rich and poor.

Sutherland examined 70 of the largest corporations in the United States and their subsidiaries (their average existence was 45 years). He noted such violations as restraint of trade; misrepresentation in advertising; infringement on patents, trademarks, and copyrights; unfair labor practices; rebates; financial fraud and violation of trust; violations of war regulations; and miscellaneous offenses. He found 950 adverse decisions against the 70 corporations, each averaging about 14 decisions.[3] He observed therefore (Cohen et al., 1956: 94–95) that violations are frequent and persistent, even more common than prosecutions indicate.

Sutherland contends that white-collar crime results from an anomic form of social disorganization, relating to the change from free enterprise to government regulation. Both businesspersons and the public are uncertain about appropriate business behavior, including acceptable standards regarding violations of law. "Business has a rather tight organization for the violations of business regulations, while the political society is not similarly organized against violations of business regulations" (Sutherland, 1961: 255). Businesspersons often feel contempt for legal regulations, and even prosecution does not cause them to lose status among their associates. According to Sutherland, white-collar criminals are quite like professional thieves in all these respects. The major difference is their higher status in society at large.

Sutherland concludes that white-collar crime, like all crime, originates in the process of differential association. Businesspersons learn the techniques and appropriate circumstances for law violation and the ideology to support this. He contends that the diffusion of illegal practices from one corporation to another substantiates his theory, as does the fact that businesspersons are not only in contact with criminal patterns but isolated from definitions unfavorable toward such behavior. He asserts (Cohen et al., 1956: 96) that if his information is correct:

> The criminal behavior of businessmen cannot be explained by poverty, in the usual sense, or by bad housing or lack of recreational facilities or feeble-mindedness or emotional instability. Business leaders are capable, emotionally balanced, and in no sense pathological. We have no reason to think that General Motors has an inferiority complex or that the Aluminium Company of America has a frustration-aggression complex or that U.S. Steel has an Oedipus complex, or that the Armour Company has a death wish or that the DuPonts desire to return to the womb. The assumption that

an offender must have some such pathological distortion of the intellect or the emotions seems to me absurd, and if it is absurd regarding the crimes of businessmen, it is equally absurd regarding the crimes of persons in the lower economic class.

Sutherland's analysis of white-collar crime has been severely criticized, but most of this is peripheral to our main concerns. His attempt to use white-collar crime as an illustration of differential association is, however, crucial. Hermann Mannheim (1965: 477) maintains that Sutherland's evidence (including material on the careers of businesspersons, and the diffusion of illegal behavior from one corporation to another) does not prove the validity of differential association. Similarly, Karl Schuessler (1974: xix) contends that "in his analysis [Sutherland] made an effort to show that white-collar criminals undergo the same process of learning as blue-collar criminals, but that effort is so incidental as to slur the importance of differential association." Mannheim disputes Sutherland's claim that white-collar crime indicates the relative unimportance of poverty as a cause of crime. He argues that poverty, combined with other factors, is frequently a valid explanation of crime. To maintain that since white-collar offenders are not poor, poverty is not a cause of crime, is simply unclear thinking. (Actually Sutherland only rejects poverty as a single and total explanation of crime.)

Mannheim also criticizes Sutherland's use of white-collar crime to dispute psychological explanations of criminality. He asserts that it is unjustified to assume that businesspersons either do or do not have psychological problems. (Differential association does not deal thoroughly with personality traits, but Sutherland is accurate in the sense that the stereotype of the offender, often viewed as lower-class and psychologically disturbed, does not fit white-collar businesspersons.)

Sutherland's other research efforts reflect similar themes and concerns, particularly his interest in a general theoretical explanation of crime. He wrote little on juvenile delinquency, in part because he believed the process of a juvenile becoming delinquent was essentially similar to an adult becoming criminal. He studied penology and crime prevention, examining the social determinants of policies and practices, but this never matched his interest in crime causation.

CRITICISMS OF DIFFERENTIAL ASSOCIATION

Differential association is criticized for being unclear and imprecise (Cressey, 1960b; Gibbons, 1977; McCaghy, 1976). The nine propositions are stated simply and briefly, resulting in much ambiguity about the intended meaning and accuracy of each statement. Sutherland's writings indicate he was aware of the criticisms of his theory and accepted the validity of some of them.

The best single source for reviewing the vast critical literature on differential association is Donald Cressey's 1960 article, "Epidemiology and Individual Conduct: A Case from Criminology." Originally a Presidential Address read before the Pacific Sociological Association in April 1960, this organizes and thoroughly documents the controversy surrounding the theory. Cressey begins by listing criticisms based on misinterpretations of Sutherland's position. He realizes Sutherland is partly to blame for these errors, since his meaning is not always obvious; but some readers also simply failed to understand him. For example, it is commonly believed that differential association refers solely to criminal behavior patterns, whereas it actually encompasses both criminal and noncriminal behavior and attempts to explain both. Also, certain critics still believe the theory only explains "systematic" criminal behavior, ignoring Sutherland's emphatic rephrasing to include all criminal behavior. Another example of such misconceptions is the notion that excessive contact with criminals inspires criminal patterns of behavior, whereas Sutherland explicitly spoke of contact with criminal patterns of behavior — which could be transmitted by criminal or noncriminal persons.

Differential association has also been criticized for its limited applicability: it cannot explain some types of criminal behavior. Cressey documents various charges that the theory does not apply to rural offenders, naive check forgers, murders, crimes of passion, and so forth. He rejects this, however, and insists that many of these criticisms are not based on research, but simply assume that differential association cannot provide an explanation. This, however, requires proof. Moreover (as Vold, 1958, notes), the theory does not necessarily have to apply to every type of crime. There can be exceptions to any theory.

I will now examine the major limitations of differential association. Although these are divided into three categories, they are intimately related to one another.

The Roots of Crime

Sutherland argues that individuals become criminals when overexposed to definitions of behavior that favor violating the law. He sees criminal behavior, then, as rooted in the particular associations a person has with criminal patterns. Pinpointing a person's associations as the crucial variable has been criticized in two respects: first, because it ignores individual differences; and second, because it disregards structural factors.

Differential association does treat psychological variables inadequately, and this is problematic insofar as such variables affect behavior. Sutherland himself acknowledged this criticism and attempted to deal with it. In a lecture given in 1942 ("Development of a Theory," Cohen et al., 1956), he claimed his theory would have to be revised to overcome this difficulty, but his statement published in 1947 did not reflect any substantial changes. In fact, in *White Collar Crime* (1949: 264–265), he notes the logical inadequacy of using "personality traits" to explain a criminal condition without indicating precisely how they relate to crime. He asked critics of differential association three questions: What personality traits are significant? Are these traits that differential association does not include? Can differential association (a processual theory) be combined with personality traits, which are basically a product of learning?

For Sutherland, these questions indicate the difficulty and perhaps the uselessness of dealing specifically with personality traits. He believes differential association can explain why, for example, some "aggressive" people commit crimes and others do not: it depends on their associations. Thus, he chooses to deemphasize individual differences, although he admits that they may be important.

Closely related is the criticism that differential association fails to explain why people have the particular associations they do. Sutherland dismisses this, saying it involves another level of analysis (Sutherland and Cressey, 1960: 79). And yet, this issue is at the heart of the problem of criminality. By ignoring it, Sutherland overlooks crucial differences between criminals and noncriminals, not simply in terms of individual differences, but regarding structural patterns. He claims that structural variables are worthy of analysis but (like Cressey) contends that omitting them is not a defect. At the very least, however, it establishes the limitations of this theory.

Sutherland recognizes that modern society is complex and diverse, with conflicting norms. While differential association concerns the transmission of criminal and noncriminal behavior, the concept of differential organization elucidates the existence of conflicting norms and variations in crime rates, thus approaching structural considerations. According to Cressey (1960a: 48, 55), Sutherland was deeply concerned with explaining crime rates and believed high crime occurs in those sections of society conducive to the development of criminal subcultures. He did not, however, offer an exacting analysis of the origins of these subcultures. His concept of differential organization is extremely underdeveloped, thus precluding a serious structural analysis of the roots of crime.

Determinism

Sutherland analyzed a person's association in order to explain criminal behavior, deemphazing (though acknowledging) the importance of structural features and psychological variables. His view of the deviant learning to violate the law has been criticized. He seems, at times, to regard individuals as determined by their environment, accepting definitions presented to them in a thoroughly passive manner. "The individual does not choose a type of behavior because it has meaning and purpose to him — he is merely 'templated' with the meanings prevalent in his social environment" (Taylor, Walton, and Young, 1973: 128). Sutherland's concept of differential organization pictured social reality as diverse — thus allowing the possibility of human choice in terms of action — but differential association did not incorporate this insight in a systematic fashion. Rather, it made the behavior of individuals seem almost inevitable, depending on their immediate associations.

Sutherland approaches a positivistic view of human behavior as totally constrained by the given surroundings. He disregards individuals making decisions, troubled by conflicting choices, or acting purposefully. To incorporate this, differential association would have to emphasize differential organization, where these conflicts and choices are rooted. Sutherland's theory should not, however, be dismissed as mere positivism, for it reaches beyond such narrow confines. Cressey (1960a: 50) ridicules the idea that Sutherland was only concerned, for example, with a simple ratio of criminal versus noncriminal associations. He explicitly discusses the variables of frequency, duration, priority, and intensity. Differential association, however, oversimplifies the learning process and ignores criminality "independently invented" by an individual. This implies a mechanistic tendency on Sutherland's part, and some of his statements can certainly be interpreted this way. For example, presenting the sixth (and major) principle in his theory, which claims a person becomes delinquent because of an excess of definitions favorable to violating the law, Sutherland states, "Any person inevitably assimilates the surrounding culture unless other patterns are in conflict" (Cohen et al., 1956: 9). Thus, he does not consider independently created deviance. In addition, there is a brief discussion by Sutherland on the relationship between personal traits and criminal behavior: "Susceptibility and Differential Association" (Cohen et al., 1956: 42–43). Unfortunately, this fragment is not dated, but in it Sutherland claims that a person with a great deal of susceptibility will need relatively few associations with criminal patterns to then engage in crime, whereas a person with low susceptibility will need many more criminal associations for the same result. This, in itself, sounds somewhat mechanistic, but it is quickly followed by a more damaging statement (Cohen et al., 1956: 43):

> This explanation makes persons substitutable. If a person is self-determinative, science is impossible and criminal behavior cannot be explained. But if a person with a given amount of susceptibility can be assumed, any other person with the same susceptibility can be substituted, and the same behavior will result. It is necessary to state the personal factor in that manner. The person in this sense is passive.

Possibly, this essay was written before 1942 when "Development of a Theory" was written, since the latter paper indicates that Sutherland initially believed susceptibility was an important consideration but later came to realize susceptibility itself was "largely if not wholly" the result of earlier associations (Cohen et al., 1956: 25). Sutherland remained discontent with his treatment of personality characteristics, but nevertheless I find that his statements still contain a view of human beings and human behavior that is disturbing.

Fortunately, there are other facets to Sutherland's work. He discusses individual meaning and definitions of the situation; he is unwilling to reduce the motivation for crime to mere rationalizations that are psychologically rooted. In his statement of differential association, for example, he claims that "the situation which is important is the situation as defined by the person who is involved"; and, while tendencies and inhibitions are largely the result of a person's earlier biography, "the expression of these tendencies and inhibitions is a reaction to the immediate situation as defined by the person" (Cohen et al., 1956: 7, 8). Criticizing his own theory, Sutherland asserts that people do not become involved in crime solely because of association with criminal patterns, but this must be connected with one's desire to satisfy the needs of a particular situation. Such statements seem less positivistic and deterministic.

This issue can be put in a broader framework through the insights of David Matza. In *Becoming Deviant* (1969), Matza insists that scientific notions of the physical world (particularly the idea of prediction) are frequently imposed on the study of social behavior. Sutherland's work reflects this, since it does not successfully repudiate positivistic notions of human behavior in favor of the human subject, the willing subject. But Sutherland did move in this direction, refusing to see antecedent circumstances as thoroughly dominant. When differential association is combined with differential social organization (as Sutherland intended), ideas of conflict and, ultimately, choice are able to emerge. Matza (1969: 107) crystallizes the limitations and the virtues of Sutherland's work brilliantly:

Though sensitive to pluralism, as manifested in the central place accorded the conception of differential social organization, Sutherland was not always appreciative of the movement of ideas and persons between deviant and conventional worlds. Partly obsessed by the idea of ecology, Sutherland nearly made his subject a captive of the milieu. Like a tree or a fox, the subject was a creature of affiliational circumstance, except that what Sutherland's milieu provided was *meaning* and *definition of the situation*. Sutherland's subject was a creature, but he was half a man. Had Sutherland appreciated the interpenetration of cultural worlds — the symbolic availability of various ways of life everywhere — and more important, had he appreciated that men, but not trees and foxes, intentionally move in search of meaning as well as nourishment . . . if, in other words, he had rejected the doctrine of radical cultural separation along with an ecological theory of migration well-suited for insects but not man, his creature would have been wholly human.

Sutherland often left his subject without alternatives, or the capacity to choose; but according to Matza (1969: 108), he succeeded in bringing this creature to "the brink of humanity," by observing the meaning individuals give a situation. Although much of Sutherland's work gives the impression of people totally constrained by their environment, there is some opportunity for their interpretation of the situation. Thus, his theory is less mechanistic and deterministic than first appears. Still, it is incomplete. As Laurie Taylor (1971: 87–91) points out, it is unacceptable to view individuals as mere "recipients" of information. They do not simply ingest external elements — human beings play an active role choosing, rejecting, and reinterpreting what is presented to them.

Matza claims the central difficulty is the tendency to treat individuals as objects that merely react. This ignores that people engage in meaningful behavior, are able to create their world, and participate in it as subjects, not objects. A theory that neglects this aspect of deviance demonstrates an incomplete understanding of human behavior.[4]

Quantification and Testing of Differential Association

Sutherland viewed his formulation of differential association as tentative and hoped it would be either supported or revised in light of empirical findings. Researchers, however, complain that the theory is untestable and poses serious difficulties for those who would operationalize its concepts.[5] How is an "excess of definitions" measured? Can the impact of varying associations, from early childhood on, possibly be grasped or quantified? How can concepts like priority and intensity be operationalized?

Differential association, perhaps more than any other theory, has been consistent with the findings of empirical research (Short, 1957, 1958; Voss, 1964; Glaser, 1960; etc.), but as James Short (1960) points

104 WOMEN, CRIME, AND SOCIETY

out, this does not necessarily mean the theory is valid. Short criticizes it for being difficult to test and suggests it be restated in more "verifiable" propositions. Even Donald Cressey, a strong proponent of differential association, regards this as a most damaging criticism and supports those who maintain that differential association should be altered to allow for empirical testing.[6] However, Cressey remains committed to the theory (1964: 164):

> Despite the defects in the theory of differential association . . . it may be concluded that the theory remains as a valid guide for those who would rehabilitate criminals, as well as for those who would explain delinquency and criminal behavior and the distribution of crime and delinquency rates in society.

Thus, he contends that Sutherland's theory can still explain the distribution of deviance, regardless of whether it is untestable or even incorrect in individual cases.

Attempts have been made to revise differential association so that it might be tested. Melvin DeFleur and Richard Quinney (1966) use set theory to reformulate Sutherland's principles, but the most notable effort is that of Robert Burgess and Ronald Akers (1966). They argue that modern behavior theory can be utilized to explain how differential association produces individual criminality. The concepts of learning theory can be operationalized, and by applying them to differential association, the difficulty with testing this theory is, supposedly, overcome. Although differential association must be reformulated with the introduction of concepts from learning theory, Burgess and Akers contend this is simply a restatement of differential association, not an alternative theory. Sutherland's nine principles are rewritten to seven new ones including, for example, number one: "Criminal behavior is learned according to the principles of operant conditioning" (Burgess and Akers, 1966: 137). Burgess and Akers conclude that modern behavior theory solves the problems of differential association by enabling it to be empirically tested, once reformulated.

If, however, the revisions suggested by Burgess and Akers are unacceptable, the problem remains. I believe there are serious difficulties with merging reinforcement theory and differential association, and even attempting to do so reflects criticisms of differential association introduced above.

Taylor, Walton, and Young (1973: 130–133) offer a biting criticism of Burgess and Akers' desire to "transplant" behaviorist learning theory onto differential association. They totally reject behaviorism and its implications. Burgess and Akers view crime as behavior learned through positive and negative reinforcements. Human choice is not at issue and is not discussed. According to Taylor, Walton, and Young (1973: 133), Burgess and Akers are repeatedly "forced back on the tautology of stating that people pursue that which is reinforcing." Very simply, values and meaningful behavior cannot be discussed "in terms of automatons propelled through their lives like Skinnerian rats." I share this disdain for behaviorism, and the belief that it distorts the spirit of differential association, a theory conceding that human beings make choices and act meaningfully. I agree with Taylor, Walton, and Young (1973: 130), however, that it is not purely accidental that differential association was reformulated in this manner. "Because of the conception of human nature as passive and the rudimentary taken-for-granted nature of differential organization, Sutherland's theory exposes itself to revisionist takeovers from behaviorism." Human choice is not written into the theory as clearly as it might be. It raises questions of determinism and ultimately leaves itself open to the positivism of behaviorist theory. Thus, attempts to solve the dilemma of testing differential association have resulted in revisions of the theory, which distort its fundamental principles. These misconceptions, in turn, spring from Sutherland's lack of a full discussion of the importance and meaning of structural variables, but more importantly of the meaning of human behavior itself.

Theory Construction

Finally, a related issue (not really a criticism) concerns the appropriate scope of theoretical explanations of crime. Differential association purports to explain "all crime," which obviously includes a tremendous variety of behavior, ranging from minor offenses to extremely serious crime. Since petty crime accounts for the vast majority of offenses, any theory that only applies to serious crime is totally inadequate. By viewing crime as normal learned behavior, differential association is better equipped to explain the bulk of crime, and the fact that a substantial portion of our population (including every social class, race, religious group, and so on) is involved in some crime.

George Vold (1958) argues, however, that, considering the immense variety of crime (ranging from sex offenses to refusing to file income tax reports), one theory cannot be expected to explain everything. Questions have been raised about the utility of a theory that includes all misbehavior. Extreme eclecticism, on the other hand, negates the purpose of theoretical explanation, which always analyzes beyond the particular. The task, then, is to decide which types of criminal behavior can logically be united and to offer explanations for each of these types. To a certain extent, Sutherland would agree. He was willing to supplement his analysis, claiming differential association explains crime in general, but particular types of criminal behavior might need further elaboration. Vold concedes that unless we generalize about criminal behavior, we cannot construct scientific theory, but he asserts that the theory should aim at categories of crime, not crime in general. If Sutherland is correct, however, a common framework exists for all crime (differential association), even if additional factors are also involved. I feel Sutherland's generalized approach offers the greatest potential and, by accepting supplements, can avoid the more serious limitations of either exceedingly general or specific theoretical models.

Conclusion

Differential association is helpful in organizing the data on crime and explaining many of the variations in crime rates, without resorting to psychological variables. It does, however, need elaboration and revision, particularly in regard to the problems outlined above. The insights of this theory are a testimony to the intellectual creativity of Sutherland; its limitations reflect problems facing not only differential association, but criminology in general.

APPLICATION TO WOMEN

According to Sutherland, differential association applies to all criminal and noncriminal behavior. It should therefore be particularly suitable for explaining female criminality (and noncriminality). In fact, Sutherland specifically mentioned (Cohen, Lindesmith, Schuessler, 1956: 19) that differential association seems to explain "why males are more delinquent than females." Unfortunately, he did not pursue the matter.

As noted above, Sutherland was dissatisfied with conventional theories of crime, particularly those emphasizing poverty as the cause of crime. His analysis of white-collar crime attempted to correct this imbalance and to generate a more comprehensive sociological theory. In *White Collar Crime* (1961: 6), Sutherland asserts that treating poverty as the cause of crime ignores the fact that approximately equal numbers of boys and girls are poor, yet the vast majority of those adjudged delinquent are males. A detailed analysis of the relationship between women and crime could substantiate Sutherland's ideas and assist in his quest for a more inclusive theory.

Sutherland insists that individuals learn different definitions of the legal code, depending on their associations. When applied to a group (such as women), this becomes a sociological theory pertaining to varying rates of crime. Sutherland (Sutherland and Cressey 1960: 80) emphasizes that individual and group explanations must be consistent, "since the crime rate is a summary statement of the number of persons in the group who commit crimes and the frequency with which they commit crimes." I will utilize his theory to discuss crime rates since he was (according to Cressey, 1960a: 48) seriously, if not primarily, interested in this. Unfortunately, this aspect of his work is incomplete. However, both Sutherland (Cohen, Lindesmith, Schuessler, 1956) and Cressey (1964, chap. 3) apparently feel differential association can explain female rates of crime, so I will analyze his nine principles in terms of women.

Nine Principles

Sutherland's assertion that criminal behavior is learned, immediately frees his theory from assumptions of biological or psychological illness and makes its application to women particularly challenging, given traditional explanations of female criminality and noncriminality. The notion that criminal behavior is learned by interaction with other people through verbal communication and gestures raises the possibility that what is communicated to males and females might vary enormously. In fact, differential socialization and diversified social roles might assist in explaining the low crime rate of females.

Sutherland maintains (principle 3) that most criminal behavior is learned within intimate personal groups. This is useful, for several reasons, in discussing the lack of female criminality. First of all, the family has traditionally been the group with which females are most intimately connected, even during adolescence. They are also likely to have their behavior and activities more strictly controlled and to be more carefully supervised within the family. If crime is learned within intimate personal groups, and for most females the crucial primary group is a restrictive family, they are much less likely to learn criminal behavior. This might explain why the sex ratio varies among young criminals with the degree of family integration (Cressey, 1964: 55). The sex ratio is lower among delinquents from broken homes, where females presumably receive less supervision than they typically encounter. Cressey indicates (1964: 55) that the sex ratio is also lower in families where males outnumber females. Here, too, is a situation in which females have more opportunity to resist traditional expectations (and possibly learn criminal behavior) through continuous contact with dominant male patterns in the household.

Given that the socialization of females is stricter than that of males, and that traditionally they are more tightly bound to the family, it should also be mentioned that they lack the opportunities males have for contact with other "intimate personal groups." Perhaps the most appropriate example is involvement with adolescent gangs. Most females would find their efforts to participate in such groups severely curtailed by family pressure, which is more likely to be successfully exerted against females than males. Women are also frequently excluded from the circles that generate white-collar crime. Thus, they have less opportunity to learn criminal behavior, and, if Sutherland is correct, impersonal agents like newspapers and films do not play a pivotal role. This might explain why shoplifting is more frequent among women, since most pilferers are not involved in a criminal subculture. Usually those arrested are first offenders who do not view themselves, prior to arrest, as thieves. They do not expect group support after being caught and, typically, feel disturbed and isolated. According to Cameron, "The fear, shame, and remorse expressed by arrested pilferers could not be other than genuine and a reflection of their appraisal of the attitudes they believe others will take toward them" (Clinard and Quinney, 1967: 117).

Sutherland's fourth principle asserts that criminal behavior involves learning both the techniques of crime and certain attitudes, motives, and rationalizations regarding crime. Sutherland claims this learning must take place through association with others. Although Cameron observed that shoplifters do not belong to criminal subcultures, she contends they probably associated with law-breaking groups in the past, where they learned the rationalizations and techniques of the crime (Clinard and Quinney, 1967: 111). It is equally possible that shoplifters devise their own techniques of crime, but neither Sutherland nor Cameron mentions this.

Generally speaking, women are shielded from criminal learning experiences. Even within the same groups as males (like the family), their social position is unequal, and they are frequently taught dissimilar attitudes. More isolated from criminal norms and techniques, they are also more consistently taught law-abiding behavior and are expected to act in accordance with the law. Scarcely any tolerance exists for behavior referred to as "sowing wild oats" or "boyish pranks" among females. Their misbehavior is never dismissed with an unconcerned sigh and a remark that "girls will be girls." Boys and girls are taught quite different standards and, with this, subtly differently attitudes toward law breaking.

Boys are certainly not encouraged to break the law, but what is explicitly taught does not encompass all that is learned. Subtle messages are absorbed; attitudes that at least excuse, if not expect, a certain amount of male misbehavior.

Cressey (1964: 54) asserts that the sex ratio in crime varies from one nation to another, and from one group to another, depending on the social position of the sexes. More equality between men and women typically results in a lower sex ratio regarding crime. Likewise, the crime rates of males and females are closer in larger communities, as opposed to smaller ones. Understandably, in populous communities and within groups that treat women more equitably, greater opportunity exists to learn the techniques and rationalizations of crime, since it is more difficult to control or protect women in these situations.

Principle 5 states that individuals learn to define the legal codes as favorable or unfavorable. American society, according to Sutherland, has conflicting norms, enabling individuals to learn reasons for both maintaining and breaking a law. Certain groups (like professional thieves) can, to some extent, be isolated from the rest of society and surrounded by unfavorable definitions of the legal code. Others (like women) can, to some extent, be separate from larger society but taught to emphasize favorable definitions of the legal code.

Although women (as compared to men) are more likely to learn values conducive to law-abiding behavior, this statement must be qualified in light of the factors mentioned above (social position, nation of origin, community size) and the extremely important variables of race and class. Here again, the reliability of the statistics must be questioned. Although serious problems are associated with criminal statistics, they are probably accurate at least in terms of general patterns of crime regarding males and females. Women might be less likely to be suspected of a crime or arrested, but the discrepancy between male and female crime rates is apt to be basically correct. Although the variables of race and class further complicate the reliability of the statistics, minority and lower-class women might have higher rates of crime than other women, although much lower than that of men.[7]

Class and race probably influence opportunities to learn various definitions of the legal codes, with working-class and minority women less protected and controlled, thus having more opportunity for contact with definitions favorable to the violation of the law than their white, upper-class sisters. The statistics also report that the sex ratio is less extreme among blacks, possibly because black men and women are closer in social standing than white men and women.

Sutherland's major principle of differential association (principle 6) proposes that a person becomes delinquent because of excessive contact with criminal as opposed to noncriminal patterns. The differential treatment of males and females outlined above would culminate, then, with women exposed to an excess number of definitions, norms, and patterns of behavior *un*favorable to violating the law. Sutherland supports this (Sutherland and Cressey, 1960: 115) in a discussion of the sex ratio in crime when he and Cressey state, "Probably the most important difference is that girls are supervised more carefully and behave in accordance with anti-criminal behavior patterns taught to them with greater care and consistency than in the case of boys." While girls are taught to be nice, boys are expected to be "rough and tough." Sutherland suggests these differences might have originated because females become pregnant and, hence, require more supervision. While males and females are certainly supervised differently, pregnancy alone does not explain this. Viewing pregnancy outside of marriage as problematic, and specifically the problem of the female, reflects socially constructed attitudes toward males and females. Furthermore, it is difficult to believe that the great differences in behavioral expectations for males and females could rest on this. A deeper analysis of the social inequalities between men and women is needed.

Sutherland notes (principle 7) that both criminal and noncriminal associations may vary in frequency, duration, priority, and intensity. By discussing this, his theory can explain the low rates of delinquency among females in high delinquency areas. Although he did not develop this, Sutherland mentioned (Sutherland and Cressey, 1960: 115) that the crime rate varies for males and females despite the fact that they come from the same homes, neighborhoods, and conditions of poverty. What varies is their social position, which "either determines the frequency and intensity of the delinquent and anti-delinquent patterns which impinge upon them or determines the frequency of opportunities for crimes which are available to them."

The socialization of females ensures that they will encounter more anticriminal patterns (within the family where they are more isolated and controlled) and over a longer period of time (due to extended supervision) than males. Given such training, criminal patterns are less likely to be encountered early in life (priority), and would probably hold much less prestige (intensity) for females. Cressey asserts (1964: 55) that sex ratios vary in different areas of a city, and the higher the crime rate, the lower the sex ratio. Perhaps females in high crime areas are simply exposed to more criminal patterns than other females, but differential socialization and expectations still result in lower female crime. Females also tend to commit crimes at later ages than males (Cressey, 1964: 51), when they are comparatively freer from the supervision that usually prevails.

Sutherland maintains (principle 8) that no unique process is involved in learning criminal or noncriminal behavior patterns: we simply learn by association. I will only add that males and females are exposed to different learning experiences, which result in different behavior.

Sutherland concludes (principle 9) that criminal behavior is not explained in terms of general needs and values (such as happiness, social status, recognition, and so on). These factors can motivate both criminal and noncriminal behavior, and indeed both male and female behavior. Sutherland correctly notes that such variables explain little, since they can be utilized to explain virtually everything.

Thus, differential association interprets the low crime rate among women in terms of their associations, which tend to ensure they will learn patterns of behavior favoring adherence to the law. Males, although frequently members of the same groups as females, are taught quite different patterns of behavior. The intensity of these differences varies in terms of one's nation, class, community, race, and so on, but the general pattern that males and females are socialized and supervised in divergent ways seems (remarkably!) to cut across these variables so that, despite different social settings, male crime exceeds that of females, with very few exceptions.

Increases in Women's Crime

Differential association explains the limited involvement of women in crime in terms of their associations. This assumes women are still tied to traditional roles and the family, with few significant changes in this regard. As Cressey notes, however, there is evidence the sex ratio is decreasing — that changes have occurred over time (Cressey, 1964: 55). He contends that as the social position of women begins approaching that of men, the crime ratio will decline. (This implies the sex ratio in crime indicates sexual inequality, as in fact it does in certain respects.) The social position of women has changed somewhat, and female crime has also increased slightly. To a large extent, differential association can account for these increases.

There have been undeniable changes regarding women in modern society. Traditional expectations have not collapsed, but they have certainly been weakened. Young females are still controlled and protected, but perhaps not as rigidly as before. If their behavior is less restricted, they will be able to come in contact with patterns of behavior that account for male delinquency and crime. As their social position changes, as expectations for males and females begin to blur (even slightly), definitions of behavior, once suitable only to males, will also begin to blur. Forms of illegal behavior, once unthinkable for females, might become a possibility, since expectations for females are no longer as clear as they once were.

The increasing employment and higher education of females (Simon, 1975) has enabled them to have contact with various groups, both legitimate and illegitimate. Certainly the opportunity for women to commit white-collar crimes had to wait until they had the educational requirements and employment opportunities to do so. Weakened restrictions over females might also lead to increased involvement with delinquent friends for drug use, shoplifting, et cetera.

Broader social trends also affect the criminal opportunities of females. As mentioned earlier, the sex ratio in crime is lower among those from broken homes. The intensifying changes in the modern family could profoundly affect females, who are more oppressed by this institution and might make gains in both freedom and crime through its weakening, if not demise. Lower sex ratios also prevail in larger communities, and increasing urbanization might play a role in expanding female crime. To some extent, then, differential association seems more capable of explaining the data of female crime than any theory discussed thus far. There are, however, serious difficulties with its explanations, and I will mention these before assessing its value in analyzing women and crime.

PROBLEMATIC ASPECTS

Certainly the problems mentioned in testing differential association, and in understanding precisely what Sutherland meant, pertain to any attempt to apply the theory. But other limitations strike me as more compelling.

Discussing female patterns of crime in terms of differential association establishes a reasonable explanation for the limited participation of women in crime, although it is not a complete analysis of the phenomenon. Sutherland asserts it is unnecessary to explain why a person has certain associations. I disagree. Perhaps one theory cannot be charged with explaining everything, but the issue of women and crime is unresolved if structural issues are not addressed. Who do males and females have different associations and, given the *same* associations, such different definitions of the legal code? Sutherland tells us the study of differential social organization can help explain varying associations, but unfortunately he does not do this. Moreover, he ignores an explication of why the behavior patterns of males and females differ so widely, given the same associations. He recognizes that men and women share the same neighborhoods, the same homes, the same parents, but he claims they are subject to different degrees of care and supervision. His ultimate explanation is that women get pregnant. This is totally unsatisfactory and a thoroughly inadequate analysis of the different social conditions of men and women. Differential association is a valuable explanation of the process of learning criminal and noncriminal behavior, up to a certain point. But it fails to address issues vital to understanding not only how certain behavior is transmitted, but why such patterns exist in the first place, and why they vary so much from one group to another.

Differential association's inherent determinism also hampers an analysis of women and crime. The theory implies that individuals are crudely affected by their various associations. Women, however, are not simply and directly affected by the number and type of associations they have; they also react and respond in divergent ways. As Sutherland noted (although he did not expand on this), the social world is diverse and conflicting. This does not mean that people are merely affected in different ways (like objects!), but that they have the possibility of choosing between alternatives. Women, as a group and as individuals, have played a part in their destiny. The struggle against an objectionable situation requires a conscious recognition of the problems involved and a belief that changes can and should be made. In modern society, at least, many women have reached this understanding, particularly since World War II, which entailed a breakdown of rather rigid norms.[8] Women have begun to perceive the oppressive conditions of their lives and the possibility of choosing to alter these conditions. As valuable as differential association is to an understanding of women and crime, it deemphasizes (at the very least) wider historical and structural changes, and the responses of women to these changes. The seeds of such an analysis are found in Sutherland's work, since he mentions that individuals define the situation and the social world is full of conflict; but a rich and thorough analysis of women and crime requires that these elements be fully explored and developed. We must examine precisely how associations affect women, how they create their own reality, and the choices and decisions that make them human subjects, not objects.

Differential association attempts to explain *all* crime. Sutherland was willing to accept supplementary explanations for particular types of crime, and this, in part, remedies the problems connected with an all-embracing theory. The deficiencies listed above are, in this sense, much more crucial. However, if a theory purports to explain crime in general, we should expect its explanation to be consistent with the data on women and crime. Most of our theories fail in this respect. Although Sutherland's work is more acceptable in this regard, he simply does not follow through on this analysis. By treating women's participation in crime as a crucial variable, we can refine our theories, set them within the proper limits, and move toward a clearer understanding of crime itself. (The variables of race and social class should function in much the same way.) But existing theories are frequently so inconsistent with female realities, that specific explanations of female patterns of crime will probably have to precede the development of an all-inclusive theory.

CONCLUSION

Sutherland's treatment of white-collar crime aims to reform theories of criminal behavior by focusing on a pattern of crime previously neglected. The study of women and crime offers the same opportunity to pinpoint erroneous, or at least incomplete, explanations of crime. Analyzing white-collar crime also assisted Sutherland in locating those factors (discussed in differential association) that are essential to a general theory of crime. The application of differential association to women partially supports the theory, since it provides a framework that, in general terms, explains not only the crime of the rich and the poor, but the criminality and noncriminality of men and women. Regarding women and crime, it is particularly helpful in emphasizing that criminal behavior is learned, not psychologically or biologically determined; and that association with criminal or noncriminal patterns are essential, and vary from one group to another. It reminds us that women are not permitted the same associations as men and, even within the same groups, are treated unequally. Thus, their crime rate can be expected to vary from that of men.

Differential association, however, does not explain why the situation of men and women varies so profoundly. The analysis it offers is sound — in and of itself — but extremely restricted. It leaves us with essentially the same puzzling questions regarding women and crime. It clarifies that women have different associations than men, but does not say why. It asserts they are more controlled and differentially socialized, but offers a flimsy explanation for this. Thus, we learn (and this is important) that associations are critical in the emergence of criminal behavior, that women are forbidden certain associations and treated differently within others, but we never learn why this is so. As mentioned regarding labeling theory, a structural as well as processual explanation is absolutely essential.

Differential association also neglects the meaning of behavior, the active role an individual or group can play in shaping his or her destiny, as opposed to merely reacting to a given situation. Addressing this would result in a richer analysis of women and crime. Thus, Sutherland's theory offers a framework to explain crime in general, but this framework must be expanded to discuss structural variables and refined to examine the particularly human aspects of behavior.

NOTES

[1]According to his student, Donald Cressey (1964: 11–12), Sutherland deleted the word "systematic" because his readers believed this referred to a limited amount of crime, while Sutherland himself intended it to include almost all criminal behavior.

[2]This was Albert Cohen's suggestion (Cohen et al., 1956: 21).

[3]Sutherland seemed most disturbed by certain war crimes, which indicated the willingness of corporations to use a critical emergency for profit. He commented (1961: 175): "This evidence raises a question whether these corporations are not driven by self-interest to such an extent that they are constitutionally unable to participate in cooperative life of society."

[4]Matza is highly complimentary of Becker's study (1963) of becoming a marijuana user, which makes it apparent that "*anyone* can become a marijuana user and *no one* has to" (Matza, 1969: 110). This, of course, implies a conscious, willing subject.

[5]For specific references regarding this criticism see Cressey, 1960a: 58.

[6]Cressey's work on embezzlement, *Other People's Money*, substantiates these criticisms. Specifically, he notes that the ratio of behavior patterns cannot be determined in individual cases. He found it unclear whether criminality depends on the ratio of contacts with criminal or anticriminal behavior patterns in cases of embezzlement. The techniques of this crime can be learned apart from contact with criminal behavior, and, moreover, it is difficult, if not impossible, to know enough about a person's contacts with rationalizations supporting crime to enable the prediction of such behavior.

[7]I am much less comfortable relying on the statistics when it comes to issues of race and class. I find arguments describing the statistics as severely distorted by race and class biases infinitely more persuasive and intellectually sound than those claiming similar (although advantageous) biases regarding women (such as Pollak).

[8]See Chafe, 1972, for a more complete discussion of this.

CHAPTER SIX

Subcultural Theory

INTRODUCTION

The study of criminal subcultures has played a major role in theoretical explanations of crime. Rooted to a large extent in anomie theory, the writings of Albert Cohen, Walter B. Miller, Richard Cloward, and Lloyd Ohlin exemplify theories that concentrate on the criminal behavior of lower-class, adolescent boys in gangs. Their explanations are fundamentally sociological, stressing the relationship between the structure of society and human behavior. Unlike Edwin Sutherland, they do not attempt to explain all crime but emphasize (implicitly or explicitly) their interest in lower-class male delinquency.[1]

Most discussions of gangs begin with Thrasher's classic work, *The Gang* (1963), a survey of 1,313 Chicago gangs first published in 1927. Thrasher did not analyze delinquent subcultures, but his work is a forerunner of such theory and has yet to be surpassed in comprehensiveness. Although gang delinquency interested sociologists since the 1920s, work on the subject waned until the publication of Cohen's *Delinquent Boys* in 1955. With this, the topic became enormously popular once again. Cohen's book focused on the concept of subculture, not simply gang membership. The groups he, Miller, Cloward, and Ohlin describe conflict with larger society. (Thrasher deemphasized this and viewed gangs as arising in play activities, providing fun and excitement.) The study of subcultures advanced criminological theory but also limited its focus in dramatic ways.

MAJOR THEORISTS

Many theorists could be included in a study of subcultures, but I will concentrate on the most influential of these: Cohen, Miller, Cloward, and Ohlin. Others will be examined briefly in the following section, as criticisms of the major theorists are presented.

Albert Cohen

Robert Merton's discussion of anomie laid the foundation for the analysis of delinquent subcultures by observing the structural impediments to success within the lower class. Cohen expanded on this, examining the content of the delinquent subculture, which he regarded as different from and even opposed to the larger culture. Instead of explaining how a particular individual becomes delinquent (Sutherland's major concern), Cohen questioned why the delinquent subculture exists and why it is found in some communities and not others. His explanation revolved around the class structure of American society: gang delinquency is a group solution to status frustrations experienced by lower-class males who are denied status in middle-class terms and seek it in the delinquent subculture. Cohen is not arguing that only working-class youngsters have difficulties but simply that their problems are very different from those of a middle-class child, and more likely to result in delinquency (Mannheim, 1965: 508).

Cohen recognized Sutherland's impact on his work, especially the idea that individuals learn delinquency through contact with delinquent groups. Instead of exploring this learning process, however, he discusses the origins of delinquent subcultures in *Delinquent Boys*. He (1955: 22) cautions that his theory will not include all crime, not even all adolescent crime: "We will thus have limited our undertaking and cannot be held responsible for failing to explain that which clearly falls outside of the task area we have staked out." The subculture Cohen analyzes is described as nonutilitarian (stolen objects are often destroyed or discarded, obviously never intended to be of practical use), malicious (evident in the delinquent's thrill at breaking taboos and seeing others disconcerted), and negativistic (in that it turns the values of the larger culture upside down).

These subcultures are also versatile (involved in a variety of offenses) and characterized by "short-run hedonism" and group autonomy, which rebels against any external restraint.

While Cohen acknowledges the problems surrounding official statistics on delinquency, he (1955: 37) nevertheless insists that "juvenile delinquency and the delinquent subculture in particular are overwhelmingly concentrated in the male, working-class sector of the juvenile population." He claims gang delinquency is a working-class phenomenon, although delinquent behavior occurs in all classes and an "adequate system" of theoretical criminology ultimately has to explain this.[2] He wonders how subcultural solutions can develop, given the powerful influences to conform, and maintains (1955: 59) that "the crucial condition for the emergence of new cultural forms is the existence, *in effective interaction with one another, of a number of actors with similar problems of adjustment.*" This process proceeds in an extremely tentative fashion, almost as though everyone changes simultaneously, and only through mutual support.

Cohen notes that social class status for both men and women centers on the family and basically depends on the occupation of the male. Men and women therefore achieve status in different ways: for women, status depends on marriage to a successful male; men, however, must be occupationally successful. Thus, expectations are different for boys and girls, and Cohen (1955: 88–91) briefly summarizes middle-class standards "primarily applicable to the male role." These include ambition, individual responsibility, tangible skills and achievements, worldly asceticism, rationality, manners, control of aggression, "wholesome" recreation, and respect for property.

Cohen (1955: 98) maintains that in the middle class, socialization is "conscious, rational, deliberate and demanding," whereas in the working class, it is more relaxed, and adolescents are more dependent on peer groups. Due to class differences in training and values, working-class boys encounter status problems when confronted with middle-class expectations. "To the degree to which [the working-class boy] values middle-class status, either because he values the good opinion of middle-class persons or because he has to some degree internalized middle-class standards himself, he faces a problem of adjustment and is in the market for a 'solution'" (Cohen, 1955: 119).

Unable to gain access to the middle-class world, a boy turns to the delinquent subculture for status. "The hallmark of the delinquent subculture is the explicit and wholesale repudiation of middle-class standards and the adoption of their very antithesis" (Cohen, 1955: 129). Cohen argues that "reaction-formation" occurs, and the drastic response of the delinquent protects him against any inner qualms. The gang not only violates middle-class norms, it "expresses contempt for a way of life by making its opposite a criterion of status" (Cohen, 1955: 134). The delinquent solution is a group solution: it enables individuals to perform actions that would be difficult if not impossible without group legitimization.

Toward the end of his book, Cohen again questions why the delinquent subculture is predominantly working class and responds that "it is in the male working-class sector that there exists a *common core* of motivation, more specifically, of status discontent, to which the delinquent subculture is an appropriate solution" (Cohen, 1955: 153). This need not be the only motivation for participation, but it is basic, and moreover it originates in fundamental American expectations for achievement. Cohen claims his work draws attention to a critical, and largely ignored, aspect of what motivates delinquency. It also stresses the importance of the availability of groups to tackle joint solutions to adjustment problems. Psychological difficulties alone do not explain delinquency. Finally, most theories of delinquency concentrate on the role of the family, ignoring vital outside influences. Thus, Cohen feels his work contributes significantly to the study of delinquency by focusing on the origins of the male, working-class, delinquent subculture.

Walter B. Miller

My discussion of Walter B. Miller will center on his seminal article, "Lower Class Culture as a Generating Milieu of Gang Delinquency," published in 1958. This article is both a criticism of Cohen and a major development in subcultural theory. Miller challenges key assumptions in *Delinquent Boys* by arguing that lower-class delinquent gangs result from efforts to conform to long-established and durable traditions of the lower-class community. Gang delinquency is not a reaction to middle-class norms, but a positive attempt to achieve status in lower-class terms. The street gang is a normal phenomenon in lower-class life, not oppositional. Miller denies that gang delinquency could persist if it were based solely on motives of rejection. Rather, its explanation lies in cultural elements and conformity to central themes that inform the actions of lower-class people.

Miller, like Cohen, focuses on the delinquent activities of lower-class gangs but discusses lower-class life as distinguished by certain "focal concerns" — "Areas or issues which command widespread and persistent attention and a high degree of emotional involvement" (Miller, 1970: 271). These concerns characterize lower-class Americans in general but are particularly prevalent among street corner gangs and delinquent gangs. He lists six of these and claims they differ significantly from those of the middle class. The first, *trouble*, is a major issue for everyone in the lower-class community. Unlike middle-class emphasis on achievement, the status of a lower-class person is often judged in terms of law-abiding or law-violating behavior. Lawful activity is valued, but getting into trouble can, at times, bring prestige and assist in attaining other goals. Running a racket can, for example, bring great wealth and power despite (or perhaps because) it is illegal behavior. *Toughness* involves physical ability, manliness, and courage. Miller believes the emphasis on tough-ness might result from the fact that many lower-class males are raised in female-based households and feel compelled to assert their masculinity. *Smartness* is the ability to outwit others, without being tricked oneself. It involves mental, not physical, gymnastics. This ability, displayed in bril-liant repartee, frequently confers more prestige than does toughness. *Ex-citement* is also a focal concern and is usually associated with drinking, gambling, or having a night on the town. The lower classes are intensely concerned with *fate*, fortune, or luck. They often feel their lives are beyond their control — subject to forces they cannot alter.[3] Finally, *autonomy* is crucial, and lower-class people frequently verbalize their re-sentment of restrictions or oppressive authority. Miller notes, however, that they often associate authority with nurturance and are therefore ambivalent regarding protection or care from others. This ambivalence is demonstrated when they seek protective environments (like the armed forces, mental hospitals, disciplinary school), while apparently rejecting such control.[4]

Miller contends that the one-sex peer group is a significant aspect of lower class and is probably related to the widespread female-based household. He argues, "it is the *one-sex peer unit* rather than the two-parent family unit which represents the most significant relational unit for both sexes in lower-class communities" (1970: 277). The adolescent street gang is just such a unit, and the delinquent gang is a subtype of this. Adolescents have the same focal concerns as the general commun-ity, with two additions: belonging (membership in good standing), and status (obvious possession of lower-class qualities — toughness, smart-ness, et cetera). Miller asserts that status is always a crucial concern, but whether it is gained by maintaining or violating the law is a major ques-tion. He recognizes that the explanation for this is complex but maintains that adolescent crime is motivated by the attempt to achieve what is valued and to avoid what is disvalued within lower-class culture, given available means and ends.

Miller claims it is possible to demonstrate explicitly the connections between illegal behavior and lower-class focal concerns, but he chooses to summarize this in three statements (1970: 279–280). First, adhering to lower-class cultural patterns violates certain legal norms. Second, even when alternatives are available, law breaking often produces more immediate results, with less effort. Third, illegal behavior is, in fact, the expected response to certain common situations in lower-class life. Thus, lower-class delinquency is an attempt to achieve what the lower-class community values. It involves conformity, not rebellion. Miller questions Cohen's description of such behavior as negativistic, spiteful, or malicious. He claims (1970: 280), "Such characteristics are obviously the result of taking the middle-class community, and its institutions as an implicit point of reference." The adolescent street gang (and lower-class culture) has a distinct tradition of its own; it cannot be viewed merely as an inversion of middle-class culture.

Richard Cloward and Lloyd Ohlin

Richard Cloward (1959) contributed to the development of anomie theory in his article "Illegitimate Means, Anomie, and Deviant Behavior," by acknowledging the strain imposed on lower-class people, due to the disjunction between cultural goals and (the absence of) legitimate means. Anomie theory implied that illegitimate opportunity is either readily available or of little concern. Sutherland, on the other hand, recognized that illegitimate means are not always accessible, but he offered little discussion of differential legitimate opportunity. Cloward combined the two traditions and stated that both legitimate and illegitimate means are, first, limited, and, second, differentially available depending on one's location in the social structure. Cloward explores the concept of "differential opportunity structures" by combining major traditions in criminological theory. This work was continued and deepened in Cloward and Ohlin's book, *Delinquency and Opportunity*, first published in 1960 and appropriately dedicated to Robert Merton and Edwin Sutherland. It deals with class as a decisive element in delinquency and specifically focuses on delinquent gangs in lower-class areas, as Cohen did, but criticizes his emphasis on the negative component of delinquency. Cloward and Ohlin's work is an alternative to Cohen's, not simply an addition or qualifying discussion, and its originality lies in its discussion of the different types of delinquent subcultures, dictated by opportunities available.

Cloward and Ohlin explain not only how delinquent norms develop but the varying content of delinquent subcultures. "In this book we shall suggest that the milieu in which actors find themselves has a crucial impact upon the types of adaption which develop in response to pressures toward deviance" (Cloward and Ohlin, 1960: x). They explicitly assert that their book analyzes the delinquent subcultures of lower-class, adolescent, urban males, not of the isolated offender. This type of delinquency is most likely to be frequent, persistent, and difficult to control. They claim there are three basic types of delinquent subculture: criminal, conflict, and retreatist — all most frequently found in lower-class areas of large cities, and particularly among adolescent males.

Drawing heavily on Merton, Cloward and Ohlin discuss the structural problem of culturally induced goals and limited legitimate means, leading to adjustment difficulties among lower-class adolescents, and the eventual formation of delinquent subcultures. They take exception to Cohen, claiming that although the lower-class delinquents want to improve their economic position, this need not include a change in their way of life, nor an acceptance of middle-class values. Their behavior is not so much a reaction-formation (as Cohen asserts), as a refusal to recognize the legitimacy of certain norms. Cloward and Ohlin (1960: 106) conclude that "widespread tendencies toward delinquent practices in the lower class are modes of adaptation to structural strains and inconsistencies within the social order."

Given the strain experienced by lower-class youths, a delinquent subculture evolves as they begin to question the legitimacy of various norms and join with others to solve mutual problems. Cloward and Ohlin (1960: 125) hypothesize that "collective adaptations are likely to emerge when failure is attributed to the inadequacies of existing institutional arrangements; conversely, when failure is attributed to personal deficiencies, solitary adaptations are more likely."

Cloward and Ohlin claim that the content of a particular delinquent subculture depends on the milieu in which it exists, in particular, the presence or absence of illegitimate opportunities. They proceed to describe the three delinquent subcultures in terms of the environment in which each will develop. The *criminal* subculture involves stealing, extortion, et cetera, as a means of achieving success and gaining prestige. This pattern usually occurs in areas where delinquents and adult criminals are closely connected, as are criminal and conventional modes of behavior. Illegitimate opportunities are available, and adult criminals provide role models for adolescents. The *conflict* subculture uses violence to gain status and requires courage and bravery of its members. It arises when both conventional opportunities and stable criminal patterns are unavailable. Tremendous frustration is rampant and inadequately controlled. "Violence comes to be ascendant, in short, under conditions of relative detachment from all institutional systems of opportunity and social control" (Cloward and Ohlin, 1960: 178). *Retreatist* subcultures involve the use of drugs and the search for ecstatic experiences. They are found when legitimate opportunity is restricted, and illegitimate opportunity (including violence) is also unavailable either because of internalized prohibitions on the adolescent's part, or because he has tried and failed all illegitimate routes. Cloward and Ohlin refer to these boys as "double failures" and declare it is not surprising they reject both the goals and means in society, given the pressure they experience.

This discussion treats delinquency as rooted in social systems. Cloward and Ohlin assert that the prevention of delinquency will require the reorganization of poverty areas. Just as Merton suggested more than 20 years earlier, legitimate opportunities must be available in lower-class communities, if, crime, violence, and retreatism are to cease.

Although Cloward and Ohlin explain why delinquency might arise among lower-class, as opposed to middle-class, adolescents, they do not discuss sex differentials. They merely mention that gangs of girls are occasionally associated, in a subordinate way, with groups of male delinquents. They suggest the sex differential (like the class differential) might be a good starting point for explaining gang behavior: "If we know that an adaptation occurs disproportionately among males, we may wish to inquire about the influence of sex roles upon the emergence of such a pattern" (Cloward and Ohlin, 1960: 33). They do not, however, pursue this "potentially fruitful" line of inquiry.

CRITICISMS OF SUBCULTURAL THEORY

Albert Cohen

Cohen himself observed that the theory presented in *Delinquent Boys* has been so "severely mauled" that it cannot stand without modification. This is a harsh assessment on Cohen's part, since his work has generally been favorably reviewed. Criticisms and revisions were likely, however, since much of Cohen's work was speculative, with little basis in empirical data (Gibbons, 1976: 117). A major discussion of Cohen's work is found in an article by Gresham Sykes and David Matza, "Techniques of Neutralization," published in 1957. This criticizes Cohen and offers a substantial addition to subcultural theory.

Sykes and Matza praise Cohen's work but assert that viewing juvenile delinquency as an inversion of the values of larger society is open to serious question. If delinquents believed their behavior were acceptable (which an inversion of values implies), they would not feel guilty about it — but evidently, they do feel guilty. Delinquents often admire law-abiding people and clearly distinguish between acceptable and nonaccept-able victims, implying an understanding that such behavior is "wrong." It is doubtful they can completely ignore the demands of larger society; more likely, certain expectations are internalized. Sykes and Matza claim the demands of society may be overcome, but understanding how this is accomplished is essential in explaining delinquency. They view delin-quents as at least partially committed to larger society, and they thus must develop their own analysis of what occurs. They assert that delin-quents commit illegal acts by rationalizing their behavior in advance. "It is our argument that much delinquency is based on what is essentially an unrecognized extension of defenses to crimes, in the form of justifica-tions for deviance that are seen as valid by the delinquent but not by the legal system or society at large" (Sykes and Matza, 1957: 265). The de-linquent does not radically oppose the system but is more aptly an "apol-ogetic failure." Sykes and Matza refer to the delinquent's rationalizations as "techniques of neutralization" and claim these are akin to Sutherland's "definitions favorable to the violation of the law."

Sykes and Matza describe five major types of neutralization: *denial of responsibility*, when the delinquent claims his behavior is beyond his con-trol, due perhaps to a poverty-stricken environment, negligent parents, and so on; *denial of injury*, claiming, for example, that no one has really been hurt by his actions; *denial of the victim*, insisting that the victim deserved the injury, or that it was justified revenge; *the condemnation of the condemners*, whereby the delinquent overlooks his own behavior by criticiz-ing those who condemn him as hypocrites, spiteful, or corrupt, and by viewing conformity as based on connections or luck; *the appeal to higher loyalties*, whereby the delinquent claims the importance of supporting his group, even if it (unfortunately) involves breaking the law. Sykes and Matza (1957: 268) conclude, in opposition to Cohen, that "these 'defini-tions of the situation' represent tangential or glancing blows at the domi-nant normative system rather than the creation of an opposing ideology; and they are extensions of patterns of thought prevalent in society rather than somethiing created *de novo*."

Sykes and Matza argue that the techniques of neutralization are in-strumental in lessening social control and thus underlie much delinquent behavior, even if they are not fully effective, or not always necessary. They suggest more research on these techniques as they relate to age, sex, social class, ethnic groups, and so on. Sykes and Matza obviously altered the main proposition of Cohen's theory — that delinquency is based on values and norms opposed to larger society. They claim, in-stead, that delinquents internalize the standards of larger society but neutralize them to engage in delinquent behavior. To some extent, the work of Sykes and Matza is compatible with Cohen's, which recognized (in part) the sensitivity of lower-class boys to middle-class standards. It can be viewed as a clarification and addition to *Delinquent Boys*, which is how Cohen (1958) perceives their criticisms. He and James Short incorporated Sykes and Matza's insights by suggesting that reaction-formation is actually a technique of neutralization, as are subcultures themselves, supporting delinquents and alleviating their self-doubts.

Cohen and Short acknowledge that there are a variety of delinquent subcultures. They now call the subculture examined in *Delinquent Boys* the "parent male subculture," since it is most common. In addition, they discuss the conflict subculture of large gangs, and the subcultures of drug addicts, semiprofessional thieves, and middle-class delinquents. They claim that a theory of subcultures must explain the social structural conditions leading to problems of adjustment and, in turn, must determine the various forms of delinquent solutions. Although this sounds similar to Cloward and Ohlin, Cohen asserts that oppositional values result in delinquent behavior, no matter what variety it assumes; whereas Cloward and Ohlin stress that the social environment affects the particular delinquent response, no matter what the original motivation (Taylor, 1971: 176).

A more thorough criticism of Cohen's work came in 1959, with the publication of Kitsuse and Dietrick's article, "Delinquent Boys: A Critique." They argue that Cohen's theory is not convincing when it asserts working-class boys value the opinions of middle-class people and measure themselves in these terms. They reason that class differences should protect these boys from the opinions of the middle class. It is as plausible to assume that they reject middle-class standards as that they accept them. Kitsuse and Dietrick also quarrel with Cohen's concept of reaction-formation, which is fundamental to his explanation of the delinquent subculture. This concept assumes working-class boys are deeply concerned about achieving status in middle-class terms, but this notion is highly speculative. Even Cohen recognized that working-class boys have difficulties in school because they have *not* been socialized in middle-class terms.

Kitsuse and Dietrick also argue that Cohen's description of delinquent subcultures is inaccurate. The activities of delinquents are far more serious than Cohen implies. Moreover, "There is no absence of rational, calculated, utilitarian behavior among delinquent gangs, as they exist today" (1970: 242). Many of the actions Cohen describes occur among middle-class — not lower-class — youths. Kitsuse and Dietrick contend that Cohen's theory presents serious testing difficulties regarding the emergence of the subculture and is unclear about the relationship between its emergence and its persistence.

Thus, Cohen has been criticized on a number of grounds. Most important is the assertion that his description of the delinquent subculture as oppositional to middle-class society and as homogeneous, is inaccurate. His analysis is helpful in noting structural sources of strain and in indicating that the culture as a whole is not homogeneous but varies, particularly in terms of class. Cohen, like Merton, criticizes a system that induces such strain, although the critique he offers is (like Merton's) rather limited.

Walter B. Miller

The conflict between middle- and lower-class values is not as deep or persistent as Miller claims. According to Cloward and Ohlin (1960: 71), "Serious delinquencies, such as burglary, robbery, assault, gang killings, and drug addiction, violate lower-class as well as middle-class values." Taylor (1971: 183) agrees that lower-class individuals are simply not as insulated as Miller suggests. They are aware of middle-class standards and values and frequently conform to them in schools, jobs, et cetera. Thus, Miller's challenge to Cohen's notion that lower-class boys are sensitive to middle-class standards is ineffective.

Miller's characterization of the lower class as highly insulated leads to another difficulty. He states that lower-class culture is "centuries old," but does not examine its origins. According to Taylor (1971: 183–84), "focal concerns must have arisen because they were associated with specific problems which were encountered in working-class life." Miller's analysis, then, is too static — ignoring the origins of focal concerns and preventing any explication of changes in working-class culture. Moreover, it is never clear at what point focal concerns become "delinquent prescriptions."

Miller also ignores the variety of delinquent subcultures (Cloward and Ohlin, 1960: 74), as well as the variety that exists within the lower class as a whole (Gibbons, 1976: 123). Female-based families, for example, are not prevalent among all disadvantaged groups. Finally, Miller would have difficulty explaining the delinquencies of middle-class groups that fit his definition of the delinquent subculture. His concept of culture conflict simply could not explain their activities, and he does not offer any other explanation.

In summary, Miller, too, has been criticized for theoretical inadequacies although his sensitive description of the focal concerns of lower-class culture added much to discussions of delinquency.

Richard Cloward and Lloyd Ohlin

Although *Delinquency and Opportunity* was initially received very favorably, there have been criticisms. I will concentrate primarily on a well-known article by Clarence Schrag, "Delinquency and Opportunity," originally published in 1962.

Schrag notes that Cloward and Ohlin do not present a general theory of delinquency but concentrate on sociocultural variables that affect gang delinquency. They propose to explain the different types of subcultures in terms of access to legitimate and illegitimate opportunity. Although the theory of differential opportunity is logically sound, Schrag finds the description of retreatism inadequate to allow for predicting this behavior. As a result, it is merely a residual category that does not have the explanatory power of a dependent variable within the larger theoretical scheme.

Schrag also points to difficulties in operationalizing many concepts of the theory. He mentions, for example, perception of opportunity, denial of legitimacy, and double failure as troublesome concepts. This necessitates certain theoretical improvements as the theory is untestable unless concepts can be operationalized. Schrag suggests refinements he considers vital, including, for example, specifications as to what is required for a gang or community to fall within the theoretical framework.

Schrag complains Cloward and Ohlin's theory is not always empirically accurate. Differential opportunity assumes that within certain areas specific subcultures should predominate, given the social structural conditions. But, empirical evidence does not support this. Some neighborhoods, for example, have several types of subcultures, and, moreover, as Taylor (1971: 176) notes, empirical data indicate that gangs themselves are diverse (rather than distinct) in their delinquent activities.

Schrag also doubts whether delinquents and nondelinquents share the same goals. Taylor, Walton, and Young elaborate on this, claiming that Cloward and Ohlin are heirs to Merton's notions of consensus. Like Merton, they stress the all-encompassing goal of monetary success. They ignore the possibility that anyone with access to legitimate means might still reject the values and ideas associated with them. "At no time is the cultural diversity of goals and means, and the multitude of gradations of acceptance and rejection of utilitarianism, existing in modern industrial societies, fully encompassed" (Taylor, Walton, and Young, 1973: 135). Clinard (1964) seems to concur, asserting that Cloward and Ohlin overemphasize economic and educational goals among lower-class boys and assume these success goals are shared throughout society.

Finally, Schrag notes that Cloward and Ohlin's description of retreatists as "double failures" is open to empirical doubt. Since there are few examples of retreatist subcultures, this pattern is likely to be much more individualistic (Suchar, 1978: 97). Perhaps retreatists are unable to maintain the bonds necessary for a subculture. Moreover, not all retreatists have failed in illegitimate pursuits. Schrag (1970: 261) summarizes the difficulties with this category: "The evidence is that there are several alternative paths to retreatism and that retreatism by no means prohibits access to opportunity or achievement by illegitimate means."

Despite these criticisms, Cloward and Ohlin have analyzed a previously neglected aspect of delinquent behavior: the delinquent's perception of available access to legitimate and illegitimate opportunities. Schrag (1970: 259) claims that the theory makes a unique contribution to the study of delinquency since it has "considerable deductive potential and . . . is rich in its implications for social control."

Conclusion

A great deal of research exists on delinquent subcultures, documenting their rich variety and making it difficult for any one theory to explain their origins and persistence. Don Gibbons (1976: 125–139) discusses and evaluates this complex literature. His comments on Cohen, Cloward and Ohlin, and Miller are of particular interest. According to Gibbons, research indicates that gangs predominate in lower-class, urban environments. Although the relationship between the environment and delinquency is admittedly complex, empirical data cast doubt on Cohen's discussion of delinquent gangs. His arguments "are seriously undermined by findings which appear to show that lower-class youths do not reject middle-class values" (Gibbons, 1976: 138). Cohen's concept of the parent subculture does, however, withstand empirical testing. Gangs are characterized more by internal diversity than by specialization. Thus, Cloward and Ohlin's clearly differentiated subcultures are hard to find. Certain aspects of Miller's work do not fare much better, since his claims about female-dominated households, as well as focal concerns, are overstated (Gibbons, 1976: 138).

In general, Cloward and Ohlin's work is most widely supported by empirical studies. "The available data do bear out their arguments concerning the part played by illegitimate opportunity structures in delinquency, and they also lend support to the claims regarding discrepancies between expectations and aspirations" (Gibbons, 1976: 138). However, opportunity theory is not fully substantiated. Besides the absence of evidence for clearly differentiated subcultures, Cloward and Ohlin's idea that lower-class youth are disinterested in middle-class values is not supported by existing data. Moreover, there is no explanation for those boys subject to strain, with few legitimate opportunities, who nonetheless remain nondelinquent. Obviously, other variables are involved, but they escape careful analysis.

Research supports the conclusion that different issues and concerns drive youths to the delinquent subculture. Gibbons (1976: 139) mentions, for example, status concerns, pervasive deprivation, personal protection, anxieties about masculinity, et cetera, and concludes that "there is no one route to the gang." While sociologists still argue about many aspects of delinquent subcultures, there is agreement on certain points. Criminal traditions are obviously persistent, offering juveniles deviant role models and frequently confounding community efforts at control. Pressures to succeed financially, coupled with limited legitimate opportunities, play an important role, as does the distribution of illegitimate opportunities.

The subcultural theories attempt to explicate the connections between social class and criminal behavior, particularly subcultural delinquency. They share the assumption that lower-class individuals, particularly young males, are significantly predisposed to crime or, at least, gang delinquency. This assumption is challenged by those who note that illegal activity is not confined to a particular class. Even if gang delinquency predominates among urban lower-class males, attention should be drawn to the fact that illegality is rampant among adults in all social classes. Thus, the theoretical explanations offered are, at best, extremely limited.

APPLICATION TO WOMEN

Subcultural theory is primarily concerned with (urban, working-class) male delinquency. Cohen (1955) explicitly states that his work concerns young males, and he only discusses females briefly. Cloward and Ohlin (1960) have even fewer discussions of female delinquents and also explicitly focus on males. Miller's work (1958) neglects even mentioning females. It is perfectly acceptable for theories to be specific, but Cohen's statement (1955: 22) that he "cannot be held responsible for failing to explain that which clearly falls outside of the task area we have staked out," is only partially accurate. When a theory focuses on the criminality of the lower classes as opposed to the upper classes, it is imperative to explain how and why class situations differ. Likewise, a theory cannot simply state that it will focus on males without explaining why it is insufficient regarding females. This is an unacceptable omission since the theory is left in a rudimentary and unclarified form. (Why is the focus on males necessary? Why, and in what ways, does their behavior differ from female behavior?) A more complete theory would explain its specificity and clearly acknowledge the problematic aspects of discussing the criminality of one group in view of the noncriminality of another group that shares so many of the same conditions (the same families, communities, poverty, etc.). Cohen attempts this, and his work comes closest to being most thorough. (He will, however, be severely criticized for the explanation he proposes.) Cloward and Ohlin state that they will focus on males but never bother to explain why their situation differs from that of females. Miller, worst of all, simply speaks of lower-class culture and never even recognizes that his analysis is inapplicable to half that population. I will proceed, then, and see what, if anything, these theories offer in illuminating female patterns of crime. Similar efforts have been encouraged by these theorists. Cloward and Ohlin note (1960: 33) the utility of inquiring into the influence of sex roles on patterns of behavior that occur disproportionately among males. Likewise, Cohen (1955: 71) claims that a complete theory has to explain why subcultures arise or fail to arise. This can be interpreted as proclaiming the necessity of elucidating the lack of female involvement in delinquent subcultures.

Albert Cohen

Cohen argues that delinquent male gangs are a solution to status problems suffered by working-class boys being measured in middle-class terms. The delinquent gang provides a means of attaining status, while repudiating middle-class standards. Anthony Harris (1977: 8–9) makes a brief attempt to consider the sex variable in terms of subcultural theory. He claims that since subcultures are, as Cohen states, a response to the blockage of legitimate opportunity, we should logically expect women to have higher rates of crime since their opportunities are more limited than those of males. Harris assumes, however, that women have the same goals as men, an assumption neither Cohen nor I am willing to make. Status frustrations can lead to participation in delinquent gangs, but the frustrations and blocked opportunities Cohen describes apply to young males, not necessarily females.

Cohen states that the delinquent subculture is specifically male, especially regarding versatility — he asserts that most female offenses are sexual delinquencies. Official statistics, and studies of hidden delinquency, certainly indicate a disproportionate criminal involvement among males.[5] However, property offenses are actually most common among both women and men, and moreover many of the "sexual delinquencies" of females can be attributed to different standards imposed on female adolescents.

Although research is scarce on female delinquent subcultures, Cohen is correct in observing that they are likely to be quite different from those of males. This reflects, at least to some extent, that female status depends heavily on marriage to a successful male, compared to a male's need to achieve occupational success. Cohen discusses sex differences regarding problems of adjustment (1955, 137–147) and asserts that males and females have different problems that require different solutions. He claims both the respectable middle-class pattern and the delinquent response are masculine in their stress on achievement, daring, mastery, et cetera. Man is measured by his performance vis-à-vis other men. Although delinquent behavior is viewed as "wrong," it is attractive and affirms a boy's masculinity. Boys are most concerned with their achievements compared to other boys; girls are interested in their relationships with males. Cohen admits that this is not necessary or "natural," but girls are typically fulfilled through relationships with the opposite sex (1955: 142). From this, Cohen draws two major conclusions: first, adjustment problems leading to delinquent subcultures are mainly male problems, and, second, the delinquent subculture is completely inappropriate for female role problems. "It is inappropriate because it is, at best, irrelevant to the vindication of the girl's status as a girl, and at worst, because it positively threatens her in that status in consequence of its strongly masculine symbolic function" (Cohen, 1955: 143–144).

I have serious reservations regarding Cohen's explanation. He claims a female's status depends on her relationships with men. "A primary determinant of the female's 'peace of mind' and feeling of security is her assurance of her sexual attractiveness" (1955: 144). He also notes that being sexually attractive is not the same as being sexually available. "Sexual accessibility, however, has this virtue: it pays the most immediate and certain dividends by way of male attention, male pursuit, male company and the wasteful public expenditure of the male's resources on the female — one of the most socially visible and reassuring evidences of success at the job of being a woman" (Cohen, 1955: 145). Accessibility, however, makes women vulnerable in terms of finding a marriage partner, so they must be discreet in bestowing sexual favors.

Cohen admits this is oversimplified but claims there are socially structured motivations for females both to give and to withhold sexual activity. "It is suggested that the problem of explaining female sexual delinquency may be viewed as a problem of accounting for choices and compromises between these socially structured alternatives" (1955: 147). Cohen does not elaborate; he merely proposes that the delinquent

subculture he is analyzing is not in tune with female problems of adjustment and that sexual delinquency is one response to the central problems
of females: establishing satisfying relationships with men.

My major dissatisfaction is that Cohen deals with women in such a
stereotypical manner. As frequently occurs, he sexualizes female behavior and refuses to examine given assumptions about women. These
attitudes are inexcusable, even if the perfunctory nod has been given toward the impact of social structure. His analysis is severely limited and
obviously the product of an implicit acceptance of the status quo: a
white, male, classist interpretation of the sexual activities of women and
the "dividends" they pay. Cohen's analysis is characterized as "white"
because he ignores varying expectations for behavior among minority
groups; "male," because he never considers female attitudes or understandings regarding their behavior; and "classist," because the standards
he imposes are not necessarily shared across class lines.[6] Differential law
enforcement, which brings young females to court on charges rarely
leveled against boys, such as ungovernability, immorality, or wayward-
ness (Gibbons, 1976: 77), is ignored. Although obvious discrimination
occurs, Cohen does not address this issue.

I agree with Cohen that, first, males and females have different problems; second, they experience different expectations (marital success versus occupational achievement); and, third, the delinquent response is
more "masculine" than "feminine." But any further acceptance of his
theory is extremely problematic, especially when he asserts that female
sexual delinquency is the "solution" to difficulties in establishing relationships with males. Since female delinquency rates (even for sexual
"misbehavior") are extremely low, what are we to assume? That females
do not have as many problems as males? That most of them have satisfactory relationships with men? Cohen disregards the subjugation of
women and the fact that even when they achieve what is commonly
expected of them (marriage and a family), they are still regarded as inferior to the male half of society. He also ignores class differences among
women. His analysis of female crime might be the best that can be
accomplished within his framework, but this is obviously inadequate. It
fails to explain the lack of criminality among women, particularly those
women who have not married (or have not married successful males),
and those whose relationships are unsatisfactory even within marriage.
Likewise, it ignores female property crime and how this could be connected with their relationships with men.

Cohen's analysis does not offer insights beyond those we were able
to glean from earlier work. It does, however, emphasize that males and
females share fundamentally different cultures. His work reinforces my

belief that a valid analysis of women and crime will not come from a framework constructed to deal with males simply altered to include females. This will distort our understanding of the phenomenon since it involves premises frequently inapplicable to women and prevents the consideration of essential variables. Cohen at least recognized the delinquent subculture he analyzed as basically male.

Walter B. Miller

Miller (1958), as we have seen, takes a different tack and argues that the delinquency of lower-class gangs is primarily an attempt to achieve what their culture values (and not a repudiation of middle-class standards). Unfortunately, Miller's article makes no attempt to deal with the sex variable, and his thesis simply breaks down when applied to women.

Miller criticizes Cohen for viewing subcultural delinquency as an inversion of middle-class values, rather than as an outgrowth of lower-class culture. He claims Cohen takes middle-class values and institutions as an implicit frame of reference, blinding him to the distinctive culture of the lower class. However, Miller's focal concerns, which supposedly characterize lower-class life, are not particularly relevant to females. Given their different location in society, they are unlikely to be as concerned as males about trouble, toughness, smartness, excitement, fate, and autonomy. Miller ignores women and assumes a male point of view, which is quite comparable to Cohen's middle-class assumptions and lack of attention to lower-class culture. Once again, a sociologist has described a situation — in this case the focal concerns of an entire culture — which neglects to consider half the population. Miller's analysis is perceptive in terms of men, but incomplete. Recognizing that lower-class culture differs from that of the middle class is important; a similar awareness is needed regarding men and women. His descriptive analysis of male lower-class culture should be matched by a similar analysis of females. Knowing their focal concerns requires a close and detailed analysis of the lives of women, lower class and otherwise. A better understanding of female patterns of criminality will emerge from such material. Miller astutely noted class differences and applied them in his study of delinquency. The sex variable awaits this kind of perceptive analysis.

Miller asserts delinquent subcultures are a means of achieving what the lower class values, but there is little here that lends itself to an explanation of female patterns of crime. If the focal concerns of males and females were the same, and this alone explained delinquent subcultures, their crime rates would be similar. If, on the other hand, their concerns are very different (as I believe), Miller's analysis is simply inapplicable to women.

Cloward and Ohlin

Cloward and Ohlin (1960) claim that male delinquent subcultures result from the extreme frustration experienced by boys faced with limited legitimate opportunity after internalizing conventional success goals. They add that illegitimate opportunities are also differentially available, depending on one's position in the social structure. Harris (1977) contends that differential opportunity theory is amenable to a consideration of the sex variable. In certain respects, this analysis offers more potential for understanding the criminality of women than either of the other subcultural theories because Cloward and Ohlin consider the blockage of both legitimate and illegitimate opportunity. Harris claims that women find legitimate opportunity blocked, but they are also limited in illegitimate opportunities, thus explaining their lower participation in crime. He (1977: 7) notes, however, that this overlooks the absence of violent crime among women, which restriction to domestic roles should not effect (the sex ratio for violent crime is twice that of property crime), and that economic crimes are increasing among young females (under 18 years of age), a group which has *less* opportunity for crime than older females.

However, Harris is assuming common goals for males and females. I believe it is more accurate to revise this theory (as I did with anomie theory) and discuss the primary goals of women as marriage and a family. The analysis might then proceed as follows. Although denied access to traditional male success goals, women are usually able to achieve what is expected of them: marriage and a family. They are not subject to the same strain as men, since their goals, though limited, are rather easily achieved. Moreover, women subject to strain, or those who find these goals unacceptable, will not easily fall into patterns of criminal behavior. They are likely to find, more so than men, that their illegitimate opportunities are severely restricted. Cloward and Ohlin (1960: 125) assert that delinquent subcultures are more apt to develop when failure is defined as the result of institutional arrangements, not personal inadequacies. Women, however, are less likely to fail (given their goals), and more likely, if they do, to view this in personal terms (although the reemergence of feminism has begun to alter this). Cloward (1959: 173) acknowledges that women are frequently excluded from criminal activities, although he maintains class differences are probably most important regarding access to illegitimate opportunities.

Ruth Morris offers a similar analysis, arguing that males are more concerned with status goals, whereas females emphasize relational goals. In two articles (1964, 1965), Morris applies Cloward's theory (that delinquency occurs most frequently with blocked legitimate opportunities and open illegitimate ones) to females. She hypothesizes that: (1) problems maintaining positive personal relationships will lead to female delinquency, (2) females have more access to their particular goals, and (3) they have less access to illegitimate opportunity. She tested her first hypothesis (1964) with a study of 56 boys and girls and concluded that female delinquents are likely to have relational problems, such as broken homes, tense family situations, or problems regarding personal appearance. She proceeded to test her third hypothesis (1965) and found that delinquent girls are more ashamed about their delinquency, that less tolerance exists for female delinquency, and that girls have fewer friends who are delinquent. She concludes: "All girls, delinquents and nondelinquents, are continuously faced with a relative absence of subcultural supports for delinquency and a much more stringent social disapproval of delinquency than are boys" (1965: 265). For Morris, this is significant in explaining the lower rates of female delinquency. I agree, to a certain extent. Let me outline what I regard as the difficulties with this.

Although Cloward and Ohlin's theory is enhanced by a consideration of illegitimate opportunities, they still fail to overcome problems with anomie theory, and my revision of their theory, as well as Morris' application of it, reflects these difficulties. The emphasis on common cultural goals, whether for men or women, disregards the diversity of modern life. Social reactions are totally ignored, and crime among women who have apparently achieved their societal goals is unexplainable. Although women avoid the strains typically associated with being male, they are subject to the suffering caused by being viewed as inferior to one half of the population and to the disappointments that ensue when alternative goals are not available. The limited number of women retreatists is puzzling, given this lack of alternatives, the fact that not all of them marry, and that certainly not all who do marry have successful personal relationships. Morris does not sexualize female behavior, but neither does she question why such differences exist in the behavior and expectations of males and females. The structural reasons for this are unexplored; this, perhaps, is the theory's most serious inadequacy.

When Cloward and Ohlin describe the three delinquent subcultures, their strictly male orientation and its inapplicability to females becomes increasingly apparent. The criminal pattern, for example, is said to predominate in areas where criminal behavior is a means of achieving success and can bring prestige to those involved. Such patterns, however, are unacceptable for women. Likewise, the conflict subculture symbolizes physical strength and masculinity. Violence is not an avenue of status for females. Even the retreatist subculture, which might lend itself to an analysis of females since it is nonviolent, is discussed in terms of the "successful cat," the male who has a lucrative "hustle." Cloward and Ohlin indicate that when both legitimate and illegitimate opportunities are restricted, retreatism is a strong possibility. They imply it is available to everyone, yet pervasive social control can block even this alternative, especially for a group as restricted as women. Each of these subcultures develops as a result of blocked legitimate opportunity, viewed primarily as male success goals. Cloward (1959: 174) expressed the hope that differential illegitimate opportunity would clarify the varying rates of crime among many groups, including men and women, but an extensive portion of his theory is inapplicable to female concerns.

Increasing crime among women is difficult to explain in terms of Cloward and Ohlin's analysis. Simon (1975) suggests that it can be attributed to increased female participation in the labor force, which gives them more opportunity for fraud and embezzlement. This is problematic, however, since these women by definition have legitimate opportunities and should not be driven toward criminal involvement. Moreover, embezzlement has more recently declined among women. Cloward and Ohlin basically discuss lower-class crime, and the existence and pervasiveness of white-collar crime challenges their theory. (It is also ironic to consider labor force participation as illegitimate opportunity. This, in itself, indicates that the problem is far deeper than restricted access to legitimate opportunity.)

One final point — Cloward asserts class differences are more influential than sex regarding access to illegitimate opportunity. I disagree. Class certainly determines the types of illegitimate opportunity available to males, since lower-class males have little chance of involvement in corporate fraud, while upper-class males are unlikely to find themselves burglarizing. But women are subject to these kinds of class restrictions, and more. The domination of females is vigorous and pervasive, regardless of their social class. The crime available to them does not simply vary in kind (as it does with males across class), it also varies more profoundly in terms of any involvement at all. Cloward demonstrates his blindness regarding female patterns of crime by asserting in this instance that class differences are more important.

CONCLUSION

The application of subcultural theory to women is extremely difficult primarily because these theories are aimed implicitly or explicitly at males. Moreover, the lack of research on female subcultures makes a parallel analysis virtually impossible. Insights can be gleaned from these theories, however. Perhaps most important is the conclusion that males and females do not share the same problems, although they live under similar conditions. The sex variable affects values, roles, socialization, expectations, and opportunities. This emphasizes that society is diverse and conflicting, not homogeneous.

Miller's characterization of gang delinquency as an extension of low-er-class values is more acceptable than Cohen's insistence that the entire phenomenon is a reaction to middle-class standards. Miller, however, fails to realize that the lower-class is not totally insulated from the upper classes, nor is it homogeneous in and of itself. His obliviousness to women when discussing lower-class focal concerns is indicative of this difficulty.

The subcultural theories leave the mistaken impression that crime is entirely the domain of the poor. This is totally inaccurate and illustrates the unwillingness of these theorists to entertain the possibility that more profound contradictions exist within our society. Cloward and Ohlin are perceptive when they discuss varying legitimate and illegitimate opportunities, and their framework is helpful in understanding the criminal patterns of women. They overcome a major difficulty in Sutherland's work (his lack of a structural analysis) by incorporating Merton's understanding of anomie. However, they inherit Merton's limited critique of the system and accept his consensual view, which is at odds with the class, race, and sexual distinctions prevasive in our society. They overlook the variety of goals people seek and neglect to explain why individuals who have access to legitimate opportunity still engage in crime. Thus, the criminal participation of various social classes must be examined in a more complete fashion, and — equally imperative — the sex variable must be treated consistently and thoroughly.

NOTES

[1]These theorists had a tremendous impact on public policy. Cloward and Ohlin, in particular, stressed that available legitimate opportunities would lessen juvenile involvement in illegitimate enterprises. This renewed empha-

sis on treating communities, not simply individuals, and was incorporated in *Mobilization for Youth*, which became a model for "War on Poverty" programs in American cities. See Edwin Schur, *Our Criminal Society*: 112.

[2]Cohen briefly discusses (1955: 44–48) the sex distribution of the delinquent subculture and describes it as "overwhelmingly male." I will examine his comments thoroughly when applying his theory to women.

[3]This accurately describes much of lower-class life — the powerlessness they experience is quite real, especially given the absence of political organization.

[4]I find this aspect of Miller's analysis totally unsatisfactory. There are much more compelling explanations for the involvement of lower-class individuals in "protective environments," including their lack of opportunity to avoid them.

[5]For example, referrals to juvenile court are four, five, and six times as frequent among boys (Gibbons, 1976: 169).

[6]I am not arguing that there is absolutely no basis for the stereotypes Cohen maintains. Moreover, I realize that notions as to precisely what women think and value are bound to be speculative at this point in time, pending future research and analysis. What is required, however, is a reassessment of Cohen's arguments in light of our current understandings as to the role of women in society, their socialization, and the way social structures impinge on them. Such an assessment always runs the risk of being unduly harsh on those who wrote and published before the widespread acceptance of feminist views and perspectives.

CHAPTER SEVEN

Marxist Approach

INTRODUCTION

Recently, a unique perspective has emerged within criminology and deviance theory. Referred to as the "new criminology," "radical criminology," and sometimes "critical criminology," it incorporates diverse contributions which, however, generally share a Marxist framework. This approach poses crucial questions and reintroduces (within criminology) some of the most compelling issues in sociology. A definite theoretical progression led to the debates that engage these particular criminologists. The perspective emerged from attempts to overcome what is lacking within labeling theory, particularly its failure to develop a structural analysis. It also grew out of the liberal brand of conflict theory, which emphasizes the unequal distribution of power in society. Attempts to analyze the larger structural situation and to deal adequately with the issue of power increasingly propelled these theorists in the direction of Karl Marx, and a thoroughly radical social analysis.[1]

The new criminology focuses on rule making and rule breaking. Previously, criminology and criminal law were treated separately, particularly in the United States, leading to unfortunate consequences for both fields (Sykes, 1974: 207–208). By the 1960s, however, this gap began to narrow, and by the 1970s the connections between law, crime, and society were being explored, and major assumptions of American criminology were being challenged in the process.

The new criminology views law as intimately related to the interests of the law makers. Criminal law does not reflect the values of the majority, as the liberals would have it, but serves the interests of the ruling class. Taylor (1971: 59–61) explains that as part of the "superstructure" in society, law corresponds to existing economic conditions, although law makers need not be self-consciously aware of this.[2] This perception of criminal law makes any extensive concern with crime secondary among Marxists. Since the law is so biased, they are discontent with simply asking why someone breaks the law. The focus necessarily shifts toward an analysis of law itself, with questions of crime causation assuming a subordinate position.[3] However, they generally view crime as resulting from contradictions inherent in capitalism. Individualistic theories of crime causation are soundly rejected, and agencies of social control are regarded as inherently unjust and functioning to maintain the interests of those in power. The solution to crime does not lie with the treatment or punishment of individual criminals, but with a new type of society. Critical criminology therefore demands widespread change in the political-economic structure of American society, not merely reform.

In sum, critical criminology is not simply a change in emphasis, but "new" in that it challenges liberal ideology by portraying modern capitalist society as a fiercely stratefied society, in which law controls the powerless and secures the interests of the dominant class.

A fully developed critical criminology has yet to emerge in the United States or elsewhere, but work is progressing, and deeply important issues are being confronted. The new criminology asks to be judged by its effectiveness in shattering the ideological pretensions of an unjust society and encouraging debate about change and alternatives. Criminologists are regarded as having a responsibility to take knowledgeable and humanistic stands on issues of crime and social control. This requires a serious commitment on their part to pose "fundamental and consistent challenges to the everyday political assumptions, practices and implications of one of the most influential and State-dominated branches of applied social 'science' — the 'science' of criminology" (Taylor, Walton, and Young, 1975: 5).

I will begin by examining the writings of Marx and Engels on crime, as well as the work of an early Marxist, Willem Bonger. Following this, I will discuss the contributions of the new criminologists.

Marx and Engels

Karl Marx argued that society is profoundly affected by its economic institution, and indeed the centrality of economic activity justifies such an assumption. It logically follows that the key to the problems of a society (including crime) might lie in its economic arrangements. Although Marx wrote little on crime, the new criminology reaches out to his work for analytical guidance and inspiration. His social theory has been tapped for core themes regarding human nature and social relations under capitalism.

Marx asserts that the owners of the means of production have vast control in society, not merely over working conditions but, for example, legal norms. Since the ruling class dominates the creation and implementation of law, it is bound to serve their interests. Law, however, is frequently envisioned as embodying the will of the people. Both Marx and Engels contend such hypocrisy must be unmasked. The new criminologists have incorporated this desire to strip away such myths and to increase awareness about the dominant impact of the political economy. Marx's insistence that individuals be viewed within their social context has also influenced the new criminologists. They regard individuals as social products and products of history; social relations are necessarily examined in an historical context. Finally, given the importance of economic relations and the contention that crime is inherent in capitalism, both Marx and the radical criminologists call for widespread change to remedy crime, specifically the destruction of the existing economic substructure.

In *Theories of Surplus Value*, Marx apparently refers to crime in functional terms, but many (Taylor, Walton, and Young, 1973; McCaghy, 1976; Hirst, 1972) contend that these statements are meant to be sarcastic. Marx writes:

> A philosopher produces ideas, a poet verses, a parson sermons, a professor text-books, etc. . . . The criminal produces not only crime but also the criminal law; he produces the professor who delivers lectures on this criminal law, and even the inevitable text-book in which the professor presents his lectures as a commodity for sale in the market (Marx, 1956: 158).

Marx asserts the criminal also produces police, judges, juries, and a host of mechanical inventions to deter crime. Crime perks up monotonous bourgeois life and contributes to economic stability: "Crime takes off the labour market a portion of the excess population, diminishes competition among workers, and to a certain extent stops wages from falling below the minimum, while the war against crime absorbs another part of the same population" (Marx, 1956: 159). Marx (1956: 160) also sarcastically notes that increasing crime "calls into existence new measures of defence, and its productive effects are as great as those of strikes in stimulating the invention of machines.''

No one can doubt the irony intended in these statements, and just as certainly they are accurate criticisms of bourgeois society. Marx surely did not intend to characterize crime as necessary.

Marx realizes that the bourgeois view of crime is intimately connected with the belief that law reflects the will of the people. In *The German Ideology*, he insists that more than this be considered. He argues: "The material life of individuals, which certainly does not depend on their mere 'will,' their mode of production and their form of intercourse, which reciprocally influence each other, are the real basis of the State" and hence of law (Marx, 1956: 225). The material basis of power, not a consensus in society, accounts for the form and content of law. Material conditions exercise the same influence on crime. According to Marx (1956: 226):

> Crime, i.e., the struggle of the single individual against the dominant conditions, is as little the product of simple caprice as law itself. It is rather conditioned in the same way as the latter. The same visionaries who see in law the rule of an independent and general will see in crime a simple breaking of the law.

For Marx, crime is a struggle against society and is conditioned by that society. "A dialectical tension is apparent between man as a determining actor (exercising free will) and man as an actor whose 'will' is a product of his times" (Taylor, Walton, and Young, 1973: 215). This interplay, not a simplistic economic determinism, gives depth and sophistication to Marx's work.

In an article on "Capital Punishment" written for the *New York Daily Tribune* in 1853, Marx again discusses crime (Marx, 1956: 228–230). He argues that basic conditions of bourgeois society produce crime and asks (1956: 230), "is there not a necessity for deeply reflecting upon an alteration of the system that breeds these crimes, instead of glorifying the hangman who executes a lot of criminals to make room only for the supply of new ones?"[4] Marx recognized the detrimental effects and the arbitrariness of social control processes. In an essay entitled "Population, Crime and Pauperism" (*New York Daily Tribune*, 1859), he states that official sanctioning "so far from being indifferent, decides on the fate of thousands of men, and the moral tone of society. Law itself may not only punish crime, but improvise it" (Taylor, Walton, and Young, 1973: 217).

Marx regarded criminals as concentrated in "the dangerous classes," the *Lumpenproletariat*. He described them as unproductive parasites, living off other workers. Their criminal activity represents false consciousness,

and is necessarily prepolitical.[5] Although he did not systematically develop his ideas about crime, he saw it as resulting from demoralization and
false consciousness, and insofar as he and Engels assume a direct relationship between crime and economic conditions, "they go close to adopt-
ing a form of economic determinism which, despite many claims to the
contrary, they do not exhibit in other areas of their work" (Taylor, Walton, and Young, 1973: 219). A basis for understanding crime in society is
therefore more likely to be found in Marx's general social theory rather
than in his specific statements on crime, as limited and fragmentary (even
misleading) as they are.

Engels also wrote relatively little on crime, although he discussed it
more fully than Marx, particularly in his book *The Condition of the
Working Class in England*. He describes the extreme competition inherent
in capitalism, an economic system which winds through booms and
slumps, requiring a reserve of workers for the high periods, who are then
unemployed during recessions. Engels refers to this pool of unemployed
as the "surplus population," and contends "When they are out of work
these people eke out a miserable existence by begging and stealing [sic], by
sweeping the streets, by collecting horse-dung, by pushing barrows or
driving donkey-carts, by hawking and peddling and by turning their
hands to anything that will bring in a copper or two" (Engels, 1958: 98).
He paints a vivid picture of the disastrous effects of industrialization and its
toll on the "bodily, intellectual and moral conditions" of the workers
(1958: 108). He does not strictly concentrate on the criminality of the
poor, but explicitly recognizes the class-based definition and implementation of criminal law. Engels defines the early death of workers, for example, as murder at the hands of the capitalists responsible for these conditions and claims this is as violent and as culpable as murder committed by
an individual. He depicts the brutal conditions under which the workers
exist and insists they "retain their humanity only so long as they cherish a
burning fury against the property-owning classes" (Engels, 1958: 129).

According to Engels, life offers little to a worker, who thus has little
fear of the law. He (1958: 130) questions why a worker should restrain
himself, why he should leave the rich man "in undisturbed possession of
his property." "What reason has the worker for *not* stealing?" Engels
maintains the condition of the working class leads to their demoralization:

> The clearest indication of the unbounded contempt of the workers for the
> existing social order is the wholesale manner in which they break its laws. If
> the demoralization of the worker passes beyond a certain point then it is just as
> natural that he will turn into a criminal — as inevitably as water turns into
> steam at boiling point (Engels, 1958: 145).

This statement indicates a deterministic view of crime on Engels' part, and a willingness to accept the notion that the working classes are indeed overly represented in crime. He later states explicitly (1958: 147) that statistics "prove" the workers are responsible "for nearly all the crimes in the country." Property offenses predominate, and Engels attributes this to poverty. He contends this is the logical result of competitive capitalism: "In short, everyone sees in his neighbor a rival to be elbowed aside, or at best a victim to be exploited for his own ends" (Engels, 1958: 149).

Willem Bonger

While Marx and Engels were mainly absorbed by questions of political economy and only incidentally interested in crime, Willem Bonger (1876–1940), a Dutch criminologist and a self-proclaimed Marxist, explicitly attempted an explanation of working class and bourgeois crime, based on Marxist concepts and understandings.

Bonger published his major study, *Criminality and Economic Conditions*, in 1916. He begins his analysis by discussing the concept of altruism, maintaining that people are born with social instincts. He claims (1969: 33) that the mode of production either develops or destroys this "social predisposition." Primitive people (for example) are altruistic, mutually helpful. They produce for personal consumption, not exchange; they have neither wealth nor property. As a result, they are not egoistic. Capitalism, on the other hand, "has engendered cupidity and ambition, has made man less sensitive to the happiness and misery of his fellows, and has decreased the influence exercised upon men's acts by the opinions of others. In short, it has developed egoism at the expense of altruism" (1969: 40). Bonger maintains that the "criminal thought" is rooted in an economic system (capitalism) that weakens altruism and encourages egoistic tendencies by emphasizing profit making and competition. The class structure inhibits notions of mutual helpfulness, fosters social irresponsibility, and leads to crime among both the bourgeoisie and the proletariat (although the proletariat are subject to more severe demoralization). Bonger (1969: 85) contends that in a conflict-ridden economic system, "compassion for the misfortunes of others inevitably becomes blunted, and the great part of morality consequently disappears." Social sentiments become weak, and people no longer value the good opinion of others.

Bonger emphasizes that economic conditions cause crime, but, moreover, that crime occurs among rich and poor. Within capitalism, the means of production are owned by a few, who then force the propertyless to sell their labor and work frantically for the barest necessities of life. This situation elicits, on the part of the powerful, "the spirit of domination, and of insensibility to the ills of others, while it awakens jealousy and servility on the part of those who depend upon them" (Bonger, 1969: 195).

Economic conditions lead to virtually all types of crimes: economic, sexual, and political crimes, as well as crimes of vengeance. Bonger is optimistic about solving the problem, although this necessitates changing the economic system. He contends that in a socialist system, material poverty would be unknown, and economic crimes eliminated. Greed would have no basis once great contrasts in wealth were abolished. Speaking of socialism, Bonger (1969: 200) writes: "Such a society will not only remove the causes which now make men egoistic, but will awaken, on the contrary, a strong feeling of altruism." Such a society will only suffer the few crimes of pathological people, best handled by physicians, not judges.

THE NEW CRIMINOLOGY

Taylor, Walton, and Young

A group of British theorists, Ian Taylor, Paul Walton, and Jock Young, are perhaps most central in the development of a new criminology. Their widely known book, entitled *The New Criminology* (1973), is a penetrating analysis of existing criminological theory and an initial step in the construction of a critical criminology. It is impossible to review the many arguments of this book, since it presents detailed criticisms of virtually the entire scope of criminological theory. Moreover, this analysis is strictly preliminary since it lays the groundwork for a critical understanding of crime and deviance, rather than actually "doing" critical criminology. It is, however, insightful and does much to illuminate essential issues in criminology. In addition, although the work is preliminary, a better understanding of critical criminology emerges from discussions of the inadequacies of existing theory.

While reviewing the state of the field in *The New Criminology*, Taylor, Walton, and Young propose the development of a political economy of crime and suggest exploring the links between interactionist theory and theories of social structure implicit in Marxism. They (1973: 221) hope this will enable criminology "to escape from the strait-jacket of an economic determinism and the relativism of some subjectivist approaches to a theory of contradiction in a social structure which recognizes in 'deviance' the acts of men in the process of actively making, rather than passively taking, the external world." This combination of Marx and Mead suggests an implicit rationality in deviant behavior, rather than innate pathology.

Taylor, Walton, and Young conclude by briefly delineating the formal requirements of a fully social theory of deviance,[6] and calling for the development of a politically aware criminology based on critical theory. They assume crime will be defeated only in the wake of a new social order. Therefore, they (1973: 281) contend "a criminology which is not normatively committed to the abolition of inequalities of wealth and power, and in particular inequalities in property and life-chances, is inevitably bound to fall into correctionalism."[7] Their approach, with its obvious political concerns, departs dramatically from the bulk of criminological theory.

An additional contribution of Taylor, Walton, and Young is their more recent edited book, *Critical Criminology* (1975). This work demonstrates the variety characteristic of early efforts to contribute to a radical criminology. Although common concerns (and an increasing tendency to rely on Marxian understandings) unite these theorists, they have chosen different emphases and diverse directions as they elucidate a new criminology. Their diversity will become apparent as this chapter progresses; within *Critical Criminology*, it is obvious in the selections by authors such as the Schwendingers, Platt, Chambliss, Quinney, and Young.

I will examine the first chapter of this book, "Critical Criminology in Britain: Review and Prospects," written by Taylor, Walton, and Young. This further explicates the new criminology and the part these theorists have played in shaping it.

According to Taylor, Walton, and Young, varying concerns and assumptions have informed the development of theoretical frameworks within criminology. For example, conservative criminological theory is characterized by description, a view of individuals as needing protection and care, a belief in hierarchy and dominance as necessary for law and order, and an acceptance of consensus within society. Liberal theory, on the other hand, is more prescriptive, suggesting institutional reforms to improve human life, although basically accepting existing social arrangements. Most contemporary criminology is founded on liberal understandings. Radical theory, however, is quite different. Human beings are seen as having unlimited potential given certain social conditions, determined by the arrangements of production. Human life can be self-directed, egalitarian, and richly diverse, but radical change is needed for this to occur. When calling for change, or discussing crime, Taylor, Walton, and Young turn to the political economy. They claim (1975: 20) that it is the basic determinant of the social framework, and that "the processes involved in crime-creation are bound up in the final analysis with the *material* basis of contemporary capitalism and its structures of law."

This view of society and crime causation necessarily has implications for scientific work: radical social science should not merely describe reality or offer liberal prescriptions for change but should *encourage* fundamental change through its very research procedures. How else, they ask, can crime be eliminated? Criminologists are therefore expected to reject the status quo, to take sides, to stop pretending to be value free, which is viewed as a useless attempt. In stark contrast to the apolitical descriptive work of traditional criminology, Taylor, Walton, and Young (1975: 26) argue:

> The point is not that one wants the world to hold still whilst one researches it; it is that one's purposes are to reveal the ways in which the constant flux of social conflict and the taken-for-granted repression of ordinary men in such conflicts can be transcended not in terms of further accumulation of descriptions of repression, but only in terms of an adequate radical politics.

This is a fundamentally different vision of criminology and criminologists.

Taylor, Walton, and Young are thus inviting criminologists to transcend the old criminology by acknowledging what they view as a more valid approach to the problem of crime and deviance. Briefly, critical criminology insists that deviance is meaningful to the actor, and values are diverse. It rejects both correctionalism and "scientificity," which views the deviant as totally determined.[8] It demands a new criminology, which will qualitatively surpass earlier brands of criminology. Taylor, Walton, and Young (1975: 8) state that positivistic criminology

> denied the deviant any consciousness, interpreting his actions from the perspective and ideology of the dominant class, whilst the idealist inversions of positivism granted him a welter of subjectivity, yet imparted to this consciousness no social or ideological significance, in that this consciousness was seen to exist unrelated to the total society, and independently of any historical setting.

Critical criminology will move beyond these limitations. In doing so, it will necessarily involve a theory of the state and the total society.[9]

Taylor, Walton, and Young counsel, however, that little can be expected by way of radical research in the near future. By necessity, debate is presently focused on deciding what has to be done. Research thus far has concentrated in three areas. First, "expose criminology" discusses behavior patterns of the powerful that could be defined as illegal, but are not, or if so defined, are not prosecuted. This destroys the myth of a crime-free ruling class and shows the inequities in our criminal justice system. Taylor, Walton, and Young feel, however, that this research is frequently based on moral indignation, not solid theoretical analysis. It must be demonstrated that the crimes of the powerful are not the work of a few deviant individuals, but "that such rule-breaking is institutionalized, regular and widespread amongst the powerful, that it is a given result of the structural position occupied by powerful men" (Taylor, Walton, and Young, 1975: 30).[10]

Second, radical criminology examines the inequities and class-based nature of crime and law in capitalist society. The criminal justice system is criticized for its ideology of equality coupled with differential law enforcement. These radical criminologists frequently choose to ignore official statistics on crime, since they claim they are so obviously distorted. Taylor, Walton, and Young (1975: 34) assert, however, that the statistics can serve a political purpose, if properly used — to examine, for example, who complies in modern society, and who rejects the current distribution of property. They note most crime is property crime. Again, theory construction, not simply data collection, is essential.

The third type of radical criminology research is the one Taylor, Walton, and Young obviously favor. It is a materialist criminology, which aims to abolish the present distribution of power and wealth and to create a just society allowing for "human diversity." They maintain that the work of Marx contains a superior method of analysis and, therefore, insist that crime be examined within a Marxian framework. Orthodox Marxist theory has avoided issues relating to crime control, but Taylor, Walton, and Young assert that troublesome questions about a socialist criminology should not be ignored within the movement.

Marx claimed that social relationships are best examined through the method of historical materialism, arguing that "there are only distinct, historically bound, forms of production, specific to given times and given conditions" (Taylor, Walton, and Young, 1975: 50). Crime must, therefore, be analyzed in light of the given mode of production. One's position in society (class) must be studied, and the historical dimension kept clearly in focus. This implies that any explanation of crime is not meant to be valid for all societies, but rather for a given society, at a given historical time.

In a materialist criminology, law must also be examined in historical terms, since material conditions lead to changes in criminal and legal norms. Taylor, Walton, and Young carefully assert that Marx is not a crude economic determinist. Although legal relations originate in material conditions, legal conflicts are not thereby reduced to economic conflicts; they are not a mere reflection of economic conditions. Every phenomenon has to be seen as part of a system of on-going social relationships, and this includes legal relations. Material conditions, however, shape social relations, and therefore law. Marx soundly criticizes those who see law as playing a similar role in all societies. According to Taylor, Walton, and Young (1975: 52):[11]

> Marx is here enjoining us to engage in the study of the specificity of legal relations (and hence of crime), the agencies of social control and all the related apparatuses of the State — precisely because it must be the case that the legal system serves in a crucial way to legitimize and to enforce a particular mode of production.

Analysis of the connections between crime, law, and production is far from accomplished in criminology. The task, as Taylor, Walton, and Young see it, is to develop a materialist analysis of law in capitalist society. They conclude (1975: 56) that such a criminology must explain legal and social norms in light of the interests and functions they serve within propertied societies. This implies a recognition "that the legal norms in question are inextricably connected with the developing contradictions in such societies."

Richard Quinney

Richard Quinney has moved from conflict theory to a Marxist model of law creation and crime, and is presently one of the most prolific contemporary Marxist writers in the field of criminology. He proposes an approach known as "critical philosophy" to, as he puts it, question everything, unmask the pretense of existing society, and create a new society and a new way of life. Most criminology emphasizes normative consensus while deemphasizing conflict. Quinney, however, concentrates on power, which he contends is unequally distributed in society and consequently enables certain (powerful) individuals to control public policy and create a particular "reality" of crime. Quinney wants to demystify the official reality of crime and demonstrate that crime and its interpretation springs from conflict and power. He proposes a socialist state as the ultimate solution to the crime problem and supports the Marxian notion that an authentic human being will arise under conditions of liberation. I will examine a brief selection of Quinney's recent writings to demonstrate how these themes are stated and supported.

In a 1972 article, "The Ideology of Law: Notes for a Radical

Alternative to Repression," Quinney criticizes the consensus image of law in capitalist society. This view assumes society is basically homogeneous and static and that law reflects the will of the people and operates for the good of all. Quinney finds such attitudes not merely uninformed, but dangerous. Society in fact is diverse and continuously changing, while law basically serves the interests of a select group. Rather than protecting all citizens, law "starts as a tool of the dominant class and ends by maintaining the domination of that class" (Quinney, 1972: 4). It operates, for the most part, to control behavior that challenges the established order. As such, it is oppressive and must be abolished. Communities could create their own systems of law, if indeed law is necessary at all.

In his textbook, *Criminology*, Quinney (1975: 37–41) explains how the legal order defines the crime problem and proposes a theory he calls the *social reality of crime* to explain crime and our notions of it. This "theory" has six propositions. (1) Official descriptions of crime are created by the ruling class, and (2) behavior is defined as crime when it conflicts with the interests of that class. Moreover, (3) the dominant class not only formulates definitions of crime, they are also powerful enough to shape the enforcement and administration of criminal law. So, (4) the probability of a law being enforced depends on whether its enforcement is in the interests of the powerful. It follows that the behavior of the powerless is more likely to be criminalized. In addition, (5) the ruling class creates an ideology of crime that serves its interests. The images of crime and the criminal, portrayed through the mass media and diffused throughout society, are predominantly the ideas of the ruling class. Finally, Quinney (1975: 40) concludes that (6) the social reality of crime is constructed by the above propositions, that is, "by the formulation and application of definitions of crime, the development of behavior patterns in relation to these definitions, and the construction of an ideology of crime."

Quinney insists that the ruling class benefits from the legal system, and crime control is, in reality, class control. Research on crime and criminals indicates that the vast majority of citizens are controlled by those few with power. Thus, the root of crime, according to Quinney, will not be found in individualistic explanations of deviance, but in an exploration of the political nature of crime-defining procedures.

Quinney's arguments are further developed in another article, "Crime Control in Capitalist Society: A Critical Philosophy of Legal Order" (1973). This article is explicitly Marxist and draws on the Frankfurt School. Quinney attempts to construct a critical philosophy of legal order, resulting in a Marxian theory of crime control in capitalist society. He claims that this involves destroying existing myths and assisting in the development of a new consciousness. Drawing on Habermas and Marcuse, Quinney notes that critical philosophy demolishes the myth of objectivism and helps us surmount the ideology of a rational science and technology to question our experience. Although critical theory necessitates thinking negatively, Quinney argues that we must proceed to notions of what society should be, and this makes a Marxist perspective essential, since Quinney claims (1973: 85), "In the Marxian notion of the authentic human being we are provided with a concrete image of the possible."

Quinney praises Marxism for focusing on the oppression caused by capitalism, and for providing a means of analysis that historically locates problems in economic class relations. Perhaps, most importantly, it helps us transcend existing society. Quinney notes that Marxism is extremely creative and open to various interpretations (he has, however, been criticized for his interpretation. See Denisoff and McQuarie, 1975), which enables him to offer a Marxian theory of crime control. Such a theory "views criminal law as the coercive instrument of the State, used by the State and its ruling class to maintain the existing social and economic order" (Quinney, 1973: 87). The ruling class will use force and violence to control society, and official crime rates merely stand as evidence of the extent to which they must exert such coercion. Critical criminology is intended to expose the true meaning of law within capitalism, and hence the true meaning of crime.

Quinney (1973: 94–95) concludes his article with six summary propositions. He asserts that America is an advanced capitalist society, and that the state is organized to serve the capitalist ruling class. Criminal law is an instrument of the state and the ruling class to maintain the status quo. Within this society, crime control is dominated by the agencies of the elite, in order to maintain domestic order. The contradictions inherent in advanced capitalism dictate that the lower classes remain oppressed, especially through legal means. Finally, crime will only be solved with the collapse of capitalism and the creation of a socialist society.

Quinney concludes by stating that to think critically and radically today necessarily implies being revolutionary. To do otherwise, he contends, is to be on the side of oppression.

Anthony Platt

Anthony Platt is also associated with critical criminology, although he has not been as prolific as Quinney, nor as influential as Taylor, Walton, and Young. He authored a fine book examining the origins of the juvenile justice system, *The Child Savers*,[12] but I will examine a particular article of his, since it discusses "Prospects for a Radical Criminology in the U.S." His introduction states that a radical criminology has been developing in the United States since the early 1960s, rooted in political struggles, including the civil rights, antiwar, and student movements. Platt aims to assess the basic assumptions of this new criminology, and its development.

He begins by outlining the assumptions of liberal criminology, which includes a belief in the ability to reform the criminal justice system within the existing economic and political order. In addition to being antitheoretical, Platt claims this dominant brand of criminology is cynical and as he puts it, "dry, without passion, and replete with technical jargon" (Platt, 1975: 98). It seems to exhibit a certain amount of defeatism regarding humanity and social change:

> This focus serves to exclude or underestimate the possibility of a radically different society in which cooperation replaces competition, where human values take precedence over property values, where exploitation, racism and sexism are eliminated, and where basic human needs are fulfilled" (Platt, 1975: 99).

Platt maintains liberal ideology has prevailed for several structural reasons, including the fact that scholarly work is typically done by the privileged, and often funded by agencies sharing this perspective.

Discussing the prospects for a radical criminology, Platt insists that the dominance of earlier criminology must be broken. This will be accomplished by criticizing existing work (as *The New Criminology* did) and by attempting to reconstruct radical traditions (examining, for example, the original socialist writings on crime). Platt also claims the subject matter of criminology must be reconsidered in light of crucial issues and commitments. This necessitates a new definition of crime, since the present legal definition implicitly incorporates the myth of an unbiased law.[13] The new definition must recognize that the legal system is based on power and privilege, only then can criminology increasingly address the issues of how society defines and controls exploitation. Platt calls for a criminology based on a class and materialist perspective and raises the issue of practice or participation in political struggles, which he views as essential. He contends (1975: 105) that political involvement is difficult "because criminologists, like intellectuals generally, in advanced capitalist societies, suffer from elitism and arrogance as a result of our socialization, specialized training, and privilege which insulates us from working people." He suggests initiating political struggle within the university, through social relationships, for example, or radical course work. The new criminology should explicate the connections between the political economy and crime, construct new definitions of crime, examine the coercion of the state, and help develop a people's criminology. Platt concludes by noting the problems and dangers involved in this, including academic repression and liberal cooptation.

The Schwendingers

I noted Anthony Platt's suggestion that the new criminology construct definitions of crime more appropriate to existing political realities and radical concerns. In an article entitled "Defenders of Order or Guardians of Human Rights?" (1970) two criminologists attempt to do this. Herman and Julia Schwendinger assert that most American criminologists define crime and the criminal in "legalistic" terms, as behavior so defined by the state or sanctioned by the state. Adhering to this notion of crime eliminates the possibility of viewing the phenomenon in a very different way (in ethical terms, for example). More importantly, however, the legalistic definition of crime is controlled by the powerful, who shape the law, and it therefore serves their purposes. According to the Schwendingers (1970: 137), "If the *ethical* criteria, of 'social injury,' 'public wrong,' or 'anti-social' behavior are not explicated, then the existent *ethical standpoint of the State is taken as a given* when the criterion of sanctions by the State is also used in the definition of crime."

The Schwendingers question why American sociologists have not challenged legalistic definitions and find their answer in the corporate liberal and technocratic ideologies of the existing order. Many criminologists maintain a social control perspective, viewing all deviance as abnormal, and threatening to the social order. Wittingly or unwittingly, they are the advisors and consultants of those who control the dominant social institutions. They are frequently blind to the connections between their own scientific behavior and the political ideology that shapes the legalistic definitions they use. In fact, according to the Schwendingers (1970: 142), the support of ideological neutrality "was one of the great myths which prevented principled scholars from being aware of the ideological character of their basic theoretical assumptions."

The Schwendingers do not propose a definitive definition of crime but make suggestions about what criminology should seek. Having demolished the pretense that legalistic definitions of crime are value free, they contend that value judgments should be part of the definition of crime and moral issues squarely faced. They maintain that the concept of human rights has expanded throughout history and claim (1970: 145), "All persons must be guaranteed the fundamental prerequisites for well-being, including food, shelter, clothing, medical services, challenging work and recreational experiences, as well as security from predatory individuals or repressive and imperialistic social elites." It then becomes the task of the criminologists to identify individual and institutional behavior that violates these rights and to define such behavior as crime. Much of this will overlap with existing criminal law, although significant changes will be required.

The Schwendingers suggest criminology focus on social conditions that elicit crime, and they insist that these conditions — not simply individual criminals — be the object of social research and social policy. They assert the right of individuals to racial, sexual, and economic equality, and argue (1970: 148):

> If the terms imperialism, racism, sexism, and poverty are abbreviated signs for theories of social relationships or social structures which cause the systematic abrogation of basic rights, then imperialism, racism, sexism, and poverty can be called crimes according to the logic of our argument.

The legalistic definition of crime does not come close to capturing the kinds of social injury inflicted by these conditions, and the Schwendingers suggest that criminology begin exploring these concerns rather than continually concentrating on petty criminals.

The Schwendingers propose, in conclusion, that crime be defined by combining traditional notions of it with the concept of egalitarianism. They maintain (1970: 149) that, "In the process of redefining crime, criminologists will redefine themselves, no longer to be the defenders of order but rather the guardians of human rights."

David Gordon

David Gordon, a Marxist economist, has also contributed to the development of a radical criminology. In "Capitalism, Class, and Crime in America" (1973) he presents a radical economic analysis of crime as rooted in our social and economic institutions. His summary of the nature and extent of crime in America will not be reiterated;[14] but his radical analysis is particularly interesting.

Gordon notes the general assumptions of a radical perspective, beginning with the belief that social and economic institutions shape individual behavior. More specifically, the social relations of production within capitalism define an economic class system, which, in turn, structures individual opportunity and must be grasped in order to understand behavior. The state serves the interests of the capitalist class by directly benefiting them and by preserving the class system on which they depend. Finally, social problems are difficult to remedy within the existing system since their solution would disrupt capitalism. Gordon insists a fundamental reallocation of power is required to alleviate social problems. He illustrates this by referring to sexism and racism, which capitalists did not invent, but which serves their interests by providing cheap labor and dividing the working class. Truly equal opportunity would threaten capitalism.

Gordon contends that many crimes (particularly white-collar crime, organized crime, and ghetto crime) are simply rational responses to the competitiveness and inequality of capitalism. Unlike other radical criminologists, he is not suggesting crime would cease to exist in a communist society, but simply (1973: 174), "that one would have to analyze crime in such a society with reference to a different set of ideas and a different set of institutions."[15] Gordon claims many crime patterns are readily understandable in terms of the class system, which structures opportunities for different types of crimes, and in terms of differential law enforcement, which radicals regard as state protection for the ruling class.[16]

Gordon maintains that the crime problem is not easily solved except through radical change, since the very causes of crime (competition, insecurity, inequality, racism) are basic to capitalism. Likewise, our system of justice reflects vested interests and supports the capitalist system by reinforcing the ideology that individuals are strictly to blame for crime, by handling potential opposition to the system as though it were a legal (criminal) problem, not a political one,[17] and by helping us ignore the dreadful effects of our institutions by labeling criminals as social misfits, undeserving of concern.

Steven Spitzer

Steven Spitzer's 1975 article, "Toward a Marxian Theory of Deviance," marks another attempt to establish a new criminology. He claims that a critical theory of deviance must incorporate an understanding of structure and process in order to know "why capitalism produces both patterns of activity and types of people that are defined and managed as deviant" (1975: 640). Such a theory must study the origins of deviant images, what they reflect about class society, and how this relates to both structural and ideological change. Since deviants are problem groups for those who rule, it is imperative to study who they are, how their membership and behavior changes, and why they are controlled. Spitzer contends that groups become eligible for treatment as deviants when they challenge capitalist standards or expectations. For example, promoting alternative life styles or denying the validity of family life would be sanctioned because, as Spitzer notes, the family is essential to capitalism due to its role in consumption, socialization, and reproduction.

Spitzer notes that within a Marxian theory of deviance, the impact of the existing socioeconomic organization on the rest of social life must be examined, and the contradictions of capitalism related to the production of deviance. He argues, for example, that capitalism must increase its productivity in order to survive, thus requiring increased reliance on machines rather than people. Consequently, the surplus population expands and becomes more entrenched. This has, according to Spitzer, serious implications for intensifying deviance production, as problem populations become troublesome and in need of more state control.

Conclusion

The new criminology is obviously neither unified nor conclusively elaborated. On the contrary, it more precisely resembles a patchwork slowly being sewn together. Common themes unite these theorists, however, and enable us to discuss their work in generalized terms. Among these themes is the explicit dedication to a fundamentally *new* criminology, one which departs from liberal (mis)understandings in significant ways. Critical criminologists reject the frequent use of their discipline to bolster the status quo. They reject the possibility of a value-free science, within traditional or critical criminology. Flowing from this, they suggest new definitions of crime founded, for example, on notions of social injury rather than strictly legalistic conceptions.

The new criminologists exhibit a keen concern with the suffering capitalism entails. They discuss the contradictions of capitalism in human terms, and their writings frequently contain a fervor absent in other scientific publications. They sympathize with those who experience the painful alienation of work and the effects of distorted social relationships. They perceive the suffering which exists in a world that does not measure up to expectations, and they refuse to engage in abstract science while the world — as Yeats so vividly describes — "is full of troubles, and is anxious in its sleep." These criminologists are explicitly concerned with social justice and maintain that this concern should be incorporated in their research.

Given an awareness of the problems in modern society, the new criminology attempts to study ways to alleviate them. They typically assert that their task is to elaborate a Marxist analysis of crime. They are virtually unanimous in arguing that the crime problem will only be solved through widespread change. Crime is intimately connected with the day-to-day workings of capitalism, and until capitalism is fundamentally altered, crime as we know it will continue. The new criminologists accept the Marxian notion of the unlimited potential of humanity and propose a socialist society as the means of unfolding this potential.

Finally, the critical criminologists call for political involvement in the struggle against oppression. They see the role of criminologists as necessarily political, involving humanistic stands, and an attempt to unite theory and practice. The new criminology thus departs from existing theory and offers a fundamentally different perspective on the problem of crime in contemporary society.

CRITICISMS

This section will concentrate on the work of the new criminologists. Since Marx and Engels were not specifically concerned with crime or criminals, their brief writings on these matters have not received extensive attention or criticism. Perhaps it is even unfair to entertain a thorough criticism of their work on the subject, since it was so peripheral to their main interests. Taylor, Walton, and Young (1973) have, as mentioned above, commented on the inadequacies of Marx's treatment of the criminal. Specifically, they claim that it is too individualistic, not in fact "Marxist" at all, and one would do much better to seek the foundations of a theory of crime in Marx's general theoretical work, rather than in his scattered statements about crime.

Bonger's work, *Criminality and Economic Conditions*, has been extensively criticized. I will mention only the most pertinent remarks, since I am mainly concerned with the new criminology. Specific problems are repeatedly mentioned regarding Bonger, and they prevent the acceptance of his work as a general theory. One such problem noted by Turk (1969) is that Bonger attributes all crime to capitalism and claims it will be eliminated under socialism. Capitalism is beyond reform, while socialism will not require any coercive social control. Turk questions why socialism will have such beneficial effects and argues Bonger does not explain this. Turk (1969: 14) concludes that "Bonger's thought founders largely because he was unable to escape the confines of his Marxism, i.e., to see that the political, conflict processes through which definitions of deviance (criminality) are created and enforced are not peculiar to 'capitalist' societies, but are generic to social life." Taylor, Walton, and Young agree Bonger is simplistic, but they insist his vision of socialism differs from that of Marx — which pictures an end to the struggle over the means of production, and the attainment of a classless society. Bonger sees socialism as superior because it is more effective than capitalism in controlling people. Marx, however, does not regard socialism as a more powerful control system, but as an opportunity for people to freely develop their humanity. According to Taylor, Walton, and Young (1973: 222), Bonger has done Marx a disservice, and unfortunately this is not an isolated misunderstanding within his work: "Bonger's efforts appear, for us, not so much the application of a fully-fledged Marxist theory as they are a recitation of a 'Marxist catechism' in an area which Marx had left largely untouched." More specifically, they criticize Bonger's discussion of egoism as totally un-Marxist with its emphasis on a particular moral climate. They note the irony of a writer who claims to be a Marxist beginning his analysis by examining an individual trait, and only later exploring the social conditions that impinge on this quality. Bonger's work is more conceptual, lacking historical and structural explanations. This is decidedly un-Marxist.

Barry Mike (1976) agrees Bonger "reduces" Marx by misrepresenting him as an economic determinist. Bonger's interpretation is invalid since it ignores Marx's dialectic logic. Mike also contends that Marx is concerned with human choice, whereas Bonger views behavior as determined by outside forces and explicitly rejects "intentional" behavior on the part of human actors. While Turk uses his criticisms of Bonger to illustrate the inadequacies of a Marxist theory of crime, Mike (more in line with Taylor, Walton, and Young) contends (1976: 236) that "this is not the case: a Marxist theory of criminality is not exhausted by Bonger's theory because Bonger has barely exhausted (much less understood) the works of Karl Marx."

Bonger has been criticized for other, comparatively minor, reasons including his use of arrest data (Barlow, 1978), his ambiguous definition of egoism (Mike, 1976; Barlow, 1978),[18] and his attempt to link all crime with economic conditions (Mike, 1976; Barlow, 1978).

Most critics concede that Bonger captures the evils of nineteenth-century capitalism and offers penetrating comments on its demoralizing effects.[19] He can be praised for attempting a Marxist analysis of crime, for his concern with economic conditions, and for his sensitivity to human exploitation. This, however, does not substitute for a sophisticated analysis of the issue.

The New Criminology

I will discuss general criticisms of critical criminology and then mention more specific commentaries on the work of Taylor, Walton, Young, and Quinney, since they are perhaps the most widely known of the new criminologists.

The new criminology has been challenged for claiming that existing criminology ignores the social and economic conflicts that are the basis of law.[20] Ironically, it has also been criticized for a lack of history and (less surprising, given the assumptions of dominant society) for being doctrinaire. A common complaint, in part owing to the newness of the perspective, is the assertion that it is extremely generalized and oversimplified. I will specify the ways in which the critics believe this to be so.[21]

First, Sykes (1974) claims that the new criminologists frequently use an oversimplified model of stratification and that there is much more diversity and variation in modern society than their simple dichotomy between the poor and the powerful implies. Similarly, Lemert (1974) remarks that the new criminologists are almost as guilty of reifying power as those they criticize. Their work lacks a detailed analysis of the subleties and impact of power. Several commentators reject their interpretation and analysis of law in capitalist society. Gibbons (1977), for example, asserts that many laws are supported by the general public and are not rooted in oppressive power. The new criminologists are criticized for problems associated with labeling theory: for having litttle sense of the complexity of law, which frequently operates to constrain the law maker as well as the general public, for failing to recognize the accommodations that are frequently part of social control situations, and for viewing law too strictly in terms of manipulation, rather than according it any legitimacy. Sykes (1974) adds that they tend to treat unintended and unrecognized functions as though they were intended and recognized by the actors. This implies that lawmakers, for example, are operating much more consciously in their own interest than they actually are.

Moreover, the new criminologists do not carefully describe the processes of law making and the exercise of power (Gibbons, 1977), nor have they specified the connections between capitalist exploitation and various forms of deviance (Gibbons and Jones, 1975). Rock (1973) notes that their lack of comparative analysis hampers any claim that social conflict and its legal effects are evident in capitalist societies alone, rather than in all complex industrial societies. (Marxists, of course, envision less class conflict in socialist societies.) As important as their focus might be, the finer points of their argument have yet to be elaborated. Gibbons (1977: 209) comments that "much hyperbole has been offered about racism, sexism, oppression, and repression, but few social indicators of the phenomena to which these labels apply have been identified."

Thus, although critics might appreciate certain contributions of the new criminologists, including their emphasis on the relationship between the political economy and crime, they view their work to date as simplistic and, ironically, accuse them of "mystification" in their accounts of the power structures of capitalism, and of "vulgar Marxism" (Gibbons, 1977). While many claim that the basic problem is a lack of detail in a relatively new orientation, the disagreements are actually much deeper. Gibbons praises the new criminology for calling attention to the relationship between crime and the economic structure, but this is not the fundamental or sole purpose of a Marxist analysis. If it were, there would be no way to distinguish Marxists from the long line of theorists who have addressed the issue of economic impact on crime. Rather, the new criminology is engaged in a class analysis of the intrinsic inequities in capitalist society, and a concern with alienation. The differences they have with mainstream criminology are not peripheral and will not be resolved, but rather deepened, as they begin the laborious task of refining the details of their framework. The following, and final, criticism of their work should clarify this point.

Sykes (1974) complains that serious criminals (murderers, rapists, burglars) can be distinguished from the rest of the population, with more than mere labeling being involved. He counsels that if the new criminology is to make an important contribution, it must resist the notion that, since legal stigmas are differentially applied, they are *necessarily* based on income and race. First of all, Sykes blurs the labeling perspective and the new criminology, but if his advice were seriously followed, the new criminology would be right back in the mainstream. It is only by focusing on the impact wealth and power have on law and its enforcement that the new criminology has something significant to offer. What lurks behind Sykes' advice is the belief that crimes are acts that offend public morality, and people are punished because they engage in these acts; that is, his is the liberal ideology. The new criminology has a different perspective, one that does not easily penetrate liberal deliberations: actions are viewed as criminal and individuals are defined as such because it is in the interests of the ruling class. Surely, at times these interests overlap with those of the general public — no one, for example, wants to be murdered — but a Marxist analysis of law goes far beyond this simplistic logic and makes such statements about common interests being served by law in a bourgeois state somewhat beside the point.

A similar problem is evident when Gibbons suggests that critical criminologists construct "social indicators" of racism or sexism. This is a reasonable request and would enhance the empirical validity of the new criminology, but, again, this is not their main concern, but that of bourgeois science. Few doubt that racism exists in our society, and the new criminology explicitly intends to go beyond endless description and cataloguing of social problems.

This does not imply that the new criminology cannot be criticized, but simply that it should be criticized in its own terms, and indeed these criticisms would be more profound since the liberals, not to say the conservatives, have much to disagree about with the radicals. Moreover, the new criminology is *not* as developed as it will become. It is still unknown whether it will avoid or duplicate the problem of existing criminology.

Taylor, Walton, and Young

Taylor, Walton, and Young explicitly intend to contribute to the establishment of a Marxist theory of crime and deviance. The creation of a Marxist criminology is, however, extremely controversial even within the Marxist camp. This serves as a reminder of the sometimes violent debates as to the correct "reading" of Marx among his followers. Paul Q. Hirst is a Marxist, and perhaps the best known of those who have denied the possibility of elaborating a Marxist theory of deviance. He is a representative of the structural Marxism of Louis Althusser, which views only its reading of Marx as acceptable.

Hirst (1972) criticizes the use of Marxism by the radical criminologists, arguing not only that Marx had a very different position on crime, but that there can be no Marxist theory of deviance. Referring to criminology, Hirst (1972: 29) concisely states:

> The objects of Marxist theory are specified by its own concepts: the mode of production, the class struggle, the state, ideology, etc. Any attempt to apply Marxism to this pre-given field of sociology (i.e. criminology) is therefore a more or less 'revisionist' activity in respect of Marxism; it must modify and distort Marxist concepts to suit its own pre-Marxist purpose.

Hirst vigorously denies that Marx is open to anyone's interpretation; he has little tolerance for Taylor, Walton, and Young's concern with socialist diversity.

Taylor and Walton (1972), in turn, reject what they view as Hirst's "idiosyncratic" use of Marxism, and his restrictive notion of the issues at hand. They criticize his limited list of Marxian concepts and his insistence on concentrating strictly on certain aspects of Marx. They state (1972: 230). "The Marxism which we believe, contrary to Hirst's caricature, to be at the base of one developing tendency in deviancy theory, is a Marxism which would be concerned to take on, and reveal, the ideological nature of social structure, and in that battle, to win people to the struggle against oppression in its various guises."

Hirst claims that the new criminology romanticizes crime and sees the criminal as an alienated rebel. The criminal class is not a revolutionary force, but reactionary, which explains Marx's antipathy toward them. Taylor and Walton deny the allegations of romanticization, although Marx's portrayal of criminals troubles them.

While I reject many of Hirst's assumptions and view Marx as more amenable to interpretation and application, Colin Sumner (1976) offers an incisive criticism of Taylor, Walton, and Young, which highlights a missing element in their work and relates to Hirst's critique. He contends that they do not have a clear conception of deviance and view it mainly as a form of rational action. They should have created a new Marxist concept of deviance (extending Marxism in ways that Hirst would disapprove), rather than trying to adapt Marxism to a given concern (crime). For Sumner, this would involve conceptualizing deviance as a form of ideology, rather than as a form of behavior. In other words, Marxism can encompass deviance by treating it as "a social censure, an historically specific, ideological formation" (Sumner, 1976: 167). A vital part of this would include examining the class foundations of such censuring policies and practices, and the role they play both formally and informally in maintaining ruling-class domination. Sumner correctly sees ideology as the link between law and deviance and overcomes a weakness in the work of Taylor, Walton, and Young, which is their limited discussion of law. According to Sumner (1976: 172), once this link is established, "the sociology of law and the sociology of deviance thus collapse as separate topics in Marxian analysis into a focus upon the dominant ideology, its institutionalization in law and its relation to class practices."

There have been many analyses of the work of Taylor, Walton, and Young, particularly of their book *The New Criminology*, but undoubtedly the most perceptive review of this book is that of Elliott Currie (1974). Although he admits that *The New Criminology* might be the best book in the field to date, he has serious criticisms of it. Previously, Tony Platt (1975), had commented unfavorably that one could read this book and be left without a sense of what the struggle is about, indicating a lack of vitality or passion, usually characteristic of traditional criminology. Currie (1974: 137) elaborates on this, commenting that *The New Criminology* was written for a select group of people, "but a major task for radicals with social science training is to develop the means for making useful ideas accessible and meaningful to other people working for social change." Certain new criminologists explicitly intend to make scientific work serviceable and to broaden the audience typically addressed in scientific research. Yet, *The New Criminology* does not succeed in this respect, since it is difficult to imagine anyone, other than serious intellectuals, approaching this book. The tone is thoroughly academic, not moral or political. The issue of the audience and purpose of science is not easily resolved and merits intensive discussion, but the work of Taylor, Walton, and Young is obviously not readily accessible to many people. The question of whether or not it should be is undecided, apparently even within the new criminology.

Sumner (1976) mentions that Taylor, Walton, and Young's model of deviance is too rational, but it is Currie who insightfully elaborates on this. He complains that they insist deviance is purposeful, and even healthy. He sees their view as approaching the romanticization of deviants as rebels, whereas a brief examination of the deviance of the powerful quickly exposes the inadequacy of this "cheerful perspective." Police brutality is not healthy diversity, corporate disregard for safety standards is not primitive rebellion. The essential point, for Currie, is that (1974: 139) "an approach to deviance that cannot distinguish between politically progressive and politically retrogressive forms of deviance does not provide much of a basis for real understanding or political action." Rape, for example, is more accurately seen as an expression of an exploitative system that oppresses women, rather than as a form of struggle against that system, however "inarticulate."

Currie insists that this overemphasis on the rational helps explain Taylor, Walton, and Young's rejection of Marx's view that crime is a result of the demoralization in capitalism. They saw a contradiction in Marx's notion that the criminal is merely "reacting," not necessarily exhibiting consciousness. Currie contends, however, that the real problem lies in Taylor, Walton, and Young's view of Marx. For Marx, consciousness is not assumed, but problematic, and a task of theory is to explain when and if it is likely to emerge. According to Currie (1974: 140):

> It follows that a main task of Marxian theory of *deviance* is to uncover the conditions in which 'deviance' becomes politically progressive and those in

which it does not; the conditions in which deviance represents the beginnings of conscious political action, and those in which it is simply the action of people ground down by a system they neither understand nor challenge.

Currie concludes that Taylor, Walton, and Young have removed the dialectical character from Marx's concept of consciousness and, instead, assert that all human action is rational.[22] This issue is vital since many forms of deviance (such as drug abuse) can be tolerated because they quiet the surplus population, which is, ultimately, destructive of Marxian political goals.

I mentioned earlier that the work of Taylor, Walton, and Young is preliminary to the development of a new criminology and does not actually *do* critical criminology. Currie recognizes this, but he charges that even their criticisms are too much like the old criminology. More specifically, they examine various theories "as isolated mental constructs rather than as ideologies rooted in the material conditions of life in advanced capitalist societies" (Currie, 1974: 135). Neither the social sources of the theories, nor their consequences, are adequately discussed. This is a serious challenge to the new criminologists from one who is extremely sympathetic to their concerns.[23]

Taylor, Walton, and Young have also been criticized for being too theoretical, and for lacking empirical research and comparative analysis. But the criticisms discussed above are paramount in the continuing development of critical criminology; a concern Taylor, Walton, and Young certainly share.

Richard Quinney

Quinney's work represents a perspective on crime and law, not really a theory of empirically testable relationships. It has been criticized for this, as well as for presenting a grand scheme, rather than a more detailed analysis of law and crime.[24] He imposes this scheme or framework on any and all issues he discusses. At times it seems rather arbitrary, and yet the very generality of the framework makes it difficult to disprove. More importantly, some of Quinney's basic concepts have been criticized and even rejected. For example, his notion of an all-powerful ruling class has been challenged, as well as his contention that law is strictly a tool in their hands. Many find his suggestions for a decentralized law or the entire elimination of law, even within socialist societies, unconvincing (Gibbons and Jones, 1975). Taylor, Walton, and Young (1973: 262) comment on his discussion of legal reform, which they feel is emphasized at the expense of a structural analysis: "All of Quinney's eclectic collection of instances of conflict produce nothing more than a sociology of civil liberties; they say little about the structure of civil society as such."

Many criticisms of the new criminology in general have been directed at Quinney in particular. These include the romanticization of criminal behavior and the lack of awareness that certain laws reflect a public consensus (Barlow, 1978). Quinney has been chastised for his simplified use of Marxism. Denisoff and McQuarie (1975), for example, contend that although he liberally uses Marxist rhetoric, he overlooks the processes inherent in Marx's theory, and thus actually misrepresents a Marxist paradigm. He certainly does not apply Marxian understandings in a subtle or exacting manner. Taylor, Walton, and Young criticize Quinney (and Marx) for conceiving of crime as pathological (very different from their own conception), and for viewing the criminal as lacking purpose or integrity (again opposed to their image). These issues have been debated earlier, but what seems indisputable is that in spite of the contribution Quinney makes, his work is extremely rhetorical, while neglecting a detailed and careful analysis that might illuminate the different points he is arguing. Thus, rather than persuading others of the merits of the new criminology, or the validity and utility of a Marxist perspective, he alienates many of those he should win as allies.

APPLICATION TO WOMEN

My application of critical criminology to women and crime will not take precisely the same format as previous chapters. In part because of the recent development of this perspective, which has yet to propose a comprehensive theory of crime, the new criminologists claim debate is still appropriately centered on points of departure, rather than on concrete radical analysis (Taylor, Walton, and Young, 1975). This makes it difficult, and somewhat unfair, to challenge or criticize them for work that has yet to be done on women and crime. Their current work can, however, be assessed in terms of their consideration of women.

In addition, radical criminology, unlike most other perspectives, is not directly interested in the causes of crime. It is concerned, rather, with broader issues, such as the role of law and its creation, definitions of crime, and the methods and purposes of social control. This makes an understanding of their notions of crime causation somewhat complicated and, likewise, complicates an application to women. Such an analysis, however, permits a more sophisticated understanding of crime and, indeed, indicates the extent to which the new criminology differs from its conventional predecessors.

Critical criminology contains themes and ideas that await an application to women, but it does not consider the sex variable any more systematically than traditional theoretical criminology. Although this neglect might be due in part to the recent emergence of this perspective, such excuses do not relieve all responsibility. Indeed, there are indications that the new criminology might fall prey to the same defects as its liberal and conservative predecessors. Frances Heidensohn (1977: 391) comments "that contemporary criminology, 'new', 'radical' and 'critical' criminology neglect women as firmly as their forebears is particularly devastating; since their common approach to conventional theories is iconoclastic and more had been expected of them."

What follows is an analysis of the work of the new criminology to date, and its relationship to an understanding of women and crime. This will be preceded by a brief examination of how the work of Marx, Engels, and Bonger applies to women.

Marx, Engels, and Bonger

Marx explicitly maintains that the roots of crime are found in material conditions and he sarcastically discusses the criminal nature of capitalism, but these comments have little to offer a direct understanding of women and crime. His awareness of the class nature of capitalism and the power of the ruling class prevents him from offering a simplistic view of crime as the product of individual will, since he recognizes the impact of these conditions on both law and crime. This, however, fails to explain the lack of criminality among women, a group who are surely as powerless and oppressed as any within capitalism. Marx's general social theory has elements that could readily be applied to an analysis of crime, and examining his general theoretical framework (rather than his specific comments on crime) is undoubtedly the best way to reach a solid Marxian understanding of crime. But such ideas about women and crime will have to be developed within the new criminology, since this is unexplored in the work of Marx himself.

Engels' discussion fails in a similar way. He wrote more about crime, but ironically this results in a more problematic analysis. He presents biting criticisms of capitalism, discussing the demoralization it involves, the collapse of humanity, the hideous working conditions, the severe competition, and the brutalizing poverty. He explicitly connects these conditions with crime among both rich and poor, arguing that the poor in particular have no reason *not* to steal. He blames these horrid conditions on capitalism and comments that workers' contempt for the system is evident in their widespread law breaking. Engels, too, has forgotten to consider women, and his analysis leaves one puzzled as to why they are basically uninvolved in crime.

Bonger (1969: 59–64) discusses the criminality of women. Remarkably, he realized his explanation of crime collapsed in light of women, a largely noncriminal portion of the population. He proposes several explanations for the disparity in crime among males and females. He claims women have less strength and courage than men, which consequently leads to their participation in fewer crimes. In addition, they are rarely involved in sexual crimes (he views prostitution as economic) because most of these crimes cannot be committed by women.[25] "Another reason is that the role of women in sexual life (and thus in the criminal sexual life) is rather passive than active" (Bonger, 1969: 60). Women seldom engage in the economic crimes poverty causes (such as robbery or burglary) because prostitution is a more lucrative alternative for them. Even across cultures women are generally noncriminal, due to their social position.

Bonger proceeds to explain precisely how the social position of women affects their criminal patterns. Regarding economic offenses, he claims (1969: 63), "the small part that woman plays in the economic life has the result that the desire to be enriched at some one else's expense is less aroused in her than it is in man, and that the opportunity to accomplish the desire is presented to her less often than to him." Since women are less involved in wider society, they are more protected from its conflicts and, hence, less likely to get involved in crimes of vengeance as well as other crimes. Limited participation in political life gives them little opportunity for political crime.

Bonger acknowledges the oppression of women but insists they are spared the directly harmful influences of capitalism.[26] Their oppression has led them to deceit and hypocrisy, often characteristic of oppressed groups, and has prevented them from developing bonds outside the family, but social factors, not higher morality, keep them from crime. According to Bonger (1969: 64), "Her smaller criminality is like the health of a hothouse plant; it is due not to innate qualities, but to the hothouse which protects it from harmful influences."

Bonger believes that the changing position of women will result in their economic and social independence. This should temporarily increase their crime rate, but once socialism is fully operative, the harmful effects of capitalism and the domination of women by men will be eliminated. So, too, will all crime — both male and female.

Bonger is to be credited for recognizing (unlike most criminologists) that patterns of female crime need explaining, and he sympathetically describes the deprivations of capitalism and the oppression of women. He is correct in assuming that women are less directly affected by capitalism, at least to the extent that the private world of the home is regarded as their principal domain. (They certainly suffer from the poverty caused by capitalism, and from the discontent it can inspire.) It is also true that women have fewer opportunities for certain crimes compared to males. I disagree, however, that women are less involved in crimes of vengeance solely because they are spared the conflicts of larger society by being in the home. Current evidence and research, often inspired by feminism, on wife abuse, child abuse, incest, et cetera make this reasoning undefendable.

Although Bonger claims to be a Marxist, his analysis is full of the same stereotypical images of women found in less radical versions of theoretical criminology (notions of female deceit, hypocrisy, lack of courage, passivity), images criticized elsewhere (Chapter 1). His discussion is as incomplete and unacceptable as earlier work. Moreover, his emphasis on egoism provides a moral and individualistic interpretation of crime rather than a class-related analysis. This calls into question how "Marxist" his work actually is. A thorough understanding of female criminality requires an infinitely more sophisticated structural analysis of women's position in capitalist society, and how this relates to their legal domination, social control, and patterns of crime. In addition, a dialectical understanding of human action and female criminality is needed in place of Bonger's rather crude determinism.

Dorie Klein and June Kress

One attempt in radical criminology that stands out from the others because it deals specifically with the issue of women and crime is a recent article by Dorie Klein and June Kress (1976), "Any Woman's Blues: A Critical Overview of Women, Crime, and the Criminal Justice System." It focuses on the crimes women commit, rather than an on analysis of their limited criminality, but it provides some insights and is a noteworthy contribution to the literature.

Klein and Kress criticize theoretical criminology for failing to consider the economic and political position of women and the part sexist oppression may play as a factor in crime. They contend that the economic system fosters crime and must be examined along with the historical and present role of women in society in order to understand female crime. Likewise, a consideration of the family is essential, since the unique economic and social position of women in capitalist society hinges on this. Klein and Kress claim that the American family has shifted from a unit of production to one of consumption, with the advent of contemporary capitalism. Moreover, (Klein and Kress, 1979: 84):

> In that the family consumes the goods, reproduces the workers, keeps them alive, and helps to inculcate children and adults alike with the values required to maintain the legitimacy of present arrangements, women's work bolsters capitalism.

Sexism, in turn, legitimates this family structure by defining the role of women as "natural." Through unpaid housework, women enable husbands and children to work; all to the benefit of capitalism. They also soften the brutality of capitalism by providing a comfortable environment for their families.

Klein and Kress observe that women are economically deprived, and one might expect a high rate of property crime among them. They (1979: 87) contend, however, that for historical reasons "most women are not sociologically, psychologically or economically in a position at this time to aggressively steal, nor do those with male providers have such a need." Women are as restricted in their criminal roles as they are in legitimate ones: "Women's lack of participation in 'big time' crime highlights the larger class structure of sexism that is reproduced in the illegitimate marketplace" (Klein and Kress, 1979: 88).[27]

Klein and Kress conclude by discussing whether current changes in women's roles will affect their crime patterns. They caution that increasing labor force participation does not mean the elimination of sexism, since women are still confined to menial, low-paying jobs, while the larger culture continues to foster and accept sexist stereotypes. This could mean the continuance of women's traditional involvement in crime. "On the other hand, if the women's movement develops a class analysis of women's oppression, and a program around which working class women can be organized, then we may witness a decrease in women's individualism, self-destruction, competitiveness and crime" (Klein and Kress, 1979: 89). Klein and Kress are careful to note that the women's movement is not criminogenic, as Adler (1975) implies. They view her analysis as simplistic and argue that an understanding of female crime must be sought in the social relations of capitalism and the particular oppression of women.

The New Criminology

Unfortunately, Marxist criminologists have rarely dealt with the issue of women and crime (the exception being the Klein and Kress article,

1976), although they have at various times commented on the oppression of women in capitalist society and even suggested redefining sexism as a form of crime. To the extent that they view capitalism as a direct cause of crime, they would have difficulty explaining why women have largely escaped being propelled into criminality. It is certainly possible that a class society oppresses men and women in different ways, and with different results, but this inevitably means that more than economic factors are at work, or at least that these economic factors translate differently in regard to males and females. The critical criminologists generally do not directly and inevitably connect capitalism and crime, but rather they emphasize the effects of an unequal and competitive society on its various members. This analysis has not been extended to women, although this could conceivably be done. In fact, the new criminology almost demands such research in order to realize its self-proclaimed goals: the desire to understand the facts of oppression within capitalism, and also the ambition to understand the facts of crime.

Although skeptical of official crime statistics, the new criminologists have exhibited a concern with the way societies report or produce certain amounts of crime. Surely, this can, and should, encompass an examination of the curious lack of female criminality, or, put differently, the disinterest of the system in "producing" female crime. Taylor, Walton, and Young (1975) claim official statistics are useful in highlighting the tremendous volume of property crime in capitalist society. Young, in particular, suggests that the statistics offer a measurement of the amount of respect for property, and conflict in society. He (Taylor, Walton, and Young, 1975: 87) sees the statistics as "the basis for a socialist analysis of the development of contradictions and conflict in a propertied society." Thus, as Taylor, Walton, and Young (1975) maintain, the statistics can help us measure the amount of compliance in industrial society among different portions of our population. Although they overlook it, the noncriminality of women is certainly important, if crime is to be used either as a measure of compliance or contradiction within capitalism. Ignoring women in such an analysis could easily lead to distorted results and assumptions, including, for example, the notion that noncriminality reflects an absence of conflict or human suffering.

Analysis of Crime.   The new criminologists generally seek a Marxist analysis of the nature of social relations under capitalism and contend that material conditions are the basis of crime, as well as law. They recommend using the framework of historical materialism to explore this relationship, and thus their explanation of crime would not be universal, but specific to a certain type of society in a given historical period. The production of crime and its interpretation are fundamentally connected with the distribution of economic and political power and historically located in economic class relations. Specific features of capitalism must be examined in terms of the role they play in crime (private ownership, for example, must be analyzed in terms of competition and exploitation, and the part this plays in crime causation). It might be discovered, as Gordon (1973) contends, that certain crimes are a rational response to the competitiveness and inequality of capitalism.

A structural analysis of the capitalist class system defines not only the opportunities for crime, but also differential enforcement practices. Thus, a Marxist analysis of class might be an excellent beginning for an understanding of crime, and the above suggestions might beneficially be applied to an analysis of women and crime. But this has yet to be done. In fact, it has barely been suggested or even recognized as a worthwhile endeavor. This should concern anyone who is apprehensive about seeing the mistakes of the old criminology paraded before us once again. Unfortunately, we have, as yet, no reason to expect anything else.

A class analysis of crime would have to be more precise and refined were it to include women. This would add considerably to our understanding of the phenomenon, and to the value of the analysis. It is also possible, however, that a class analysis might not cover all conflict in society, and criminologists must be sensitive to what might be overlooked.[28] Sexism and the criminality of women are likely to require special attention and a different analysis. Men and women have very different social positions within capitalism, and sexual oppression is borne by women across class lines, unlike the economic oppression of men (and women). This must figure in an understanding of their crime patterns.

Law and the State.   A Marxist analysis of social relations under capitalism involves an analysis of law as a means of social control and as a tool of the ruling class. Critical criminology's view of law as a creation of the ruling class helps explain their disinterest in focusing solely on why people become criminal, or break the law. Law breaking cannot and should not be treated apart from the biased and distorted nature of law itself. Their view of law is, in turn, based on a radical analysis of the state, which is also regarded as serving the ruling capitalist class. Virtually all the new criminologists explicitly regard law as reflecting material conditions and the mode of production in capitalist society, and both law and the state as protecting the ruling class and maintaining the status quo.

The new criminologists have not explicitly applied these insights to men, let alone women. Nonetheless, establishing the connections between law, crime, and capitalism regarding women promises very interesting results. Assuming that the law enables the powerful to maintain their standards of morality, protect their property, and control anyone who might threaten the status quo, it is imperative to understand how this might vary regarding males and females, and if they are restrained by law in the same way. Their widely differing criminal involvement indicates that they might not be. Apparently, women are controlled with much less criminalization than men, which necessitates a rethinking of the role of criminal law in maintaining the status quo. The effects of formal as well as informal censures have to be explored in an effort to elucidate class and sexual domination. A complete understanding of the connections between crime and law, rooted in specific economic and historical circumstances, will not be achieved until basic differences between the social conditions of men and women are acknowledged and carefully analyzed.

Definition of Crime. A thoroughly radical analysis of law and crime will entail redefining crime, presenting an opportunity to explore issues of particular concern regarding women. Tony Platt (1975) discusses the need for a definition of crime that is more than merely a legal definition and that recognizes divisions of power and privilege. This issue is intimately connected with how society defines and controls exploitation. Treating prostitution, abortion, and the sexual behavior of young females as criminal has enabled society to maintain stricter control over women. As the Schwendingers (1970) point out, sexism, however, has not been viewed as criminal, although its effects are undoubtedly much more pernicious than sexual "delinquencies." To view sexism as crime would involve redefining crime in ethical terms, as a violation of human rights. This raises compelling questions about the linkages among crime, law, and women's role in capitalist society.

Along similar lines, Spitzer (1975) suggests examining the images of deviants and how they reflect a class society, especially in terms of structural and ideological change. He contends that this would be very useful, since deviants are groups who pose special problems for the ruling class. Although Spitzer does not mention it, examining the changing image of the female deviant might be particularly enlightening. Since the portrayal of criminals in the mass media frequently reflects the interests of the dominant class, we might ask why the media have repeatedly sensationalized the growth in crime among women, often connecting this with women's "liberation," while the fact of the matter is, crime, especially violent crime, has not escalated rapidly among women. It is likely that the women's movement threatens the status quo in terms of the role of women and the family in capitalist society. Subtly blaming the movement for increases in female crime is one way of discrediting changes in the position of women. Women are oppressed apart from class, and not particularly in terms of criminalization. Nonetheless, crime is useful to the powerful as a means of social control, and this should not be ignored in a study of women and crime.

Research Suggestions.   In addition to the major considerations outlined above, critical criminology offers a wide variety of useful and challenging ideas that could be applied to a study of women and crime, as the details of this perspective are elaborated. This includes its methodology of historical materialism, discussed above, and its rejection of value freedom. In opposition to value freedom, the new criminologists are anxious that their political beliefs be reflected in their research and that their writings, in turn, serve a political purpose. They should welcome research that might further the emancipation of women by drawing the connections between their social position and their criminality in capitalist society. The new criminologists, following Marx, aim to destroy the myths of the present society, and the pretensions that bolster its injustice. In fact, they judge their research by its effectiveness at this task. A thorough discussion of women, crime, and law would challenge present political assumptions and practices and, thus, assist in the political work of critical criminology. Since critical criminology attempts to aid human liberation and fight the forces of oppression, it should carefully distinguish between the oppression of men and women, and the role of crime and law in this regard. The fact that women have low rates of crime does not mean that they are not oppressed in capitalist society, but simply that this oppression must be carefully analyzed and not subsumed under considerations of men, which in itself indicates the sexism of modern science and modern society.

The new criminology actively debates the possibility of social change and the necessity of a new society to maximize freedom and equality. Unlike its liberal counterpart it envisions a much brighter future in which social problems are conquered. It recognizes, however, that this cannot be attained without widespread structural change. Thus, the oppression of women will only end under vastly different social conditions.

CONCLUSION

Critical criminology is an extremely valuable perspective, particularly in terms of the challenges it presents to traditional criminology, and its rethinking of fundamental sociological issues: its discussion of value freedom, new definitions of crime, the debate about human suffering and revolutionary change, and so on. Presently, however, their theoretical work is seriously underdeveloped, and when they have begun to formulate the links between crime and capitalism, women's criminality is rarely, if ever, discussed. This might be corrected as the new criminology continues to develop, but it is at least as likely that it will duplicate the problems of the old criminology. Not only does sexism cross class lines, it also afflicts individuals of every political persuasion. Given the work the radicals have done to date, there is little reason to suspect that they will avoid the sexism found in other perspectives. There are, however, a few encouraging signs. The Schwendingers (1970) state that sexism might be defined as crime, and other critical criminologists occasionally acknowledge the subjugation of women. There exists, at least, an awareness and interest in the facts of oppression, and this includes the oppression of women.

On the other hand, Taylor, Walton, and Young's massive criticism of criminology (1973) does not contain *one word* about women. They thoroughly scrutinize and criticize theoretical criminology, yet they never notice the limited applicability of these theories to women. Likewise, Quinney is all but blind to distinctions between the conditions of males and females in capitalist society. Thus, it seems that the potential exists for a sophisticated analysis of women and crime from the perspective of critical criminology, but this has yet to be accomplished or even suggested. The danger is that the inadequacies that hamper traditional criminology will be repeated within a radical framework.

The development of a critical criminology of women and crime is potentially fruitful, since it offers the possibility of a political and economic analysis of a phenomenon typically handled in extremely individualistic terms. It could be rich in its analysis of stratification, law, and power, not oversimplified as current accounts even of male criminality generally are. Critical criminology could also strive to make this accessible and politically effective, not as abstract and elitist as scientific work generally is. Moreover, it could incorporate Marx's dialectical view of humanity as determined, yet determining, while making distinctions between forms of deviance that are politically progressive and those that are merely reactions to a brutalizing system.

It is impossible at present to apply critical criminology to an understanding of women and crime because, to date, as criticisms of this perspective suggest, it is extremely generalized, even oversimplified. At this stage, it should be acknowledged that the new criminology would be extremely useful in an analysis of women and crime, and it should be strongly advised that women be considered as the intricate details of this approach are articulated. The role of women in contemporary society, the changes they are experiencing, the details of their oppression, the ways they support capitalism and reject it, the necessity of structural change, and a host of other issues might be illuminated by a detailed discussion of the connections between women, crime, law, and capitalism.

NOTES

[1]Sociohistorical changes, and rapidly changing values, also played a vital role in its development (Sykes, 1974: 211–212). In addition, the political protests of the 1960s, which enabled many citizens to experience first hand the workings of political oppression and the obvious misuse of political power, had an impact.

[2]In dialectical fashion, as Taylor (1971) notes, the law does not simply reflect economic reality but may, in turn, influence the economic situation.

[3]See Laurie Taylor (1971), for a more complete discussion of this, and Karl Renner (1949), for a skillful application of historical materialism to the study of legal norms.

[4]In the course of this essay, Marx explicitly aligns himself with the positivist Quetelet, which has left him open to charges of economic determinism. His view of social reality is, however, much more complex than this, since he emphasizes material conditions, social control, and human reaction (Taylor, Walton, and Young, 1973: 216).

[5]This explains, in part, an obvious disdain with which Marx regarded criminals.

[6]Taylor, Walton, and Young (1973: 268–282) contend that such a theory would have to examine and maintain the connections between the following seven elements. First, *the wider origins of the deviant act* have to be sought in the structural, cultural, and sociopsychological conflicts of larger society. Second, *the immediate origins of the deviant act,* — what precipitates the action — must be understood. This involves a sociopsychology of crime. Third, *the actual act* must be explained in terms of choice or constraints just before action. In other words, social dynamics must be examined. Fourth, *immediate origins of social reaction* must be explored in terms of the choices available to the audience. This calls for a sociopsychology of social reaction. Fifth, the *wider origins of the deviant reaction* involves a political economy of social reaction, which is almost totally neglected in the literature. Sixth, *the outcome of the social reaction on the deviant's further action* must be studied, with the premise that this is closely connected with the conscious choices that led to the

initial action. Seventh, *the nature of the deviant process as a whole must be understood*, all the different aspects must be dialectically related to one another.

[7]Taylor, Walton, and Young (1975: 44) have defined correctionalism as "individual rehabilitation or tangential social reform." It is fundamentally related to a criminology that bolsters the status quo and unquestioningly views its role as assisting in reforming criminals, to secure the given social order.

[8]Essentially, "scientificity," for Taylor, Walton, and Young, is the ideology of positivism. Elsewhere, they (1975: 7) have discussed the basis of positivism as its insistence that the assumptions and methods of physical science can successfully be applied to the study of the social world. Given this premise, positivism has three basic aspects: "positivists have proceeded to propound the methods for the quantification of behavior, have acclaimed the objectivity of the scientist, and have asserted the determinate, law-governed nature of human action."

[9]Radical criminology involves a return to a theoretical analysis of larger society but *not* as Taylor, Walton, and Young (1975: 19) put it, "with a view to understanding the sinews of equilibrium, but with a view to identifying the institutions relevant to radical change."

[10]A materialist theory would also be interested in critiquing the perfectly legal distribution of wealth in capitalist society.

[11]This quote is made in spite of Althusserian critics who claim that such issues cannot be addressed within an authentic Marxian framework, since Marx himself was not concerned with the topic of crime.

[12]Platt's book was first published in 1969. In a new addition in 1977, he noted that the earlier version was too narrow, too reformist. He, like many of the new criminologists, had moved increasingly toward a materialist analysis. By 1977, he felt that the child-saving movement was best understood in the context of the political economy of Progressivism.

[13]This will be explained more fully below as I discuss the contribution of the Schwendingers to the new criminology.

[14]Gordon asserts, among other things, that crime is increasing and mainly economically motivated, although only selected crimes (usually those of the poor) are emphasized, while many (like white-collar crimes) are relatively hidden. He also claims that attempts to curb crime are notably unsuccessful. He discusses public attitudes toward crime, and like Taylor, Walton, and Young and Platt, outlines conservative, liberal, and radical approaches to crime. He also includes a brief discussion of orthodox economic treatments of crime.

[15]In a similar vein, Karl Schumann (1976: 293) suggests that we carefully consider if a revolutionary change of capitalism will actually eliminate crime. "If class theory does not grasp all relevant social conflicts in capitalist societies, revolution may not suspend the causes of all social conflicts either." He mentions the treatment of women as social conflict that is not class related.

[16]Barry Krisberg's book, *Crime and Privilege* (1975), contributes to critical criminology by discussing how crime relates to the privilege structure. He suggests examining the state in this regard, for he sees it as a "partner to privilege." He also suggests (1976: 26) that the new criminology explore the

connections among different privilege systems, such as racism, sexism, or class oppression.

[17]Certain behavior with obvious political implications is nonetheless labeled as criminal, and its political impact thus diffused. Ghetto riots are, perhaps, the best example of this. See Isaac Balbus, *The Dialectics of Legal Repression* (1977) for an analysis of the mid-1960s riots and their criminalization.

[18]Taylor, Walton, and Young note that egoism and altruism are not as easily separated as Bonger implies. Crime can be, and often is, more than egoistic action; it can represent an attempt to solve problems, or can be motivated by concerns for one's family, gang, et cetera.

[19]Taylor, Walton, and Young (1973: 228–229) comment that, "Notably, Bonger's discussion of the subordination of women (and its contribution to the aetiology of female criminality) and of 'militarism' (in sustaining an egoistic and competitive moral climate) seem far ahead of their time."

[20]Gibbons (1977) insists that Sutherland and Vold acknowledged the importance of conflict, although he admits most criminology portrays a pluralistic model of law, not a monopoly of power.

[21]A discussion of these criticisms of the new criminology can be found in Gibbons (1977), Lemert (1974), and Sykes (1974).

[22]Taylor, Walton, and Young are concerned with a simplistic interpretation of Marx's work as economic determinism, which would also entail an absence of any dialectical understanding.

[23]Currie's review also contains an excellent critique of the theoretical perspective that underlies the book, particularly Taylor, Walton, and Young's proposal of a "social" theory.

[24]See McCaghy (1976), Barlow (1978), and Gibbons and Jones (1975) for further discussion of these criticisms.

[25]Bonger does not explain what he means by this. The crimes he treats in this section of his book are adultery, rape, and indecent assault on adults and children.

[26]Bonger insists women are also spared the pernicious effects of alcoholism and militarism, which foster criminality among men.

[27]Klein and Kress (1979: 88) also note that racism is reproduced in the criminal world, as in the straight world.

[28]See Schumann (1976) for a brief discussion of this.

CHAPTER EIGHT

Toward
A Feminist Theory
of Crime

Theoretical criminology is unable to explain adequately the phenomenon of women and crime. Theories that are frequently hailed as explanations of human behavior are, in fact, discussions of male behavior and male criminality. In addition, as I have demonstrated, this oversight regarding women is not easily remedied. We cannot simply apply these theories to women, nor can we modify them with a brief addition or subtraction here and there. They are biased to the core, riddled with assumptions that relate to a male — not a female — reality. Theoretical criminology is sexist because it unwittingly focuses on the activities, interests, and values of men, while ignoring a comparable analysis of women.

WOMEN AND CRIME

In many respects, women have experienced tremendous social change since World War II, particularly regarding employment outside the home and increased education. This, combined with more recent exposure to feminist ideas, has begun to alter traditional sex-role expectations. However, most women still choose to marry and have children; most are still confined to low-status, low-paying occupations. This pattern of change and nonchange is duplicated in female criminal endeavors. Women's crime is increasing, particularly larceny-theft and fraud. Basically, however, women are remarkably noncriminal, and the crimes they commit are usually petty and nonviolent. Thus, in many respects, their traditional patterns of crime persist.[1] The limited criminality of women is surprising in our own crime-ridden society, and even more puzzling since it is a cross-cultural phenomenon. It fails to astound people only because it is so commonplace.

Some writers (Simon, Adler, etc.) have suggested that as women begin to assume traditionally male positions of prestige and authority, as they begin to enter white-collar jobs, their opportunities for crime and their criminal involvement will rise. Adler claims that we have no reason to expect otherwise, but I think we do. The argument that increased white-collar employment for women will lead to increased white-collar crime among them assumes that women behave the same as men, given apparently similar situations. Yet, we should know this is not so. The poverty, the unemployment, the limited opportunities that supposedly drive many men to crime, have not had the same effect on women. Perhaps the opportunity for white-collar crime will not have the same effect on them either. In fact, the *declining* rate of embezzlement among women in a decade of *increasing* female employment seems to substantiate this, Given their vastly different historical, social, and economic experiences, women should not be expected to behave like men. Even in apparently similar situations, they will behave differently. The *social* sources of these differences must be explored. Simply predicting female behavior by reference to male behavior is unlikely to work. This is precisely the problem confronting all our theories — they barely acknowledge let alone incorporate existing differences between men and women. We need much more information about the contrasting social worlds, and world views, of men and women.

SEXISM, SOCIOLOGY, AND SOCIAL SCIENCE

The problem of sexism is not limited to criminology, but readily extends to a more general discussion of sociology and social science. Exploring this issue necessarily raises concerns that are among the most fundamental and fascinating in the field of sociology — questions of what we know, and precisely how our social position affects such knowledge. Feminism has begun to have a major impact on social science by vividly describing the extent to which our supposedly "value-free" and "unbiased" science has been tainted by characteristically male approaches to social reality. This has meant the reanalysis of basic assumptions, re-search interests, and theoretical frameworks. As Millman and Kanter (1975: viii) explain, "Feminist critiques have shown us how social science has been defined by models representing a world dominated by white males, and so our studies of the social world have been limited by the particular interests, perspectives, and experiences of that one group."

A recent report by the Committee on the Status of Women in Sociol-ogy (1980) discusses various aspects of the research process where sexism is frequently found. It can occur, first, regarding problem selection, when topics are treated strictly in terms of men, or those of particular concern to women are ignored. The Committee report mentions gender-blind social theory in this regard, when gender is a significant variable but is left unexamined. This readily applies to criminology, since topics such as women and the law have previously been overlooked, or as the Committee notes, male-victim crimes have received much greater atten-tion than female-victim crimes. We have thoroughly discussed theoretic-al criminology's "gender blindness"; it might simply be added that, according to Donald Cressey (1964: 53), "sex status is of greater statistic-al significance in differentiating criminals from noncriminals than any other trait."

Sexism is also apparent in reviews of the literature, when researchers neglect to mention that earlier work refers only to a single sex, or is extremely imbalanced in this regard. Similarly, men or women are often simply omitted from study without sufficient reason for the exclusion of one sex. Moreover, differences in male-female behavior are commonly regarded as the result of biological or psychological differences, with lit-tle or no attempt to explore social factors. This certainly applies to many discussions of female crime.

Sexism also extends to the interpretation of research results. For ex-ample, studies based on single-sex samples frequently do not qualify their results in this regard, but speak in general terms as though they refer to both sexes.[2] Such studies are often incorrectly entitled. The Committee appropriately gives the example of a study of male crime being called "Crime in American Society."

The sexism of theoretical criminology illustrates the role of social theory in science and in society. Alvin Gouldner (1970) accurately notes that vital connections exist between a critique of society and a critique of our theories about society. He argues that social theorists do not simply "study" society; they themselves are products of their society. As a re-sult, the theories they create contain explicit as well as implicit (back-ground) assumptions or beliefs. Although these beliefs are not necessarily consciously chosen, they exist, and sociologists can study their influence.

Embedded in every theory are the political and personal concerns of the theorists, who necessarily tackle issues of concern to them personally. This necessitates, according to Gouldner, a "heightened self-awareness," so that sociologists can recognize the hidden social assumptions on which their work is based. He correctly asserts that sociologists are no more likely to be automatically free from social contingencies than those they are inclined to study. Everyone operates within a social framework. Gouldner illustrates this with a few examples that ironically point to some of his own "background" assumptions. Imagine a sociologist, who happens to be a woman, and perhaps a feminist, reading Gouldner (1970: 57): "Like other men, sociologists also have sexual lives," which affects their work. "For example," he continues, "it is my strong but undocumented impression that when some sociologists change their work interests, problems, or styles, they also change mistresses or wives."

Gouldner's example enables us to realize that his critique of sociology can be recast in feminist terms. Sociological thought, as Dorothy Smith (1973) notes, has been based on a male view of the social world. All sociologists, male and female, are taught certain approaches to the study of society, in which certain concepts and topics are viewed as valid and relevant. According to Smith (1973: 8), women learn to discard their own understandings and interpretations of the world, and to "confine and focus (their) insights within the conceptual frameworks and relevances which are given in the discipline." She refers to this as a type of "conceptual imperialism," in which women are outsiders and subservient to men's social world, and their sociological reflections on that world.

A feminist critique of theoretical criminology substantiates Gouldner's claim that social theory in general is embedded in personal and political values. It also challenges the notion of value-free science and indicates the need for a reflexive sociology.[3]

FEMINIST RESEARCH AND BEYOND

The subject of women and crime must be studied in its own right, as a separate and distinct phenomenon. Existing theories will not do, nor can the topic be subsumed under these explanations of crime. What is presently indispensable is a feminist criminology to provide the thought and research required for a more complete criminology.

The ultimate goal, however, is not a "criminology of women," which is given one chapter in each criminology text, and one lecture in each criminology course. The topic requires enormous research immediately, but to continue to treat it separately would mean leaving the sexism of theoretical criminology intact. This is unacceptable, particularly since criminology, and social science in general, usually view their research efforts as cumulative. While Merton or Cohen are justly criticized for doing sexist work in the 1930s or 1950s, it must be acknowledged that most people were blind to women's issues at that time. But for criminology to continue presenting the same theories in the 1980s, unchanged and uncriticized, is totally unacceptable.[4] Our theoretical frameworks must incorporate an understanding of both male and female behavior or, alternatively, be absolutely clear that the theory is insufficient in this regard, and explain precisely why this is the case.

Recent work on women and crime, like the literature that came before, has tended to view the phenomenon as distinct from male behavior. This implicitly separates a theoretical consideration of male and female criminality, and runs the risk of having women's issues treated as an addendum. No attempt is made to explain the separation of male and female social worlds, nor to analyze the connections between them.[5] Discussing the literature on stratification, Joan Acker (1980: 27) persuasively argues against separate conceptual frameworks, maintaining that, "The positing of two separate systems is a more sophisticated form of intellectual sexism than the conceptual invisibility of women." In either case, the man is viewed as the "general human being." She also notes that attempts to integrate women into general theoretical frameworks have elicited critiques involving the basic assumptions of these frameworks. Hence, the possibility arises of substantively improving and refining our general theories by reanalyzing them from a feminist perspective (implying, for example, a more powerful understanding of male, as well as female, criminality.)

Separate studies of women are definitely needed to move criminology toward a more satisfactory understanding of human behavior, but the goal should be a unitary science, with unitary theories that no longer ignore vast segments of society. In the meantime, the sexism of criminology must be forcefully noted.

TOWARD A FEMINIST ANALYSIS OF CRIME

The task that faces not only criminology, but social science in general, is two-pronged. Initially, critiques of existing theory and research are required to demonstrate the limitations of current material. Beyond that, new methods and theories must be constructed, methods and theories that overcome such weaknesses. Most work, at this point, centers on the first task, which must be achieved before nonsexist ways of describing social reality can evolve. However, critique, in and of itself, is insufficient. Moreover, people are anxious to examine newer, feminist models and are understandably dissatisfied when they are not forthcoming. For this reason, I will sketch a rough approximation of how a nonsexist theory of crime might evolve. It is imperative to realize that although critique is unavoidable in the development of new theories, it alone cannot be a basis for these theories. Quite simply, the understanding, the insight, the research materials required for this task are absent from current theoretical discussions. The very problem with these frameworks is what they ignore; the realities they overlook; the insights they miss. I will, however, discuss the way an adequate theory of women and crime (and ultimately an understanding of crime in general), might develop. This involves exploring the questions such a theory should be able to answer, and the available theories and bodies of literature that might be examined in such a quest. I will conclude with more questions than answers, since the construction of a satisfactory feminist theory of crime awaits future research.

In order to approach an acceptable understanding of female patterns of crime, I would recommend the following four steps:

First, examine the insights found in existing criminological theory regarding the causes and production of crime.

Although theoretical criminology does not explain female patterns of crime, this does not mean it should be discarded, nor that it has nothing to offer in terms of understanding crime. The processes it describes could be useful in building a feminist theory. Early explanations of limited female criminality are, of course, totally unsatisfactory. We are too aware of the influence of social structure to argue seriously that women are more virtuous than men and, perhaps, too disillusioned even to suggest such a thing. Likewise, contentions that physical strength limits female crime are easily countered by observing that guns at least equalize any situation, and, moreover, that women (like men) can choose victims who are less powerful, such as weaker women or children. These explanations are now rightfully scorned. Understanding the criminality of women requires a serious look at several interconnecting factors bearing on the particular situation of women here and in other cultures, and closely connected with their peculiar brand of oppression.[6] Existing theories of crime do not achieve this, although certain insights can be gleaned from their work. Anomie theory, for example, discusses structurally induced pressures that can result in criminal activity. Reinterpreted, it suggests that women are comparatively less burdened by the financial strains imposed on men in our society, due, in part, to varying traditional expectations.[7] The fact that men, not women, are still largely responsible for financial support and financial success might help explain limited female crime, particularly in capitalist societies. It can also alert us to the subordinate status of women, and their traditionally low expectations.

Differential association discusses criminal and noncriminal behavior as learned through association with others, not as biologically or psychologically rooted. This would be valuable in an analysis of female crime, which is typically viewed in extremely individualistic terms. Differential association also offers the opportunity to discuss the membership of men and women in varying groups, and the fact that they are treated differently even within the same groups. It recognizes that learning varies from one group to another and, thus, presents the possibility that women are shielded from learning crime.

Subcultural theory highlights the importance of exploring the restrictions on female opportunities, both legitimate and illegitimate. With the exception of Miller's work, subcultural theory contains at least a tacit understanding that the sex variable is crucial, and affects values, roles, socialization, opportunities, and so on. It raises the possibility that males and females have different expectations, and that females might participate in a subculture that reinforces certain patterns of behavior, while discouraging others, including perhaps criminal behavior.

Thus, these theories might provide clues regarding the limited criminality of women, although they are severely lacking in many respects. This has been thoroughly discussed above; I will simply mention that none of them (including labeling and the new criminology) rigorously considers women, and they frequently contain invalid assumptions regarding them. Moreover, since these frameworks typically refer to men, it is particularly unwise to rely solely on them when constructing an explanation of female patterns of crime. Such an analysis would be apt to incorporate the same problems that persistently hamper criminology, viewing women once again in terms of male categories. It is essential to move beyond this, which leads to our next step.

Second, the implications of the new research on women and crime should be systematically explored.

The movement beyond traditional assumptions regarding women and crime began with the discussion of differential role expectations for men and women. Female crime is viewed, in part, as the illegitimate expression of role expectations. We now recognize that women are socialized to different roles; they are subject to more social control; that, in effect, it is "unladylike" to be involved in criminal activity. To a certain extent, this is valid and useful, especially given traditional explanations of female crime, but what does it actually mean? Men are certainly not actively socialized to be burglars, robbers, rapists; and society, it seems, would gladly control such activities if it were able. The analysis of sex roles is a good beginning; the protection and supervision of women and their training to be nonaggressive, obedient, dependent, and restrained should be considered. At best, however, these explanations do not get to the root of understanding the limited criminality of women or, to put it another way, the connections that exist between socialization and social structure. *Why* are women taught to be nonaggressive? Role differentiation itself must be understood in terms of economic, political, and historical factors.[8]

More recent work on women and crime has moved in this direction, at least in terms of implicit assumptions. These assumptions merit attention, and could assist in developing a theory of women and crime. Although researchers have begun to analyze women in terms of the criminal justice system, their prison experiences, drug use, victimization, sexist laws, and so on, adequate theoretical frameworks are still forthcoming.

Carol Smart (1976) suggests that the sexual exploitation of women is connected with their economic and political dependency. Bowker (1978) advises examining both criminological theory and sex-role theory in order to explain female patterns of crime. He, like Smart, recognizes that macrostructural variables will necessarily be involved in this explanation. Balkan, Berger, and Schmidt (1980) recommend viewing female crime in terms of women's socialization and opportunities under capitalism. They recognize the importance of socioeconomic conditions as well as gender-role expectations, and emphasize the political economy and class conflict. Thus, certain newer writers are turning from individualistic explanations or inherent characteristics of women toward more structural and cultural interpretations in which women are frequently viewed as victims, not villains. The assumptions they make, the variables they emphasize, and the insights they provide, should be scrupulously examined.

It would also be worthwhile to examine case studies of women criminals, with an eye toward understanding general patterns of female crime. Earlier case studies, mentioned above, as well as more recent work, could be analyzed.[9] In addition, exceptions to traditional female patterns of crime should be explored. In Uganda, for example, females are more likely to be arrested for assault than for theft (Clinard and Abbott, *Crime in Developing Countries*, 1973).

Other bodies of research could also yield insight and information applicable to a theoretical understanding of women and crime. For example, anthropological literature on women in various cultures, or women in different ethnic groups, classes, or historical periods within the United States, could be helpful if analyzed in an attempt to understand their limited criminality. Available literature on conformity could also be useful, as well as comparisons of women and other subordinate groups within society.

Third, labeling theory and Marxist discussions of crime should be expanded in order to approach a more complete understanding of women and crime.

Although these particular theoretical frameworks are presently no more adequate in explaining female patterns of crime than those mentioned earlier, they might be particularly valuable in placing the criminality of women in a larger framework. The insights of the other theories, and recent literature on women and crime, are best based on explicit considerations of power and the political economy.

Labeling theory alerts us to the inherent biases found in the law, its relativity, and differential law enforcement. It encourages us to consider *whose* laws are in operation. These are important considerations in terms of women and crime. Labeling also allows the possibility of understanding limited female criminality in terms of the impact of social reaction on the self. More specifically, the strict imposition of informal social control on females might enable them to avoid more formal types of control, and the negative effects this often entails. Moreover, the "positive" labeling of women, both formal and informal, might assist them in viewing themselves, and having others view them, in noncriminal terms. Most importantly, labeling theory alerts us to the centrality of power in modern society. A character in a John Barth novel put it concisely: "Never mind the question, the answer is power." This insight has yet to be examined in terms of women.

Labeling theory, however, has drawbacks. It offers little understanding of initial deviance. As previously discussed, it lacks a structural explanation for crime and an adequate analysis of the role of power in society. A thorough analysis of the structures of power, and how they impinge on women, would be required. In this regard, the new criminology should be helpful.

Like labeling theorists, the new criminologists are concerned about the role of law in society, definitions of crime, and the methods and purposes of social control. However, they specifically recommend examining material conditions and the class nature of capitalism in an effort to understand the connections between law, crime, and capitalism. Their approach might be fruitfully applied to females. Women and crime could be discussed in terms of the position of women vis-à-vis the political economy, the role of sexism in a class society could be examined, the relationship between women and the family in capitalist societies could be analyzed regarding female criminality and noncriminality. The potential of such an analysis is encouraging, although at present the details of this perspective are still forthcoming, thus offering little to a contemporary understanding of women and crime.

Fourth, and I believe most important, feminist theory should be carefully examined so that its understanding and insights regarding women can be applied to an analysis of women and crime.

I stress the importance of an explicitly feminist perspective in order to avoid the pitfalls we have discussed throughout this book. Certainly, valuable insights can be gleaned from existing theoretical criminology, particularly labeling theory and the new criminology. Likewise, recent discussions of women and crime or related bodies of literature on conformity, for example, are extremely worthwhile. But unless they are approached with a solid grounding in feminist understandings of the role of women in contemporary society, I believe we would once again succumb to a partial and distorted description of women and crime. For the most part, our background assumptions (whether we are male or female) are likely to be sexist, unless we consciously strive to rid ourselves of them. This takes more than an act of will, it takes a knowledgeable assessment of the details of women's oppression.

Thus, a general examination of feminist literature is imperative.[10] Moreover, an examination of classical socialist literature on women would be useful.[11] I would particularly recommend exploring recent Marxist and socialist feminist writings, since these illuminate the role of women within a larger political and economic framework.[12] Feminism has provided a great deal of understanding regarding the political, economic, and social conditions that impinge on women, particularly in capitalist societies. The inequality of men and women, and their varying oppression,[13] should be considered when examining crime and law in terms of women. The role of women in the family as well as in the marketplace must be examined as it applies to female patterns of crime. This would mean an analysis of women's relative economic power, which is surely an important determinant of other inequalities. Again, this analysis should not only be radical, but also feminist, since radicals themselves have had difficulty locating women in their discussions of inequality and oppression and have also ignored women's issues. These considerations are to some extent challenging class theory[14] and have led to interesting analyses of capitalism and patriarchy, which could usefully be examined in terms of women and crime.[15]

CONCLUSION

A theory of women and crime should be able to answer certain questions that contemporary theoretical discussions do not address. Why, for example, are women relatively uninvolved in crime, although they are found in all social classes, including those apparently subject to the most severe strain in our society? What structural factors influence their particular patterns of crime? How do their associations affect them, vis-à-vis men? What accounts for the differences in socialization, social control, goals, and legitimate and illegitimate opportunities between males and females, and how does this affect their crime? Specifically, how does the distribution of wealth and power affect women in contemporary society, and their criminality? Why are women, who are relatively powerless, infrequently labeled as criminals in our society? What role do they play in a class society, differentiating their oppression, social control, legal domination, and patterns of crime from that of men?

A structural analysis is obviously required to provide the framework for understanding the connections between women and their patterns of crime. This will counteract the tendency to see the issue in apolitical individualistic terms, instead of focusing on how social structures shape the social position, oppression, and crime among women. Moreover, this structural analysis must be combined with an understanding of the process by which a person becomes criminal.[16] Although the work of Sutherland could be expanded to include structural considerations, I believe a reformulation and elaboration of labeling theory and the new criminology holds the most potential for examining female criminality in a wider moral, political, and economic framework. A grasp of law making and the application of law is essential (as labeling and the new criminology recognize), since an examination of crime that ignores this, and only discusses why a certain person, or group of people, become criminal, is severely limited.

Finally, although I am particularly interested in having the sex variable included in the study of crime, a complete understanding of crime (especially in American society) necessitates an analysis of how sex, race, and class interact to produce criminal patterns.[17] Sociology and criminology have barely begun to overcome the biases of race, class, and particularly sex, which have so badly warped a deeper understanding of social reality, including crime.

I hope this analysis will ultimately add to a better comprehension of the causes of crime, by focusing on a variable frequently ignored in contemporary considerations of crime,[18] by encouraging the reformulation of theoretical criminology, and by reemphasizing that the roots of crime are found in the impact of structural conditions on social behavior and human potential. I am convinced of the utility of a feminist perspective and a radical perspective in approaching a resolution to these issues and providing a more complete understanding of women and crime. Constructing theoretical frameworks that adequately analyze both male and female behavior is work for the future.

NOTES

[1]We are reminded once again that traditional assumptions about women's place in society still remain, as do patterns of discrimination. Likewise, the greatly publicized appearance of the "new female criminal" is more fiction than fact; rapidly rising crime among women is outrageously overemphasized.

[2]Pejorative labeling is also problematic in terms of research formulation. The Committee mentions, for example, the tendency to regard female behavior that violates sex-role expectations as deviant and a cause for concern (juvenile sexual activity, prostitution), whereas any behavior within sex-role limits is acceptable.

[3]A reflexive sociology would contain within it an awareness of the interests, concerns, and background of the sociologist as researcher. For a complete discussion of "reflexive sociology," see Alvin Gouldner (1970).

[4]It would be extremely interesting and valuable to analyze the structural and historical forces behind the appearance and disappearance of various theories of crime. In particular, a discussion of the emergence of a feminist theory in criminology would be welcome.

[5]These are the problems Dorothy Smith notes (1973: 7) regarding the sexism of sociology in general.

[6]Women's oppression is, at times, an odd combination of care and cruelty. Their subservience has given them some protection, amidst the powerlessness. In fact, it is here that the oppression of women and blacks varies, although comparisons are often made between the two groups: blacks are powerless, but they are certainly not protected, not even in the limited ways women are (such as freedom from military service, some expectation of financial support, dubious guarantees of chivalry, etc.). However, it should be noted that these protections are extremely limited and tenuous, and moreover, they fundamentally prevent the full growth and independence of women.

[7]It is important to avoid Merton's mistake of assuming that *one* goal has overriding significance for all of society. All women do *not* seek marriage and a family, and they are certainly interested in financial success. But, distinctions will have to be made between their goals and those of men, given the fact that they are subject to different expectations and socialization. As Juliet Mitchell (1966: 16) points out, "In bringing up children, woman

achieves her main social definition." This does not, however, preclude social change.
[8]This suggests a basically sociological explanation of women and crime. While this is not a total explanation, I would argue that it is the most powerful one, and psychological or biological variables could be added to it, to complete the picture more fully. Role theory, on the other hand, tends to slide into discussions of inadequate socialization, framing the problem once again in individualistic terms.
[9]Mary Hartman (1977) has examined French and English murderesses, while Ann Jones (1980) discusses their American counterparts. Examining women in literature, whether specifically involved in crime or not, could also provide insights regarding their criminality.
[10]See, for example, Alice Rossi (1973), Margrit Eichler (1980), Alison Jagger and Paula Struhl (1978), Marcia Millman and Rosabeth Moss Kanter (1975), and Charlotte Perkins Gillman (1898).
[11]See, for example, August Bebel (1910), Frederich Engels (1942), and *The Woman Question: Selections from the Writings of Karl Marx, Frederich Engels, V.I. Lenin, Joseph Stalin* (1951).
[12]Such an analysis might draw on Simone de Beauvoir (1953), Sheila Rowbotham (1973), Zillah Eisenstein (1980), and Juliet Mitchell (1966).
[13]Class society oppresses men and women in different ways, although this does not necessarily imply a departure from Marxist analysis. Bonger (1969), for example, regarded women as less directly affected by capitalism, in that they play a smaller role in traditional economic life.
[14]In reviewing the literature on stratification, Joan Acker (1980: 26) notes that unlike with women, the socioeconomic situation of men as men is generally not distinguished from their position in the class structure. She concludes: "This suggests to me that class, which we take to be sex neutral, is actually a concept built on understandings of the socioeconomic world as lived by men." She claims that other Marxian concepts, like surplus value, also cannot fully explain the class position of women.
[15]See, for example, Sheila Rowbotham (1973).
[16]As C. Wright Mills suggests in *The Sociological Imagination*, a structural analysis is also powerfully deepened through historical and cross-cultural frames of reference.
[17]Cressey (1964) also mentions the variables of age, nativity, and size of the community. These, although important, do not seem as critical as sex, race, and social class.
[18]Although none of our theoretical frameworks totally explain male criminality, they are obviously even more inadequate regarding females. A consideration of the sex variable could lead to a richer understanding not only of female crime, but of male criminality as well.

Bibliography

ABRAHAMSEN, DAVID, *Crime and the Human Mind*. New York: Columbia University Press, 1944.

ACKER, JOAN. "Women and Stratification: A Review of Recent Literature." *Contemporary Sociology* (January 1980) 9: 25–39.

ADAM, HARGRAVE L. *Woman and Crime*. London: T. Werner Laurie, 1914.

ADLER, FREDA. *Sisters in Crime: The Rise of the New Female Criminal*. New York: McGraw-Hill, 1975.

————, and RITA SIMON, eds. *The Criminology of Deviant Women*. Boston: Houghton Mifflin, 1979.

AKERS, RONALD L. "Problems in the Sociology of Deviance: Social Definitions and Behavior." *Social Forces* (June 1968), 46: 455–465.

ANDERSON, ETTA A. "The 'Chivalrous' Treatment of the Female Offender in the Arms of the Criminal Justice System: A Review of the Literature." *Social Problems* (February 1976) 23: 350–357.

BABCOCK, BARBARA ALLEN. "Introduction: Women and the Criminal Law." *The American Criminal Law Review* (Winter 1973) 11: 291–294.

BALBUS, ISAAC. *The Dialectics of Legal Repression*. New York: Russell Sage Foundation, 1977.

BALKAN, SHEILA, and RONALD BERGER. "The Changing Nature of Female Delinquency." In Claire B. Kopp and Martha Kirkpatrick, eds., *Becoming Female: Perspectives on Development*. New York: Plenum Press, 1979, pp. 207–227.

BALKAN, SHEILA, RONALD BERGER, and JANET SCHMIDT. *Crime and Deviance in America: A Critical Approach*. Belmont, Calif.: Wadsworth Publishing Company, 1980.

BARKER, GORDON H., and WILLIAM T. ADAMS. "Comparison of the Delinquency of Boys and Girls." *Journal of Criminal Law, Criminology, and Police Science* (December, 1962) 53: 470–475.

BARLOW, HUGH. *Introduction to Criminology.* Boston: Little, Brown, 1978.

BEAUVOIR, SIMONE DE. *The Second Sex.* New York: Knopf, 1953.

BEBEL, AUGUST. *Women and Socialism.* New York: Socialist Literature Company, 1910.

BECKER, HOWARD S., ed. *The Other Side.* New York: The Free Press, 1964.

———. *Outsiders: Studies in the Sociology of Deviance.* New York: The Free Press, 1963.

———. "Review of Cameron, the Booster and the Snitch." *American Journal of Sociology* (March 1965) 70: 635–636.

BISHOP, CECIL. *Women and Crime.* London: Chatto and Windus, 1931.

BONGER, WILLEM. *Criminality and Economic Conditions.* Abridged and with Introduction by Austin T. Turk. Bloomington: Indiana University Press, 1969.

BORDUA, DAVID. "Recent Trends: Deviant Behavior and Social Control." *Annals of the American Academy of Political and Social Science,* (January 1967) 57: 149–163.

BOWKER, LEE. *Women, Crime, and the Criminal Justice System.* Lexington, Mass.: D.C. Heath, 1978.

BROADHEAD, ROBERT. "A Theoretical Critique of the Societal Approach to Deviance." *Pacific Sociological Review* (July 1974) 17: 287–312.

BURGESS, ROBERT, and RONALD AKERS. "A Differential Association-Reinforcement Theory of Criminal Behavior." *Social Problems,* (Fall 1966) 14: 128–147.

BURKHART, KATHRYN. *Women in Prison.* New York: Doubleday, 1973.

CAMERON, MARY OWEN. *The Booster and the Snitch.* New York: The Free Press, 1964.

———. "An Interpretation and Shoplifting." In Marshall Clinard and Richard Quinney, *Criminal Behavior Systems.* New York: Holt, Rinehart and Winston, 1967: pp. 109–120.

CERNKOVICH, STEPHEN, and PEGGY GIORDANO. "A Comparative Analysis of Male and Female Delinquency." *The Sociological Quarterly* (Winter 1979) 20: 131–145.

CHAFE, WILLIAM H. *The American Woman: Her Changing Social, Economic and Political Roles.* New York: Oxford University Press, 1972.

———. *Women and Equality: Changing Patterns in American Culture.* New York: Oxford University Press, 1977.

CHAMBLISS, WILLIAM. "Toward a Political Economy of Crime." *Theory and Society* (Summer 1975) 2: 167–180.

CHESNEY-LIND, MEDA. "Judicial Enforcement of the Female Sex Role." *Issues in Criminology* (Fall 1973) 8: 51–69.

CICOUREL, AARON. *The Social Organization of Juvenile Justice.* London: Heinemann, 1968.

CLINARD, MARSHALL. "The Theoretical Implications of Anomie and Deviant Behavior." In M.B. Clinard, ed., *Anomie and Deviant Behavior.* New York: The Free Press, 1964; pp. 1–56.

CLINARD, MARSHALL, and DANIEL ABBOTT. *Crime in Developing Countries: A Comparative Perspective.* New York: Wiley, 1973.

——— and RICHARD QUINNEY. *Criminal Behavior Systems: A Typology.* New York: Holt, Rinehart and Winston, 1967.

CLOWARD, RICHARD A. "Illegitimate Means, Anomie, and Deviant Behavior." *American Sociological Review* (April 1959) 24: 164–176.
———, and LLOYD OHLIN. *Delinquency and Opportunity: A Theory of Delinquent Gangs.* New York: The Free Press, 1960.
COHEN, ALBERT K. *Delinquent Boys: The Culture of the Gang.* New York: The Free Press, 1955.
———. *Deviance and Control.* Englewood Cliffs, N.J.: Prentice-Hall, 1966.
———. "The Sociology of the Deviant Act: Anomie Theory and Beyond." *American Sociological Review* (1965) 30: 5–14.
———, ALFRED LINDESMITH, KARL SCHUESSLER, eds. *The Sutherland Papers.* Bloomington: Indiana University Press, 1956.
———, and JAMES SHORT. "Research in Delinquent Subcultures." *Journal of Social Issues* (1958) 14: 20–37.
COHN, YONA. "Criteria for the Probation Officer's Recommendation to the Juvenile Court." In Peter Garabedian and Don Gibbons, eds. *Becoming Delinquent.* Chicago: Aldine, 1970: 190–206.
Committee on the Status of Women in Sociology. "Sexist Biases in Sociological Research: Problems and Issues." *Footnotes,* January 1980: 8–9.
COWIE, JOHN, VALERIE COWIE, and ELIOT SLATER. *Deliquency in Girls.* London: Heinemann, 1968.
CRESSEY, DONALD. "Changing Criminals: The Application of the Theory of Differential Association." *American Journal of Sociology* (September 1955) 62: 116–120.
———. *Delinquency, Crime and Differential Association.* The Hague: Martinus Nijhoff, 1964.
———. "Epidemiology and Individual Conduct: A Case from Criminology." *Pacific Sociological Review* (Fall 1960a) 3: 47–58.
———. "The Theory of Differential Association: An Introduction." *Social Problems,* (Summer 1960b) 8: 2–6.
CRITES, LAURA. *The Female Offender.* Lexington, Mass.: D.C. Heath, 1976.
CURRIE, ELLIOTT. "Beyond Criminology." *Issues in Criminology,* (Spring 1974) 9: 133–142.
DATESMAN, SUSAN, FRANK SCARPITTI, and RICHARD STEPHENSON. "Female Delinquency: An Application of Self and Opportunity Theories." *Journal of Research in Crime and Delinquency* (July 1975) 12: 107–123.
DAVIS, KINGSLEY. "Prostitution." In Robert Merton and Robert Nisbet, eds., *Contemporary Social Problems.* New York: Harcourt Brace Jovanovich, 1971.
DECROW, KAREN. *Sexist Justice.* New York: Random House, 1974.
DEFLEUR, MELVIN, and RICHARD QUINNEY. "A Reformulation of Sutherland's Differential Association Theory and a Strategy for Empirical Verification." *The Journal of Research in Crime and Delinquency* (January 1966) 3: 1–22.
DENISOFF, R. SERGE, and DONALD McQUARIE. "Crime Control in Capitalist Society: A Reply to Quinney." *Issues in Criminology* (Spring 1975) 10: 109–119.
DERHAM, EDITH. *How Could She Do That? A Study of the Female Criminal.* New York: Clarkson N. Potter, 1969.
DOUGLAS, JACK D. "Deviance and Order in a Pluralist Society." In John McKinney and Edward Tiryakian, eds., *Theoretical Sociology: Perspectives and Developments.* New York: Appleton-Century-Crofts, 1970, pp. 367–401.
EICHLER, MARGRIT. *The Double Standard: A Feminist Critique of Feminist Social Sciences.* London: Croom Helm, 1980.

EISENSTEIN, ZILLAH. *The Radical Future of Liberal Feminism.* New York: Longman, 1980.

ELLIOT, MABEL. *Crime in Modern Society.* New York: Harper & Row, 1952.

ENGELS, FREDERICK. *The Condition of the Working Class in England.* Trans. and ed. by W.O. Henderson and W.H. Chaloner. New York: Macmillian, 1958.

_____. *The Origin of the Family, Private Property, and the State.* New York: International Publishers, 1942.

ERIKSON, KAI T. "Notes on the Sociology of Deviance. *Social Problems* (Spring 1962) 9: 309–314.

_____. *Wayward Puritans: A Study in the Sociology of Deviance.* New York: Wiley, 1966.

FANON, FRANTZ. *The Wretched of the Earth.* New York: Grove Press, 1968.

FELDMAN, SAUL, ed. *Deciphering Deviance.* Boston: Little, Brown, 1978.

FRANKEL, LOIS. "Sex Discrimination in the Criminal Law: The Effect of the Equal Rights Amendment." *The American Criminal Law Review* (Winter 1973) 11: 469: 510.

FRANKLIN, CHARLES. *Women in the Case.* London: Hale, 1967.

GARFINKEL, HAROLD. "Conditions of Successful Degradation Ceremonies." *American Journal of Sociology* (March 1956) 61: 420–424.

GIALLOMBARDO, ROSE. *Society of Women: A Study of a Women's Prison.* New York: Wiley, 1966.

GIBBONS, DON C. *Delinquent Behavior.* 2nd ed. Englewood Cliffs, N.J.: Prentice-Hall, 1976.

_____. *Society, Crime, and Criminal Careers: An Introduction to Criminology.* 3rd ed. Englewood Cliffs, N.J.: Prentice-Hall, 1977.

_____, and PETER GARABEDIAN. "Conservative, Liberal, and Radical Criminology: Some Trends and Observations." In Charles Reasons, ed., *The Criminologist: Crime and the Criminal.* New York: Goodyear, 1974, pp. 51–65.

_____, and JOSEPH JONES. *The Study of Deviance: Perspectives and Problems.* Englewood Cliffs, N.J.: Prentice-Hall, 1975.

GIBBS, JACK. "Conceptions of Deviant Behavior." *Pacific Sociological Review* (Spring 1966) 9: 9–14.

GILLMAN, CHARLOTTE PERKINS. *Women and Economics.* Boston: Small, Maynard and Company, 1898.

GLASER, DANIEL. "Differential Association and Criminological Prediction." *Social Problems* (Summer 1960) 8: 6–14.

_____. "The Differential-Association Theory of Crime." In Arnold Rose, ed., *Human Behavior and Social Processes.* London: Routledge and Kegan Paul, 1962, pp. 435–442.

GLICK, RUTH. "National Study of Women's Correctional Programs." Washington, D.C.: United States Department of Justice, 1974–1976.

GLUECK, SHELDON. "Theory and Fact in Criminology." *British Journal of Delinquency* (October 1956) 7: 92–109.

_____, and ELEANOR GLUECK. *Five Hundred Delinquent Women.* New York: Knopf, 1934.

GOLD, MARTIN. *Delinquent Behavior in an American City.* Monterey, Calif.: Brooks Cole, 1970.

_____, and DAVID REIMER. "Changing Patterns of Delinquent Behavior among Americans 13 Through 16 Years Old: 1967–72." *Crime and Delinquency Literature* (December 1975) 7: 483–517.

GORDON, DAVID. "Capitalism, Class, and Crime in America." *Crime and Delinquency* (April 1973) 19: 163–186.

———, ed. *Problems in Political Economy: An Urban Perspective.* Lexington, Mass.: D.C. Heath, 1971.

GOULDNER, ALVIN. *The Coming Crisis of Western Sociology.* New York: Avon Books, 1970.

GRABINER, GENE. "The Limits of Three Perspectives on Criminology: 'Value-Free Science.' 'Objective Law,' and State 'Morality.'" *Issues in Criminology* (Spring 1973) 8: 35–48.

HAFT, MARILYN G. "Hustling for Rights." In Laura Crites, *The Female Offender.* Lexington, Mass.: D.C. Heath, 1976, pp. 207–228.

HARRIS, ANTHONY. "Sex and Theories of Deviance: Toward a Functional Theory of Deviant Type-Scripts." *American Sociological Review* (February 1977) 42: 3–16.

HARRY, JOSEPH, and MARY SENGSTOCK. "Attribution, Goals, and Deviance." *American Sociological Review* (1978) 43: 278–280.

HARTMAN, MARY S. *Victorian Murderesses: A True History of 13 Respectable French and English Women Accused of Unspeakable Crimes.* New York: Schocken Books, 1977.

HARTZEN, CLAYTON. *Crime and Criminalization.* 2nd ed. New York: Praeger, 1978.

———. "Legalism and Humanism: A Reply to the Schwendingers." *Issues in Criminology* (Winter 1972) 7: 59–69.

HASKELL, MARTIN, and LEWIS YABLONSKY. *Criminology: Crime and Criminality.* Chicago: Rand-McNally, 1978.

HEIDENSOHN, FRANCES. "The Deviance of Women: A Critique and An Inquiry." *The British Journal of Sociology* (June 1968) 19: 160–175.

———. Review of *Women, Crime, and Criminology* by Carol Smart in *The British Journal of Criminology* (October 1977) 17: 390–392.

HINDELANG, MICHAEL. "Age, Sex and the Versatility of Delinquent Behavior." *Social Problems* (Spring 1971) 18: 522–534.

———. "Decisions of Shoplifting Victims to Invoke the Criminal Justice Process." *Social Problems* (April 1974) 21:580–593.

HIRST, PAUL Q. "Marx and Engels on Law, Crime and Morality." *Economy and Society* (February 1972) 1: 28–56.

HOFFMAN-BUSTAMANTE, DALE. "The Nature of Female Criminality." *Issues in Criminology* (Fall 1973) 8: 117–136.

JAGGAR, ALISON, and PAULA STRUHL. *Feminist Frameworks.* New York: McGraw-Hill, 1978.

JENSEN, GARY, and RAYMOND EVE. "Sex Differences in Delinquency, An Examination of Popular Sociological Explanations." *Criminology* (February 1976) 13: 427–448.

JONES, ANN. *Women Who Kill.* New York: Holt, Reinhart and Winston, 1980.

KANOWITZ, LEO. *Women and the Law: The Unfinished Revolution.* Albuquerque: University of New Mexico Press, 1969.

KITSUSE, JOHN I. "Societal Reaction to Deviant Behavior: Problems of Theory and Method." *Social Problems* (Winter 1962) 9: 247–256.

———, and AARON CICOUREL. "A Note on the Uses of Official Statistics." *Social Problems* (Fall 1963) 11: 131–139.

———, and DAVID DIETRICK. "Delinquent Boys: A Critique." *American Sociologic-*

al Review (April 1959) 24: 208–215. Reprinted in Harwin Voss, ed., *Society, Delinquency, and Delinquent Behavior.* Boston: Little, Brown, 1970, pp. 238–245.

KLEIN, DORIE. "The Etiology of Female Crime: A Review of the Literature." *Issues in Criminology* (Fall 1973) 8: 3–29.

_____, and JUNE KRESS. "Any Woman's Blues: A Critical Overview of Women, Crime, and the Criminal Justice System." *Crime and Social Justice* (Spring-Summer 1976) 5: 34–49. Reprinted in Freda Adler and Rita Simon, eds., *The Criminality of Deviant Women.* Boston: Houghton Mifflin, 1979, pp. 82–90.

KONOPKA, GISELA. *The Adolescent Girl in Conflict.* Englewood Cliffs, N.J.: Prentice-Hall, 1966.

KRATCOSKI, JOHN and PETER KRATCOSKI. "Changing Patterns of Boys and Girls." *Adolescence* (Spring 1975) 10: 83–91.

KRISBERG, BARRY. *Crime and Privilege: Toward a New Criminology.* Englewood Cliffs, N.J.: Prentice-Hall, 1975.

LEMERT, EDWIN M. "Beyond Mead: The Societal Reaction to Deviance." *Social Problems* (April 1974). 21: 457–468.

_____. *Human Deviance, Social Problems, and Social Control.* 2nd ed. Englewood Cliffs, N.J.: Prentice-Hall, 1972.

_____. *Social Pathology: A Systematic Approach to the Theory of Sociopathic Behavior.* New York: McGraw-Hill, 1951.

LIAZOS, ALEXANDER. "The Poverty of the Sociology of Deviance: Nuts, Sluts, and Perverts." *Social Problems* (Summer 1972) 20: 103–120.

LOMBROSO, CAESAR, and WILLIAM FERRERO. *The Female Offender.* New York: D. Appleton and Company, 1900.

MCCAGHY, CHARLES. *Deviant Behavior: Crime, Conflict, and Interest Groups.* New York: MacMillan, 1976.

MANNHEIM, HERMANN. *Comparative Criminology*, 2 vols. London: Routledge and Kegan Paul, 1965.

MANNING, PETER K. "Deviance and Dogma: Comments on the Labeling Perspective." *The British Journal of Criminology* (January 1975) 15: 1–20.

MARX, KARL. *Capital.* Vol. 1, tr. by E. Aveling and H. Moore. Moscow: Foreign Languages Publishing House, 1965.

_____. "Capital Punishment." *New York Daily Tribune,* February 18, 1853.

_____. *The Economic and Political Manuscripts of 1844.* Moscow: Profress Publishers, 1967.

_____. *Karl Marx: Selected Writings in Sociology and Social Philosophy.* Edited by T.B. Bottomore and Maximilien Rubel. London: Watts and Company. 1956.

_____. "Population, Crime and Pauperism." *New York Daily Tribune,* September 16, 1859.

_____. *Theories of Surplus Value.* Vol. 1, tr. by Emile Burns. London: Lawrence and Wishart, 1969.

_____, and FREDRICH ENGELS. *The German Ideology.* London: Lawrence and Wishart, 1965.

MATZA, DAVID. *Becoming Deviant.* Englewood Cliffs, N.J.: Prentice-Hall, 1969.

_____. *Delinquency and Drift.* New York: Wiley, 1964.

MERTON, ROBERT K. "Anomie, Anomia and Social Interaction." In M. B. Clinard, ed., *Anomie and Deviant Behavior.* New York: The Free Press, 1964, pp. 213–242.

———. "Social Problems and Sociological Theory." In R. K. Merton and R. Nisbet, eds., *Contemporary Social Problems.* New York: Harcourt Brace Jovanovich, 1966, pp. 775–823.

———. "Social Structure and Anomie." *American Sociological Review* (October 1938) 3: 672–682.

———. *Social Theory and Social Structure.* New York: The Free Press, 1956.

MIKE, BARRY. "Willem Adriaan Bonger's 'Criminality and Economic Conditions': A Critical Appraisal." *International Journal of Criminology and Penology* (August 1976) 4: 211–238.

MILLER, WALTER B. "Lower Class Culture as a Generating Milieu of Gang Delinquency." *Journal of Social Issues* (1958) 14, No. 2, 5–19. In H. Voss, ed., *Society, Delinquency and Delinquent Behavior.* Boston: Little, Brown, 1970, pp. 270–281.

MILLMAN, MARCIA, and ROSABETH MOSS KANTER, eds. *Another Voice: Feminist Perspectives on Social Life and Social Science.* New York: Doubleday, 1975.

MILLS, C. WRIGHT. "The Professional Ideology of Social Pathologists." *American Journal of Sociology* (September 1943) 49: 165–180.

———. *The Sociological Imagination.* New York: Oxford University Press, 1959.

MITCHELL, JULIET. "Women: The Longest Revolution." *New Left Review* (November–December 1966) 40: 11–37.

MONAHAN, FLORENCE. *Women in Crime.* New York: Ives Washburn, 1941.

MORRIS, RUTH. "Attitudes Toward Delinquency by Delinquents, Non-Delinquents and Their Friends." *British Journal of Criminology* (July 1965) 5: 249–265.

———. "Female Delinquency and Relational Problems." *Social Forces* (October 1964) 43: 82–88.

NAGEL, STUART, and LENORE WEITZMAN. "Women as Litigants." *The Hastings Law Journal* (November 1971) 23: 171–198.

NEWBERG, PAULA. "Female of the Species." *Interdiscipline*, (Spring 1967) 4: 29–42.

NOBLIT, GEORGE, and JANIE BURCART. "Women and Crime: 1960–1970." *Social Science Quarterly* (March 1976) 56: 650–657.

NORLAND, STEPHEN, and NEAL SHOVER. "Gender Roles and Female Criminality." *Criminology* (May 1977) 15: 87–104.

OPPENHEIM, MASON, and J. CZAJKA. "Change in U.S. Women's Sex-Role Attitudes, 1964–1974." *American Sociological Review*, (January 1976) 41: 573–596.

PARKER, TONY. *Women in Crime.* New York: Delacorte Press, 1965.

PETERS, ANNE. "Book Review — Carol Smart, *Women, Crime and Criminology.*" *Crime and Social Justice* (Spring-Summer 1978) 9: 86–89.

PEYSTER, JOHN. Transactions of the 4th International Criminological Congress, The Hague, September 1960.

PIKE, LUKE OWEN *History of Crime in England*, Vol. 2. London: Smith, Elder and Company, 1876.

PLATT, ANTHONY. *The Child Savers.* Chicago: University of Chicago Press, 1977.

———. "Prospects for a Radical Criminology in the U.S." In Ian Taylor, et al., eds., *Critical Criminology.* London: Routledge and Kegan Paul, 1975, pp. 95–112.

POLLAK, OTTO. *The Criminality of Women.* Philadelphia: University of Pennsylvania Press, 1950.

QUINNEY, RICHARD. "Crime Control in Capitalist Society: A Critical Philosophy of Legal Order." *Issues in Criminology* (Spring 1973) 8: 75–99.

———. *Criminology: Analysis and Critique of Crime in America.* Boston: Little, Brown, 1975.

———. *Critique of Legal Order: Crime Control in Capitalist Society.* Boston: Little, Brown, 1973.

———. "The Ideology of Law: Notes for a Radical Alternative to Repression." *Issues in Criminology* (Winter 1972) 7: 1–35.

———. *The Social Reality of Crime.* Boston: Little, Brown, 1970.

RASCHE, CHRISTINE. "The Female Offender as an Object of Criminological Research." In Annette Brodsky, ed., *The Female Offender.* Beverly Hills: Sage Publications, 1975, pp. 9–28.

RECKLESS, WALTER C. *The Crime Problem.* Englewood Cliffs, N.J.: Prentice-Hall, 1961.

REID, SUE TITUS. *Crime and Criminology.* Hinsdale, Ill.: The Dryden Press, 1976.

RENNER, KARL. *Institutions of Private Law and Their Social Functions.* London: Routledge and Kegan Paul, 1949.

ROCK, PAUL. "Feature Review Symposium." *The Sociological Quarterly* (Autumn 1973) 14: 594–596.

———. "The Sociology of Deviancy and Conceptions of Moral Order." *British Journal of Criminology* (April 1974) 14: 139–149.

ROGERS, KRISTINE OLSON. "For Her Own Protection." *Law and Society Review* (Winter 1972) 7: 223–246.

ROSENBLEET, CHARLES, and BARBARA PARIENTE. "The Prostitution of the Criminal Law." *The American Criminal Law Review* (Winter 1973) 11: 373–427.

ROSENBLUM, KAREN. "Female Deviance and the Female Sex Role: A Preliminary Investigation." *British Journal of Sociology* (June 1975) 26: 169–185.

ROSSI, ALICE S., ed. *The Feminist Papers: From Adams to de Beauvoir.* New York: Bantam Books, 1973.

ROWBOTHAM, SHEILA. *Woman's Consciousness, Man's World.* Harmondsworth, England: Penguin Books, 1973.

RUBINGTON, EARL, and MARTIN WEINBERG, eds. *Deviance: The Interactionist Perspective.* New York: Macmillan, 1968.

SARRI, ROSEMARY, "Juvenile Law: How It Penalizes Females." In Laura Crites, *The Female Offender.* Lexington, Mass.: D.C. Heath, 1976, pp. 67–87.

SCHRAG, CLARENCE. "Delinquency and Opportunity: An Analysis of a Theory." *Sociology and Social Research* (January 1962) 46: 167–175. In Harwin Vass, ed., *Society, Delinquency and Delinquent Behavior.* Boston: Little, Brown, 1970, pp. 256–261.

SCHUESSLER, KARL, ed. *On Analyzing Crime.* Chicago: University of Chicago Press, 1974.

SCHUMANN, KARL F. "Theoretical Presuppositions for Criminology as a Critical Enterprise." *International Journal of Criminology and Penology* (August 1976) 4: 285–294.

SCHUR, EDWIN. *Crimes Without Victims.* Englewood Cliffs, N.J.: Prentice-Hall, 1965.

———. *Labeling Deviant Behavior: Its Sociological Implications.* New York: Harper & Row, 1971.

————. *Our Criminal Society.* Englewood Cliffs, N.J.: Prentice-Hall, 1969a.

————. *Radical Non-Intervention.* Englewood Cliffs, N.J.: Prentice-Hall, 1973.

————. "Reactions to Deviance: A Critical Assessment." *American Journal of Sociology* (November 1969b) 75: 309–322.

SCHWARTZ, RICHARD, and JEROME SKOLNICK. "Two Studies in Legal Stigma." *Social Problems* (Summer 1962) 10: 133–142.

SCHWENDINGER, HERMAN, and JULIA SCHWENDINGER. "Defenders of Order or Guardians of Human Rights? *Issues in Criminology* (Summer 1970) 5: 123–157.

SHORT, JAMES. "Differential Association and Delinquency." *Social Problems* (January 1957) 4: 233–239.

————. "Differential Association with Delinquent Friends and Delinquent Behavior." *Pacific Sociological Review* (Spring 1958) 1: 20–25.

————. "Differential Association as a Hypothesis: Problems of Empirical Testing." *Social Problems* (Summer 1960) 8: 14–25.

SIMON, RITA. *Women and Crime.* Lexington, Mass.: D.C. Heath, 1975.

SINGER, LINDA. "Women and the Correctional Process." *American Criminal Law Review* (Winter 1973) 11: 295–308.

SMART, CAROL. *Women, Crime and Criminology: A Feminist Critique.* London: Routledge and Kegan Paul, 1976.

SMITH, DOROTHY. "Women's Perspective as a Radical Critique of Sociology." *Sociological Inquiry* (1973) 44: No. 1, 7–13.

SMITH, DOUGLAS. "Sex and Deviance: An Assessment of Major Sociological Variables." *The Sociological Quarterly* (Spring 1979) 20: 183–195.

————, and CHRISTY A. VISHER. "Sex and Involvement in Deviance/Crime: A Quantitative Review of the Empirical Literature." *American Sociological Review* (August 1980) 45: 691–701.

SPARROW, GERALD. *Women Who Murder.* London: Arthur Barber Limited, 1970.

SPITZER, STEVEN. "Toward a Marxian Theory of Deviance." *Social Problems* (June 1975) 22: 638–651.

STEFFENSMEIER, DARRELL. "Crime and the Contemporary Woman: An Analysis of Changing Levels of Female Property Crime, 1960–75." *Social Forces* (December 1978) 57: 566–584.

————, RENEE STEFFENSMEIER, and ALVIN ROSENTHAL. "Trends in Female Violence, 1960–1977." *Sociological Focus,* (August 1979) 12: 217–227.

SUCHAR, CHARLES. *Social Deviance: Perpsectives and Prospects.* New York: Holt, Rinehart and Winston, 1978.

SUMNER, COLIN. "Marxism and Deviancy Theory." In Paul Wiles, ed., *The Sociology of Crime and Delinquency: The New Criminologies.* New York: Barnes and Noble, 1976, pp. 159–174.

SUTHERLAND, EDWIN. *The Professional Thief.* Chicago: University of Chicago Press, 1937.

————. *White Collar Crime.* New York: Holt, Rinehart and Winston, 1961.

———— and DONALD CRESSEY. *Principles of Criminology.* Philadelphia: Lippincott, 1960.

SYKES, GRESHAM. "The Rise of Critical Criminology." *The Journal of Criminal Law and Criminology* (June 1974) 65: 206–213.

————, and DAVID MATZA. "Techniques of Neutralization: A Theory of Delinquency." *American Sociological Review,* December 1957: 664–670. In Harwin Voss, ed., *Society, Delinquency, and Delinquent Behavior.* Boston: Little, Brown, 1970, pp. 263–269.

TANNENBAUM, FRANK. *Crime and the Community*. Boston: Ginn and Company, 1938.

TAYLOR, IAN, and PAUL WALTON. "Radical Deviancy Theory and Marxism: A Reply to Paul Hirst." *Economy and Society* (May 1972) 1: 229–233.

TAYLOR, IAN, PAUL WALTON, and JOCK YOUNG, eds. *Critical Criminology*. London: Routledge and Kegan Paul, 1975.

TAYLOR, IAN, PAUL WALTON, and JOCK YOUNG. *The New Criminology: For a Social Theory of Deviance*. New York: Harper & Row, 1973.

TAYLOR, LAURIE. *Deviance and Society*. London: Michael Joseph, 1971.

TEMIN, CAROLYN ENGEL. "Discriminatory Sentencing of Women Offenders: The Argument for ERA in a Nutshell." *The American Criminal Law Review* (Winter 1973) 11: 355–372.

TERRY, ROBERT M. "Discrimination in The Handling of Juvenile Offenders." In Peter Garabedian and Don Gibbons, eds. *Becoming Delinquent*. Chicago: Aldine, 1970: 78–92.

THIO, ALEX. "Class Bias in the Sociology of Deviance," *The American Sociologist* (February 1973) 8: 1–12.

THORSELL, BERNARD, and LLOYD KLEMKE. "The Labeling Process: Reinforcement and Deterrent?" *Law and Society Review*, (February 1972) 6: 393–403.

THRASHER, FREDERIC M. *The Gang: A Study of 1,313 Gangs in Chicago*. Introduction by James F. Short. Chicago: University of Chicago Press, 1963.

TURK, AUSTIN. *Criminality and Legal Order*. Chicago: Rand McNally, 1969.

VOLD, GEORGE B. *Theoretical Criminology*. New York: Oxford University Press, 1958.

VOSS, HARWIN. "Differential Association and Reported Delinquent Behavior: A Replication." *Social Problems* (Summer 1964) 12: 78–85.

———, ed. *Society, Delinquency, and Delinquent Behavior*. Boston: Little, Brown, 1970.

WARD, DAVID, and GENE KASSEBAUM. *Women's Prisons*. Chicago: Aldine, 1965.

WARKER, ELY VAN DE. "The Relations of Women to Crime." *The Popular Science Monthly* (1875–1876) 8: 1–16, 334–344.

WEIS, JOSEPH. "Liberation and Crime: The Invention of the New Female Criminal." In Peter Wickman and Phillip Whitten, eds., *Readings in Criminology*. Lexington, Mass.: D.C. Heath, 1978, pp. 130–140.

WILES, PAUL, ed. *The Sociology of Crime and Delinquency: The New Criminologies*. New York: Barnes and Noble, 1976.

WINICK, CHARLES. "Physician Narcotics Addicts." *Social Problems* (Summer 1961) 9: 174–186.

———, and PAUL KINSIE. *The Lively Commerce: Prostitution in the United States*. Chicago: Quadrangle Books, 1971.

WISE, NANCY B. "Juvenile Delinquency Among Middle-Class Girls." In Edmund Vaz, ed., *Middle-Class Juvenile Delinquency*. New York: Harper & Row, 1967, pp. 179–188.

WOLFGANG, MARVIN. *Patterns in Criminal Homicide*. Philadelphia: University of Pennsylvania Press, 1966.

———, LEONARD SAVITZ, and NORMAN JOHNSON, eds. *The Sociology of Crime and Delinquency*. New York: Wiley, 1970.

The Woman Question: Selections from the Writings of Karl Marx, Frederich Engels, V.I. Lenin, Joseph Stalin. New York: International Publishers, 1951.

Index

59; organized, 157; perjury, 3;
poisoning, 4, 6; property, 25, 27,
31, 38, 40, 59, 131, 133, 135, 146;
prostitution, 3, 5, 8, 12, 29, 31, 35,
44–45, 59–60, 78, 81, 87–88, 169,
174; rape, 25–26, 45, 162, 165;
robbery, 25, 28, 39, 42, 169; sex
offenses, 31 (*see also* rape and
prostitution); shoplifting, 3, 59–61,
83, 108, 112; statutory rape, 45, 81;
theft, 3, 5, 28–29, 31, 35, 41, 59,
66, 123, 169, 188; vandalism, 25;
victims of, by sex, 183; violent, 25,
27, 31, 38, 40, 42, 45, 59, 135, 137,
170; welfare fraud, 43; white-collar,
8, 43, 92, 96–97, 108, 114, 137, 157
Criminality and Economic Conditions
(Bonger, 1916), 146, 159
Criminality of Women (Pollak, 1950),
3–7
criminal subcultures, 117
Criminology (Quinney, 1975), 152
Crites, Laura, 38–39, 43
critical criminology, 141–77
Critical Criminology (Taylor, Walton
& Young, 1975), 148–50
"critical philosophy" (Quinney), 151

De Fleur, Melvin, 104
delinquency, 39–40, 78, 111, 118–20,
125, 135, 138, 174
Delinquency and Opportunity (Cloward
& Ohlin, 1960), 122, 128–29,
130–31
deRham, Edith, 7, 15
determinism, 101–103, 105, 113, 170
deviance, 157–58
differential association, xii, 91–115,
187; quantification and testing of,
103–105
double standard, legal, 41, 81
drug addiction, 8, 61
drunkenness, 31, 41
Durkheim, Emile, 49

Engels, Friedrich, 14, 145, 168–70
equal opportunity and crime, 51, 57
Erikson, Kai, 70–71, 86

Female Offender, The (Lombroso &
Ferrero, 1900), 2–3
feminist theory of crime, 181–92
Five Hundred Delinquent Women
(Glueck & Glueck, n.d.), 3
free will, 144

gambling, 25, 31
Gang, The (Thrasher, 1963), 117
gangs, 117ff., 138; girl, 124
"gender blindness" of criminology,
183
German Ideology, The (Marx &
Engels, 1965), 144
Gibbons, Don C., 54
Gibbs, Jack, 73–76
Glueck, Eleanor, 3
Glueck, Sheldon, 3
Gordon, David, 156–57
Gouldner, Alvin, 183–84

*How Could She Do That? A Study of
the Female Criminal* (deRham, 1969),
7, 15

Jones, Joseph, 54

Kitsuse, John, 69–70, 74
Klein, Dorie, 37, 170–71
Kress, June, 170–71

labeling, effects of, 86–87
labeling theory, xii, 65–89, 91,
114–15, 161, 187, 189, 191
Lemert, Edwin, 67–70, 74, 76
liberal criminology, 154
liberation (of women), and rising
rates of crime, 9, 46
Lombroso, Caesar, 2–3, 15, 17
Lumpenproletariat, 144